LADIES:
A Conjecture of Personalities

By
Feather Schwartz Foster

PUBLISH AMERICA

PublishAmerica
Baltimore

First printing

ISBN: 1-59286-361-2
PUBLISHED BY PUBLISHAMERICA, LLLP
www.publishamerica.com
Baltimore

Printed in the United States of America

TABLE OF CONTENTS

Introduction by
LUCY HAYES

This is all my idea, you know. Mine and Carrie's. After a century or more of being the "non-entity" First Ladies, Carrie...Caroline Harrison...and I got the girls together and decided to write our own book. We figured thus: The "modern" Ladies, from Mrs. Kennedy forward, have had unparalleled opportunities to express themselves. Everyone knows about them. Perhaps more than enough. Some even wrote their own memoirs. But as for the "more obscure" ladies—the first thirty or so of us—the world knows little. Perhaps there was little to know. For certain, we had few opportunities to be known, or to be anything, for that matter.

So this book is for us. The "moderns" are included only in commentary, and they have many comments to make.

> **CAROLINE HARRISON**
> *We are striving for candor, of course, but let's try to be kind.*

> **JULIA GRANT**
> *You mean we can actually say whatever we like? Anything at all? No matter what?*

> **CAROLINE HARRISON**
> *Whatever you want, Julia, but do try to be kind.*

> **MARY LINCOLN**
> *Julia? Kind? It is not in her nature.*

The truth of the matter is that we were all PARAGONS for our time. We were modest. We were gracious and pious. We were excellent wives and mothers. The embodiment of every virtue that women of our day were expected to have. But if you change the rules; if you decide that the virtues of past days are inconsequential; does it make *us* inconsequential for following those rules? Of course not! We *must* be judged according to the standards of *our* times—not *your* times!

First Ladies are a very unique sorority. Two hundred and some years, and only a handful of us! Some of us were acquainted in our lifetimes: Lady Washington and Abigail Adams were always cordial. Edith Roosevelt and Nelly Taft had been acquainted for years.[1] And Lady Bird Johnson knew everyone from Eleanor Roosevelt to Hillary Clinton. But here, in eternity, we *all* know each other. We know each others' times and histories. We can tell our own stories in our own voices. We can comment.[3] We can have opinions. We can express our personalities. We can be understood. We can be ourselves. *Finally!*

> [1]**NELLIE TAFT**
> *Edith was an iceberg.*[2]
>
> [2]**EDITH ROOSEVELT**
> *Nellie was a pill.*

> [3]**NANCY REAGAN**
> *And we will!*

So Carrie and I said to the girls: If people know nothing about you, they will assume there is nothing worth knowing. Tell what you want posterity to know. Write your own stories. Become real. Since history has thrust us into the light, let us not evaporate into its pages. Some of the Ladies were thrilled. Others were shy. But all were eager to participate.

So this is for us. And for the future.

Lucy

P.S. from Caroline Harrison: Julia Tyler, Frances Cleveland and Edith Wilson are the only "Ladies" who married "Presidents." The rest of us—moderns included—married men. Just plain men. And probably at a time when the Presidency wasn't even a glimmer. Don't forget that!

- C.H.

MARTHA DANDRIDGE CUSTIS WASHINGTON
1731-1802
First Lady: 1789-1797

When I was a very old lady, Mr. Gilbert Stuart painted my portrait. I looked contented and modest. The consummate grandmama, which I was. But then, I was a very old lady.

As a young girl, however, I was lively. Nay, frivolous! I loved to dance and go to parties and wear the latest fashions. And I was willful, especially with my studies. My father always said he had his hands full with his "Patsy."[1]

> **[1]BETTY FORD**
> *How you get "Patsy" from Martha is beyond me, but it seems to be a common nickname of the age. Like Betty, from Elizabeth.*

My spelling was always poor, even in a day when nobody cared about spelling. My penmanship was worse. And while I could read well enough, I never enjoyed it as a pastime the way Mrs. Adams or some of the other Ladies did. But in Colonial days, there was little that was pleasurable for a woman to read.[2] I never did see joy in Plutarch. My education was purely domestic, and therein I excelled. I sewed

> **[2]ABIGAIL ADAMS**
> *Shakespeare comes to mind. And Dante. And Homer.*

beautifully, painted some, and amassed a fine collection of receipts for sweetmeats and pastries. I learned the usual wifely skills needed to manage a plantation house, dozens of dependencies, and of course, slaves. And that was fine with me.

At eighteen, I married Daniel Parke Custis, who was more than twice my age. I was fortunate, since I had fancied him from afar. "Older" man that he was, he had a rakish gleam in his eye that I found most attractive. Perhaps it was his roguish Irish ancestry. He was also a very wealthy planter, which pleased my father. Daniel was good to me, indulged all my vanities (which I fear were many), and I adored him. Most people think my first marriage was merely an "arrangement." It was not. I truly loved Daniel Custis. We had four children, and buried the last two near as infants. Then Daniel fell ill with a fever and died.

I was left a widow at twenty-five, with two small children and vast estates that now became my property.[3] I had no idea how vast those

> **[3]DOLLEY MADISON**
> *Most young Colonial girls were married to men many years their senior. It guaranteed their financial security. If they could survive the dangers of childbirth, fevers, accidents or Indians, they would eventually be young widows. Hopefully, wealthy ones. Then they could afford to marry for inclination.*

estates were. I came to realize how scanty my education had been and what a trial I must have been to my tutors.

There I was: one of the wealthiest widows in Virginia, and very much at a loss. Nevertheless, I set about to learn, and thus my real education commenced. First, I learned exactly what my inheritance and the trusts for my children entailed. It entailed thousands of acres of rich Virginia farmland, thriving plantations, thousands of head of livestock and more than 300 slaves. Next, I learned what my encumbrances entailed, and I discharged them promptly. I always despised debt. And finally, I learned what my responsibilities entailed, and set about to meet them in an orderly fashion. I like order.

About a year after Daniel's death, I was introduced to Col. George Washington, of the Virginia Militia. We engaged in an amiable friendship, and then affianced within six months.[4] He was tall, attractive and young. Depending on whose calendar revisions you choose, he was either a few months older or a few months younger than I. Neither of us ever knew for sure, or cared. He stood a full foot higher, however, and was a charming and most attentive companion. In addition, he had substantial property of his own, for which I was thankful. Having come into such wealth, and being an uneducated woman, I feared falling prey to someone who wooed me only for my fortune.[5]

Col. Washington was an excellent manager of my estates and a scrupulous custodian for my children's inheritance. He was a fine businessman, although more inclined toward land speculation than I might have wished. I was not one to take chances. He was a devoted, albeit stern, stepfather to little Patsy and Jackie, and it was our deep misfortune to have had no children of our own. We both loved children and were happiest when surrounded by nieces and nephews and even the children of our slaves.

To chronicle the details of my life would be dull. My days were spent in the usual routines of Colonial women. But Mrs. Hayes

---

[4]DOLLEY MADISON
Widowed people (myself included) were expected to remarry promptly in our day. Personal affection had little to do with anything. Children needed parents, spouses needed spouses. The lengthy mourning periods of the 19th century were unheard of in the 18th!

[5]ABIGAIL ADAMS
Fortune hunters were always to be feared. My daughter unfortunately married an impecunious scoundrel, and I believe it shortened her life.[6]

[6]BETTY FORD
Actually, Nabby Adams died of breast cancer. She underwent a mastectomy on a kitchen table with whiskey as the anesthetic and dirty knives as the instruments. While her unfortunate marriage may not have eased things, it did not cause her death.

said we must tell posterity the truth, so I choose to address those subjects for which posterity seems to require answers.

George Washington and I met when were both in our twenty-seventh year and I was a widow with children. He was well aware that my Daniel and I had enjoyed a felicitous union. At age twenty-six, I had to presume that the Colonel was not impervious to the charms of the fair sex. It would never have occurred to me, however, to violate his privacy with improper questions, nor would it have ever occurred to him to offend my sensibilities with unsuitable knowledge. Historians have always liked to pry into the private lives of public people, and are eager to speculate that Col. Washington "did not love me." This is foolishness. Modern readers and historians too, for that matter, were raised on fairy stories. They have no understanding of 18th century sentiment, when men and women married for ease of living. Love, if one was fortunate, came later. And that kind of love was usually the result of affectionate treatment, thoughtful provision and protection, each partner fulfilling his and her duty, and pleasant companionship by the fireside.

> **NANCY REAGAN**
> *What about passion?*

When most Colonial women had ten or more children (if she survived), you can assume there was passion.

George and Sallie Fairfax were our friends and neighbors. We valued the Fairfax society and connections very highly. Sallie was tall and slim and generously endowed with every social grace and elegance. She had many attributes I lacked. But I had one thing Sallie lacked. I had George Washington, and he would never behave improperly, nor violate the established boundaries of conduct. Never.

Many years later, when he was President, my husband became acquainted with Mrs. Eliza Powel. They were often dancing partners, since by that time, age and infirmity prevented me from all but the mildest minuet. The President, who was an excellent dancer, had so many cares of office that it would have been cruel to deny him such pleasurable and harmless relaxation. Mrs. Powel was not only a fine dancer, but an intelligent and insightful lady. Her friendship with both of us allowed the President rare moments of reflection, and in truth, he was not often inclined to reflect inward.[7] Wifely remarks are seldom valued after nearly forty years of marriage, no matter how accurate they might be. And since a woman's

> **[7]EDITH ROOSEVELT**
> *Men of great physical action are seldom men of deep reflection. It is much easier for them to bury uncomfortable self-awareness and forge on. Theodore was a man of extremely broad knowledge, but self-awareness was not among his better attributes.*

sensibilities are usually superior to a man's, Mrs. Powel provided my husband with an opportunity for the introspection that was somewhat alien to his nature. We both appreciated it.

It occurs to me that many of us "Ladies" suffered the loss of children. There is no greater grief. In the modern world, losing a child is considered "unnatural." We are intended to bury our parents, not our children. That is the law of nature. I bore four children. I lost two as infants, a common occurrence then. Sad enough, but common. Children were weak, and only the strong could survive. Losing grown children, or near-grown children, is a tragedy.[8]

[8]**JANE PIERCE**
Nothing tears at the very core of a mother's heart than losing her babies. Nothing.[9]

[9]**IDA McKINLEY**
Losing my two little babies was the tragedy of my life. It shattered my health, and I never recovered.

My Patsy died of a fit when she was sixteen. My Jackie was little more than twenty when he died of a fever. He had been a handful to raise. Willful like his mother, I suppose. And maybe like his wild Irish ancestors as well. Perhaps that was why I loved him and spoiled him so. At least that was what the General said after his many attempts at discipline failed. But Jackie was a good lad, and once he married, he became a fine and responsible husband and father.

I pined bitterly when Patsy died, but Jackie's death was devastating. Four children born; four children in graves. Jackie left a young widow and two small babies. As was the custom, in due time, my daughter-in-law saw fit to remarry. We were pleased with her choice, and we always remained as kin. But as more children were born to Eleanor and her new husband, I suggested that she permit the General and myself to raise the two that were my natural grandchildren.

Actually, adopting little Nellie and George Washington Custis was the General's idea. He knew how deeply I grieved for my children, and he feared for my health. He thought the patter of small feet at Mount Vernon would lift my spirits. He was right. I loved children, and although I was well into my middle years by that time, I had sufficient help with the necessities and more than sufficient love to give.

[10]**SARAH POLK**
But Madam, you are the best one to address this subject. And it needs to be addressed.

As to slavery. I despise discussing this subject.[10] I have great difficulty projecting two centuries hence, let alone understanding a culture so strange from mine. I can only reflect upon my own time and in my own terms. Slavery had been an institution in Virginia long before I was born. My father had slaves and my grandparents had slaves, and Daniel Custis and his family had slaves. So did the Washingtons and Jeffersons, Madisons and Monroes.[11]

> [11]**ABIGAIL ADAMS**
> *The Adamses, of course, never owned slaves.*

The truth is, if you were from the South and had property, you had slaves. There was no way a large plantation could have operated without such labor. That was the way it was. Our slaves at Mount Vernon were part of our lives. They were well fed and cared for. Many a time I myself went to nurse a sick darky in slave quarters. And since many of the Washington slaves married with Custis slaves, it was truly "family."[12] General Washington was a great believer in training, and those slaves with sufficient intelligence and industry were taught carpentry and cobbling and harness making and other skills and trades. I personally taught many of the girls to do fancywork and sew a fine seam. We also made the best gingerbread in the County.

> [12]**LADY BIRD JOHNSON**
> *It's hard for a non-Southerner to understand this attitude. Maybe you just have to be born there to have an idea of the traditions. It doesn't make it right; but then again, history isn't always right. It's like Lady Washington said: It was the way it was.*

Lucy Hayes commented that we must be judged according to the standards of our own times. She is right. Sobeit.

I had, however, one or two unfortunate experiences with our slaves, and I fear it has darkened my perceptions. There was one who I took into our house after my Patsy died. She was a likely lass of ten or twelve and I felt a true affection for her. I taught her embroidery, for which she showed a remarkable aptitude. Her fancywork was better than my own and her skill was such that I entrusted her with my finest brocades and silks. Many an evening she and I sat together, like mother and daughter, sewing by the fire and chattering away.

And how was I repaid for my kindness and solicitude? She ran off. I could understand it if a slave was mistreated.[13] But this one lived in her *own* room in *our* house. She had soft labor. She did not have to work in the kitchens or the washing room. Her clothes were made over from my own, and more than once I gave her fresh lace or buttons for trim. She ate what we ate, and food was plentiful. She was surrounded by family and friends and people who cared about her. She broke my trust. And my heart.

> [13]**ROSALYNN CARTER**
> *Concepts take years to change. Centuries, sometimes. And then they are still not completely changed.*

Some time later, the General made inquiries as to her whereabouts, and discovered that she had fled to Philadelphia, where she kept shop as a dressmaker or milliner. He asked if I wanted him to take steps for her return. No, I said, I could never trust her again. Trust is important to me.

This calls to mind another unfortunate episode. At the end of his life, General Washington wrote his will, wherein he manumitted all his slaves—after my death. He was the only "Founding Father" to do so.[14] But he reasoned that since so many of *his* slaves had married with *my* slaves, and with so many children as issue, it would have been cruel to free some and not others, and thus separate families. I imagine he expected me to follow suit in my will.

[14] **ABIGAIL ADAMS**
Naturally the Adamses had no slaves to manumit.[15]

[15] **LOUISA ADAMS**
We heard you the first time, Abigail.

I had no strong feelings about slavery other than its conventional necessity as a labor force. The "social" questions did not even exist in my mind. I believed that we, as masters, had a moral obligation to care for our slaves generously; they, in turn, were expected to serve us loyally. I did my part. I expected them to do theirs. I was also a very old lady—past seventy—and needed constant assistance. Perhaps I also suffered from the deterioration of faculties that comes with age, but I was terrified by the General's promise of manumission. I was certain that some of our slaves were plotting to poison my food or smother me in my sleep. If a slave could run off from a life of ease, all for the sake of "freedom," I could imagine what less-favored darkies might do to speed their promised liberty! I am afraid the General's kind intentions toward our dependents made my remaining days fearful and intolerable. Death, at least a soft, uncomplicated, death in my bed, was welcome.

[16] **BESS TRUMAN**
Most of us would agree with that, ma'am. I was always happiest in my own home with my own dear friends.

And finally, I suppose everyone wants to know how it was to be the very "First" Lady. That is an easy question. I hated it. I hate it still. It was intrusive, confining and worrisome.[16] Everything I did reflected upon the General—or the President, as he became.

There was a time, in those dark days of indecision after the War, when George Washington could have been made King, if he inclined. Fortunately he did not so incline, for I would have been truly discomfited being Queen Martha. Whilst General Washington and I came from propertied stock and had considerable land holdings, we were not of the true Virginia aristocracy, or the "FFVs" as they called the First Families of Virginia: the Byrds andRandolphs, the Lees and Carters[17]. Neither of us was comfortable in the limelight. He was deeply concerned that his every action would be scrutinized, not so much for himself, but for our Country, which we both held so dear.

We were in the unenviable position of setting precedents for the highest office in the land. If I was "elegant," it would be said that I was putting on airs to imitate the monarchies. If I was "plain," we would be perceived as impoverished and shabby, to be disdained and held in low esteem by the European nations, who considered us upstarts, anyway. If I was hospitable and "warm," I would be called "familiar." If I stayed aloof, the presidency would be called "remote," and again, monarchial. And everyone was so afraid of monarchies. My own personality was disinclined toward setting styles of any kind. I would have been far happier at Mount Vernon, committed to entertaining the "Virginia" way, instead of the "political" way.

> [17]**ROSALYNN CARTER**
> *No relation to Jimmy's family. My in-laws were just poor folks. And I was a "Smith," like Abigail Adams and Margaret Taylor. But we weren't related either.*

The "Virginia" way allowed us to entertain extensively at Mount Vernon. There was seldom a day we had less than ten at our table. Often total strangers passing through the area availed themselves of our hospitality. Entertaining in New York and later Philadelphia was much different. There were many people who would have been warmly welcomed at Mt. Vernon, but political restraints excluded them from the President's table. I did what was demanded of me: a weekly levee, an occasional State banquet and returning calls from those who called upon me.

> **ELIZABETH MONROE**
> *I put an end to returning the calls. It was time consuming and inappropriate for my position.*

> **DOLLEY MADISON**
> *Nonsense!*
> *Calling on people and being sociable is a large and important part of the First Ladies' duties.*

As I said, I had a "willful" streak, and since so much talk was made of my comings and goings, and what I wore and what carriage was driven, I resolved to go out as seldom as possible. I voluntarily imprisoned myself in our rented house and longed for the serenity of Mount Vernon. The "freedom" our new Country fought and bled for, obviously did not apply to me.

I deemed myself not as a setter of style and fashion, like some later Ladies, but as the wife and helpmeet of a man who, by accident of fortune, became President of a new untried country. It was my duty to supply devoted companionship and a serene home. It was my responsibility to provide the President—my husband—with a warm, happy hearth; his favorite dishes for supper; his clothes clean and properly mended, and both his Madeira flagon and pipe filled and ready for his pleasure. And it was the joy of my life to listen to him complain about the farm, the crops, the weather and his rheumatism.

It was my idea of heaven.

ABIGAIL SMITH ADAMS
1744-1818
First Lady: 1797-1801

I was surprised to be invited to participate in this endeavor. Like Mrs. Lincoln and Mrs. Roosevelt, I have been subject to a great deal of scrutiny, and there is little more I could add that is not already well documented. Recent history has been especially kind to me. I cannot think of any woman who would take offense at praise of her intelligence or strength or talents. But Mrs. Clinton is no doubt more intelligent, and I suspect increasingly aware of her own strength. And no Lady was more talented than the first Mrs. Wilson, a renowned artist in her own right. I just left a long trail. I enjoyed voluminous correspondence with many illustrious people, most of which was preserved by our family. Posterity has mined a rich vein with the Adamses. We were a family of prolific letter-writers and we discarded nothing.

History has treated me even more kindly than it has my dear John, and he was the finest man I ever knew.[1] But Mrs. Hayes and Mrs. Harrison inferred that we should tell something history does not already know. I am afraid that with several hundred letters written in my own hand, there is little left to be known.

> [1]**DOLLEY MADISON**
> *I believe history has treated me more kindly than my Jemmy. The scholars respect his ability and great contribution to our country. But the people remember me.*

I was brought up in a Puritan Society. My father was a minister. Complaining and bemoaning our lot in life was a sin. So was pride. We encouraged hard work and forbearance, so I worked hard and forbore.

When John served in the Continental Congress in Philadelphia in the early 1770s, I was busy at home raising the children; we had six, buried two. Our little farm in Braintree provided practically our entire subsistence, and it was left to me to make it profitable. When the little ones were bedded down for the night, and the mending was done, and the bills were tallied, and the soap and candles were congealing, and the dishes were put away for another few hours, all that remained for me was a patch of time by a dying fire, *forbearing* the deep and weary loneliness for the one dearest to my heart.

> **²MAMIE EISENHOWER**
> *Abigail is not the only Lady to endure long and often dangerous separations. Any woman whose husband served in the military, especially during wartime, underwent the same painful ordeal.*

So I wrote John and told him the necessary things. How the corn was spoiling from too much rain. How the children fared. Tommy's measles and how Nabby did not progress as quickly as Johnny with her Latin. And I told him of our neighbors' health and the news of our kin. And I answered his questions, discussed the sermons I had heard, reflected on some of the issues of the day, cautioned him to take care of his rheumatism, and occasionally hinted at the empty side of our bed, and how cold the New England nights could be.[2]

History credits me for entreating my husband to exhort Congress to "remember the ladies." History credits me poorly, since my husband did not exhort nor did Congress remember. It remained another hundred years until the ladies decided to remember themselves. I had nothing to do with it. History also credits me for the caution that "all men would be tyrants if they could." It is a bon mot worthy of our illustrious and witty colleague Dr. Franklin, but it is only the truth. All men *would* be tyrants if they could. Except for my dear John, of course.

But there was one thing I never did tell John, although it lived with me forever. I was certainly no beauty, nor was I raised to value frivolous charms.

> **³LUCRETIA GARFIELD**
> *I understand completely. My husband was also away for long periods, in the company of cosmopolitan and sophisticated women.*

But during those long, cold and empty New England nights, I sometimes caught sight of myself in the glass, and detected new lines around my eyes, and a firmness at the mouth that seemed almost harsh. I was only thirty-two, but was I ever young? And where was my husband while these lines were forming on my face? He was in Philadelphia, the gayest and most cosmopolitan city in the country, being entertained regularly by wealthy men and their worldly wives and daughters.[3]

I could picture him talking and smiling and dancing with the belles of Philadelphia, and later Holland, and worst of all, Paris! (Well, perhaps not dancing. John was not light on his feet.) I was no match for Paris women, not that I wished it. But the temptations must have been very great, even for one of John's high moral deportment.

Without question I trusted my husband's fidelity. It was inconceivable to think otherwise. But for all his fidelity, and the loneliness I know he shared, I deeply feared that I would prove disappointing upon his return. Some years passed more slowly than others, and my hair became gray, and the lines deepened around my eyes, and my waist grew thicker, and my tongue a good deal sharper. How could a New England farmeress even begin to compare to the beautiful and sophisticated ladies of fashionable Philadelphia and Paris?[4]

> **[4]FLORENCE HARDING**
> *And you wonder why I would never let my husband out of my sight![5]*

> **[5]NANCY REAGAN**
> *Obviously your husband was out of your sight on a few occasions, Florence.*

Envy is a sin, and I prayed every night that I should not envy those women who would be in my husband's company. And I worried, because I know that it *is* possible for some women to be beautiful, charming *and* intelligent.[6] It is hard to admit how deeply I needed and sought John's reassurance, not merely his devotion, which I knew was mine. I wanted him to walk with me on his arm, and have all of fashionable society turn and acknowledge that indeed, Mrs. John Adams was lovely.

> **[6]JACQUELINE KENNEDY**
> *Isn't it ironic that the women who are beautiful, charming <u>and</u> intelligent are usually only appreciated by OTHER women's husbands?*

> **LOUISA ADAMS**
> *Perhaps that was the unconscious reason for my mother-in-law's resentment of me. I was considered "lovely."*

> **BARBARA BUSH**
> *I have read a great deal about the illustrious Abigail Adams. Many compliments have been paid. But I never heard of her being called "lovely."*

Posterity also credits me with virtues I must disdain. Maintaining our farm and trying to make it profitable was nothing more than what was done by hundreds and thousands of New England wives, and, as the War progressed, widows. And as far as being my husband's confidante and intellectual "partner," again, there were many other wives whose intelligence and wit and learning were certainly equal to that of their spouse. My two sisters come to mind immediately. That John encouraged my intellectual companionship is to his credit, not mine. Most husbands relegated wives to the domestic side of their lives. John was the exception.

[7]**BARBARA BUSH**
It took two hundred years, but I understand the feeling. Unlike Abigail, I had the good fortune to be alive at my son's election. I would be hard pressed to choose which gave me more pride: my husband's election or my son's.[8]

[8]**NELLIE TAFT**
I came close to being the mother of a president as well. I still believe that Bob Taft would have been a fine Chief Executive.

Of course, there is my distinction of being the mother of a President as well as being First Lady.[7] It may be a distinction, but it is certainly not an accomplishment, especially when my other two sons took to drink, and never achieved their potential. Only one success from three sons is no cause to boast—*if* I were inclined to boast.

No. If you ask *me*, what *I* consider my greatest contribution to posterity, it would be thus: that I reflected the glory of others more worthy. But my regrets? Ah, there were many.

Thomas Jefferson had been our dear friend. I met him for the first time in the mid 1780s, when John was Minister to Great Britain, and Mr. J. ditto in France. John had known Mr. Jefferson for a decade or more; I knew him only by his esteemed reputation. We both adored him. When Mr. J. was detained in Paris, he asked us to meet the ship bringing his young daughter Polly to Europe. She was only about seven, and hadn't seen her father in two or three years. Mrs. Jefferson had died when Polly was a baby, and she had been staying with an aunt in Virginia, whilst he was abroad.

Poor little thing! Such a long trip, with no guidance save a fifteen-year-old slave girl. She was leaving the only family she had ever known and crossing an ocean to meet a father she barely remembered. And she was being met by total strangers: Mr. Adams and myself. But what a lovely, bright, warm-hearted child she was! I took her to my heart in an instant! Happily for me, she responded in kind. I lavished great affection upon her, since I dearly loved children and my own were grown or near grown at the time. I read stories to her, braided her hair, counseled her on the Bible, listened to her nightly prayers, tucked her in and kissed her tenderly. It was wrenching, a few weeks later, to turn her over to her father!

In the time we spent in Mr. Jefferson's company, I grew to admire him enormously. He was one of the best-read individuals I had ever met, and I valued his brilliant insights and opinions, as did John. We all spent many hours in deep and interesting conversation. Mr. Jefferson did not particularly care for "intellectual" women. He liked "his" women to be feminine and submissive for the most part, like the late Mrs. Jefferson. If they were knowledgeable or talented in the arts and other "womanly" subjects, that was to be admired; but if they expressed interest or aptitude about politics, economics, philosophy, government, and other worldly affairs, he was cool.

DOLLEY MADISON	**JACQUELINE KENNEDY**
I knew Mr. Jefferson better than any of the other Ladies. My husband and he were intimate friends for fifty years. I adored him as well! But Abigail is right. He did not care for a challenging woman.	*Jack Kennedy was like Jefferson in that respect. The whole Kennedy family was. Women were meant to be beautiful, charming, religious and good mothers. It was also nice if they could swim and ride and look good at parties. The Kennedys did not like "their women" to shine otherwise.*

Perhaps I was a notable exception. I had no musical inclinations, nor could I paint. And my dancing was little better than John's. But then again, I was a married woman past forty, with four nearly-grown children, so I imagine I did not quite come into the category of "his women." He did not need to find me attractive. But then again, I was not the "lovely" Mrs. Adams.

As our new country developed, and both John and Mr. Jefferson were recalled, John to serve as Vice President, and Mr. J. to be Secretary of State, it was becoming obvious that there was a deep philosophical division about how the country would, and should, develop. Alexander Hamilton, our new Secretary of the Treasury, was not quite as diversely intellectual as Mr. J., but he was six times more shrewd. His foresight was visionary. He believed the country would grow through industry, thus requiring a strong central government. Mr. J., and many like him, preferred the agrarian theory of state rule, to wit: Keep the central government weak, and let most decisions be made locally.

Perhaps it was because John and I were born and raised in the industrial north that we were inclined to believe Hamilton's thesis the wiser.[9] Certainly it had more vision for growth. We were far from wealthy. I considered myself fortunate to have a farm hand or two, and an occasional servant girl to help in the house. I cooked and cleaned,

[9]**DOLLEY MADISON**
There is much to be said about Mrs. Adams' comments. Slaves, while they were unpaid, were an enormous expense to the owner. And since Southern hospitality was generous to a fault, it was very easy to accrue large debts. I believe the expression is "land poor." Too many acres and dependents and not enough cash. We suffered from want of money as did Mr. J. So did the Monroes.

chopped the wood, kept the garden, worried about the bills, doctored the sick and missed John during his many long absences. And since our Puritan background abhorred debt, we were meticulous about living within our limited means. The agrarian society, on the other hand, thrived on slave labor and the famous Southern hospitality. How such a brilliant man as Thomas Jefferson permitted himself to incur such tangled finances is beyond me. But that is another story....

The political and personal differences between Mr. Hamilton and Mr. Jefferson grew wider and wider, and became very ugly at times. John, like President Washington, wanted to incorporate the best of both doctrines, since indeed, there was much good in each. But the great aptitude for international diplomacy that was so notable in both my husband and my son, John Quincy, disappeared completely in their national and private associations. John was never popular. Respected yes, but popular...alas, never. Neither was Johnny.

When John was Vice President, he deemed it a moral obligation to support President Washington's decisions one hundred percent all the time. They may have had private disagreements. I am certain there were times John yearned to have the overwhelming affection that the country gave so easily and heartily to the General. I am also certain there were a few decisions John might have made differently. However, it would have been unthinkable for him to do anything other than support the President publicly at all times. Therefore, when John became President, and Mr. Jefferson his Vice President, it was all the more painful to have dissension and disloyalty in the "Official Family."

When the breach became so wide as to prevent further contact let alone amity, it was a painful situation for both John and me.[10] He was deeply hurt, and I was very angry. It was a twenty-year friendship totally shattered. I believed that such good friends, and such intelligent men as John and Mr. J., should have been able to confide their differences to each

[10]**EDITH ROOSEVELT**
I remember how it was when Theodore fell out with Will Taft. They had been dear friends for so many years, and it was such a disappointment to my husband. Personally, I didn't care that much, since I thought Will was dull, and I never cared for Nellie.[11]

[11]**NELLIE TAFT**
It broke Will's heart to break with Theodore Roosevelt. Will was not a shrewd man. But he was a decent, loyal, honest and true friend. Theodore was strictly an opportunist, and Edith, well, she could have sunk the Titanic, for all her warmth.

other and resolve them rather than to let the partisan newspapers of the day make mincemeat of everything. But it was not to be. We felt the estrangement deeply. And when Jefferson challenged John for the Presidency—a situation that John would have *never* done with General Washington—it was the last straw. Mr. Jefferson's name was no longer mentioned in our home.

Some years later, during Jefferson's Presidency, his daughter Polly died in childbirth. She was only twenty-five or so. I remembered her with such great affection, that I felt compelled to write to Mr. Jefferson, offering my fond memories and sincere condolences, since I knew how devoted he was to his daughter and how deeply grieved he must have been. He responded quickly in his usual graceful style, thanking me for my sympathy, and tactfully inquiring after my husband, thus encouraging further correspondence.

> **MARTHA WASHINGTON**
> *It is interesting to note that while it was unseemly for a woman to engage a gentleman in serious conversation, it was perfectly acceptable for her to exchange views in serious correspondence. I did not correspond a great deal since my penmanship and spelling were poor, and I was embarrassed. But there were many other women of my acquaintance who corresponded freely with the men of their acquaintance—including the General.*

And herein lies one of my deep regrets. I was in a position to encourage my husband to take up his own pen and renew their old acquaintance. I did not. I was still rankled by Jefferson's duplicity. Whatever faults could be found with the Adamses, duplicity was not among them. Long grudges, I fear, were. More than a dozen years would pass before a mutual friend effected what rightfully should have been my true claim to immortality: The revived friendship and deepening understanding between John Adams and Thomas Jefferson. I had that opportunity. I let it slip.[12] The cordial and lively exchanges between them became a long afterglow in the twilight of two aging giants. One of the gold mines of history must surely be the opening of

> [12]**NELLIE TAFT**
> *Some years after their famous falling-out, Will and Theodore met by accident in Chicago. The friendship won over the feud, and their public embrace meant a great deal to Will. I doubt it meant that much to Theodore. Sincerity was never his virtue.*

their great and good hearts to each other. It brought them both much pleasure in their old age. I regret, too, that I could not be alive to share it.

> **[13]LOUISA ADAMS**
> *My mother-in-law had too much to say about too many things that were none of her concern. Her sanctimonious nature drove all her children to despair. John Quincy was the only one of them who succeeded in life—but then again, he was so much like HER.*

And finally, I imagine that my daughter-in-law is panting to take me to task for all my many failings.[13] I admit that I did not approve of my son's choice of a wife. This has nothing to do with Louisa herself; she is a fine lady. I believed, however, that John Quincy would have been better matched with a New Englander, or at least someone from New York. An "American." But an Englishwoman, with Southern ties? I felt she would be too soft for my son, especially if the task of running a household fell on her shoulders, as it had with me. I doubted that she could ever be a true helpmeet and companion. Obviously I was right; my son's marriage was not especially successful or happy. My husband liked Louisa enormously, and I believe she was very fond of him as well. But no matter what she says, I was never unkind to her.

> **LOUISA ADAMS**
> *Mr. Adams Senior was a delightful man. The austerity of his youth had become warm and mellow in his old age. I esteemed him greatly, and loved him dearly. He was the only one in my husband's family who was kind to me.*

In hindsight, however, I suppose my "matchmaking" judgment may have been less than intuitive. In her youth, my daughter Nabby had been enamored of a young man from Boston. His prospects appeared inadequate and there was some serious talk of him that reflected poor character on his part, thus I strongly discouraged further acquaintance. I insisted that Nabby come with

> **[14]LOUISA ADAMS**
> *Abigail's "wishes" could more aptly be called "demands." She was a very difficult lady to please.*

me to England, where John was Minister. She was an obedient daughter, and usually submitted to our wishes.[14] Whilst in London, John had engaged a young man as his Secretary. He came from a good family, and had served as an officer with General Washington. His references were excellent. He was soon smitten with our daughter, and we encouraged the romance. I do not know how deeply Nabby cared for Col. William Smith, but they married.

22

It was not a prosperous marriage. Col. Smith had serious flaws that unfortunately were not apparent to either John or myself early on. He was an impecunious laggard, constantly demanding unwarranted considerations because of his "connections." Our daughter never complained, but she was unhappy, and suffered a great deal. If it hadn't been for whatever assistance we could provide, and the generous support her brother Johnny gave her, she would have been destitute.[15]

> [15] **LOUISA ADAMS**
> *My husband always had a close relationship with his sister. I was fond of Nabby, although we were abroad for much of the time and did not see her often. Sometimes I think my sister-in-law was the only true friend my husband ever had.*

When she was in her early forties, Nabby took ill and somehow managed the long journey back to our home in Braintree. John and I were shocked at her appearance. She was a mere shadow. Our doctor came at once, and said it was the cancer that had arisen in her breast. He said if it wasn't excised immediately she would surely die. He sent for some colleagues, and they amputated my dear daughter's breast in our house. I brought in every spare candle and every piece of linen I could find. The doctors forced strong whiskey down Nabby's throat to help ease the pain, but she could not tolerate it, and vomited it up. We tied her arms and legs to the kitchen table, and jammed a block of wood between her teeth. When they cut, God was merciful, and allowed her to faint so as not to bear the terrible pain.

I sat with her throughout, and had hours in which to reflect on my failings. The young man she fancied in her youth had become a successful attorney and a well-respected member of the community. He was appointed Chief Justice of the Supreme Court of Vermont. He was devoted to his wife and children. Nabby would have been happy with him. It was my fault that her life took so sorrowful a turn. I regret that the most.

I believe that is all I can add. History has given me far more credit than I warrant. Thank you for inviting me to participate.

DOLLEY PAYNE TODD MADISON
1768-1849
First Lady: 1809-1817

For nearly 150 years, I was *the* "Lady" of renown. Other than Martha Washington and perhaps Mary Lincoln, I was probably the only First Lady whose first name was known or remembered. For more than a century I was "the quintessential hostess" and the "Lady of Fashion." All the women in the country copied the clothes I wore—especially my hats. Today most people only remember me from the Washington portrait story and think I invented ice cream. No matter. I don't care a bit. I am delighted to participate in Lucy's endeavor and tell my tale.

JULIA TYLER	FRANCES CLEVELAND	JACQUELINE KENNEDY
Mrs. Madison was a Lady of Fashion when I was a child. When I became First Lady, I wanted nothing more than to emulate, nay, surpass her fame, and establish a style and fame of my own.	*When I bought a gown without a bustle, it started a new look. Within two years, bustles were a thing of the past.*	*My little pillbox hats were all the rage! They were small and simple and I only wore them because I hated hats. But women had to wear hats then, so I wore one.*

I wasn't always a "Lady of Fashion." I was a North Carolina Quaker, born and raised. My father, a convert, was very strict in his observance and expected the entire family to obey. My mother, born and raised in the Episcopal Church, rebelled and named me Dolley. Father had preferred that I be called "Patience" or "Prudence," neither of which quality I possessed in great abundance. But Mother was victorious, and my sisters Lucy, Anna and Mary were equally grateful.

Everything about my upbringing was "plain." We wore the traditional Quaker gray gowns and bonnets. Food was plentiful, but plain: bread and game and vegetables. Corn meal pudding with honey was the only treat we knew. When I was ten, I stayed a fortnight with my Episcopal Grandmama. There I discovered silk and lace and jewelry. There I discovered slaves wearing bright red and yellow and blue bandanas and shirts, and they sang and danced and played the fiddle. There I discovered pies and preserves and all sorts of confections. And there I discovered it was not sinful to laugh and enjoy oneself.

Do not misunderstand. My father, although stern, was a kind man. We were a loving family—just not a merry one.

When I was sixteen, we moved to Philadelphia. The reason was twofold. My father, who still owned several inherited slaves, became increasingly disturbed by the evil of slavery and determined to release them from bondage, despite the great financial distress it would cause our family. Secondly, Philadelphia was predominantly a Quaker city. There would be other Friends and opportunities for prominence amongst the Congregation Elders. He had ambitions.

Philadelphia was a wonder! I loved it! It was the largest and most prosperous city in the country! There were scores of shops and stalls filled with beautiful things. On market days, more than a hundred wagons and carts came from all over to ply their wares. There was nothing you could not buy in Philadelphia! And, too, the country had just established its independence, and important men from every State congregated in Philadelphia! It was the capital city.

Unfortunately, the Payne family fared less well. My father's business venture failed and we were obliged to take in boarders to make ends meet. Then Father sickened, lingered for two years and died. When I was twenty-two (nearing spinsterhood by the standards of the day), I met John Todd, a struggling young lawyer who occasionally attended our Meeting House. We courted for several months. It was my father's dying wish that we marry, and although I did not "love" John Todd in the modern-day romantic sense, I knew he was a good man and would be kind to me.[1] We wed and began to raise a family. We were happy, and indeed, I grew to care deeply for John Todd.

> [1]**MARTHA WASHINGTON**
> *A good and kind man is the best possible choice for a husband. You can grow to love a kind man very easily.*

Three years afterwards, there was a terrible cholera epidemic in Philadelphia. Nearly a third of the population died, among them John Todd and my infant son. I had also been desperately ill with the fever, but I survived with my two-year-old son, mounting debts and no means of support. My mother urged me to sell my little house, pay my debts, and move back with her and help run the boarding house. And there my life began.

All the aforementioned is background. What was omitted is this: although

I always possessed a true reverence for the Deity and was an obedient daughter, I did not possess the soul of a Quaker. I loved to laugh. I loved pretty things and bright colors. I craved sweets. And above all, I enjoyed the pleasures of merry companionship.

My mother's boarding house was an important place. We housed eight Congressmen, one Senator (Aaron Burr) and the Secretary of State, Thomas Jefferson, a childhood friend of my mother's. Every important man in Philadelphia passed through our portals at one time or another.

I venture to say that the reason for the popularity of the Widow Payne's Boarding House was the fact that we treated our boarders as honored guests. If I learned that Congressman "A" fancied oranges and Congressman "B" had an aversion to walnuts, I made a point of providing oranges as frequently as possible, and avoided serving walnuts to Congressman "B." And at evening meal, I tried to ensure that all participated in conversation—even the most reticent. I never permitted "controversial" subjects to be discussed at table, claiming it was bad for the digestion. Naturally, no one wished to offend the Widow Todd. Our dinner conversations were lively, interesting and delightful.

It was Senator Burr who informed me that the "great little Madison" wished to make my acquaintance. James Madison was indeed a "great" man, having been so instrumental in drafting the Constitution. There was no one who did not esteem him highly. He also had the distinction of being Secretary Jefferson's closest friend. Mr. Madison was also "little." He and I stood nose-to-nose, and I was around five-foot-five inches in flat slippers. He was of slight build, and I fear I may have outweighed him by ten or even twenty pounds—and I was not overly portly. He was also nearly twenty years my senior.[2]

> **[2]JULIA TYLER**
> *President Tyler was nearly thirty years my senior when I married him—and it was a most felicitous match.*

His marriage proposal a few months after our meeting caused me a great dilemma. Again, I did not "love" Mr. Madison in the romantic sense.[3] But I sensed a warm, dear heart beneath the shy, scholarly exterior. I also knew the Quakers would expel me if I married out of faith. I consulted my mother, who was herself becoming disenchanted with the strict Elders. They had recently demanded that she burn several beautiful linen cloths left to her by Grandmama. "It is up to you, Dolley," she said, "but I will not desert you." With my father dead, I had no personal reluctance

> **[3]MARTHA WASHINGTON**
> *Entirely too much is made of romance. No wonder modern marriages have problems! People expect too much.*

to marry out of faith. The same good Lord who made Quakers had done an excellent job with Mr. Madison also, and I knew he would be a good stepfather to my little son Payne. I had nothing to fear from the Deity. Besides, every one of my brothers and sisters married out of faith as well. Poor Father.

But I inherited something else from Father, although it might have equally displeased him. I also had ambition. Being freed from the Quaker ban on anything resembling gaiety, I could indulge my love for color and pretty things. The Madisons had substantial property and expected to see me finely clothed. Then too, Mr. Madison was an important person. My life with him would surely be amongst interesting people. That was even more important to me than wearing a blue or yellow dress!

It was dear Lady Washington who provided the impetus. My sister Lucy had married President Washington's nephew, so we had become kin. The "First" Lady began inviting "The Widow Todd" to her regular levees, where I became acquainted with the wives and daughters of every prominent man in Philadelphia. At one afternoon reception, Lady W. took me aside and said:

MARTHA WASHINGTON
Dolley dear, we have noticed that Mr. Madison has singled you out for his special attentions. He is a fine and brilliant man, and both President Washington and I recommend him most highly. We hope you will consider his suit.

Well, with such recommendation from the Washingtons, I couldn't possibly refuse. Jemmy Madison and I married. I bought a trousseau with not one gray dress in it. He gave me a magnificent necklace that had been in his family for generations. And then he took me to Montpelier, the Madison family plantation in Virginia, where he promptly declined to stand for re-election to Congress. My Philadelphia days were over. My ambitions were dashed.

Montpelier was large and prosperous and beautiful. Jemmy's parents and siblings welcomed me with open arms, and I responded in kind. We had a loving relationship all our lives. Throughout John Adams's presidency, we remained in Virginia.[4] Jemmy was happy

[4]**ABIGAIL ADAMS**
I don't remember if I had ever met Mrs. Madison, but we certainly heard glowing reports of her charms.

there and contented himself with overseeing construction projects and carrying on a voluminous and scholarly correspondence with all the important men in the country. All he asked of me was that I be kind to his family (an easy request, since I loved them as my own), to try to "love him a little" (which I grew to do in abundance) and to "be happy."

Ah. That was a problem. I was bored at Montpelier. I was neither scholarly nor brilliant. Writing letters did not take the place of the graceful and witty environs of Philadelphia society. But the Quaker girl never died within Mrs. Madison, so I accepted it as God's will that I be grateful for all the bounty I had received.

Then the letter came from Mr. Jefferson, who had just been elected president. "Come to Washington City at earliest haste and be my Secretary of State," he begged my husband. "I cannot serve effectively without your wise counsel." Jemmy, of course, was loath to refuse his good friend, and I was walking on air! The new Capital City! Exciting and important people! We started our journey immediately.

Soon after our arrival, Mr. J. asked me to tea. "As you know, Dolley, I am a widower and so is Vice President Burr," he began. "Both my daughters have young families to attend. They cannot always be here. Will you help with our social obligations?" Would I? Do birds fly? Do fish swim? I began at once, reviewing the various guest lists and diplomatic protocol. I took complete inventory of the silver, plate and linens, and ordered what was needed. I visited every shop and stall in the area, since I believed it would be good politics for Mr. J. to distribute government business fairly. And, of course, I worked closely with "French John," the chef and maitre d' that President Jefferson had brought from Paris. It was Mr. J. by the way, who introduced ice cream to the country. I only ate it, loved it, and served it often to our guests.

Hosting for the President was a delight! I loved people. I truly did. Being surrounded by them was always my pleasure. President Jefferson preferred small, intimate, very democratic groups, unlike the big formal affairs of the European courts. This suited me as well, but when my Jemmy was elected president eight years later, we expanded commensurate with the growth and prominence of our nation.[5] I retained the same democratic style, but we invited far more people!

> [5]**ELIZABETH MONROE**
> *I only hosted at the large state banquets. Smaller dinners were for "men only" during the Monroe years.*

It was customary then to allow all well behaved, properly dressed people to "stop at the President's House." I encouraged it, and made certain that all distinguished visitors to Washington City received invitations to my next levee or dinner party. There were seldom less than two dozen at dinner every night. I am not certain that this pleased my husband, who was, by nature, very reticent in company. But he knew it made me happy, and that was his fondest wish. It was also very good for politics, since everyone wanted to be invited to Mrs. Madison's soirees.[6]

> **[6]LOU HOOVER**
> *By the time we were in the House, it had become too unwieldy—and posed serious security problems. We ended all "open houses."*

There were good reasons why my parties were popular. First, no one wished "to offend Mrs. Madison" by rude behavior, thus even the most politically opposite notables took care to be cordial in our "home." Second, I made certain that everyone was introduced to a suitable companion for conversation. And third, I made sure to introduce plenty of subjects for discourse. I made it a habit of carrying a book with me, since it was bound to attract comment and start conversation. And I always had snuff available to share with our guests.[7]

> **[7]GRACE COOLIDGE**
> *It is always helpful to a shy man if his wife is outgoing and friendly.*

Jemmy had planned to retire after a single term. He was past sixty by then, and wanted to return to Montpelier. He also did not wish to wage war with England, and events were leading in that direction. But there was no one else of sufficient stature to replace him. Young Messrs. Clay and Calhoun and their friends promised their strong support if we declared for war…so Jemmy was again President. And we went to war.

It was a foolish war. We were ill-equipped and ill-trained. Our standing army numbered only a few thousand. Our equipment—and generals—were relics from forty years prior. It went badly for us. Word came that the British were scarcely fifty miles from Washington City. Finally, my dear, sweet, unwarlike Jemmy mounted his horse and rode off to the front to lead the Army in battle.[8] He was Commander-in-Chief, and believed it to be his duty. He instructed me to wait until I received further word from him.

> **[8]ELIZABETH MONROE**
> *My James handled the duties as both Secretary of State and War. I feared for his life, since he also rode into battle.*

Twenty had been invited for luncheon that day; places had been set at the table. Our meal had been prepared. But all morning, messengers arrived expressing "regrets" from our guests, and urging me to leave at once. One friend even sent a horse and carriage for my convenience. But I waited as I was told. I packed all the important state papers and the Great Seal, and some of our best silver, and was ready to leave at a moment's notice. What else should I take? When I spied the large portrait of President Washington in the

[9]**HILLARY RODHAM CLINTON**
I don't think the portrait has ever again been moved from its place in the East Room. It's the most valuable—and popular—painting in the White House.

East Room, I insisted that it be saved from possible harm. George Washington had been so dear to both of us and my poor husband was trying valiantly to fill those illustrious shoes. I believed the General's portrait would watch over us and bring us good fortune. "French John" cut the canvas from the frame; I rolled it up and put it in my satchel. When word finally came instructing me to leave, the portrait was in my hand.[9]

The President's House was put to the torch later that day. Providence—or George Washington—must have been watching over us. Within hours there was a torrential rainstorm which kept the mansion from total destruction.

That storm also caused my driver to lose his way in the Maryland woods. Tired and drenched, we finally arrived at a small tavern. My coachman begged the woman to "provide some shelter for his Lady." She invited me in, gave me hot coffee and a warm place by the fire. We chatted amiably for nearly an hour, and finally she asked my name. When I told her who I was, she stood up abruptly and said, "No disrespect, Madam, but *your* husband has *me* husband out fightin' instead of farmin', and I'll not be givin' ye the hospitality of me house!" And she turned me out again. I was soaking wet, but I was laughing! Obviously, I was not popular with everyone! When I was able to return to Washington City, I made it a point to have some sweetmeats sent to her.

It took nearly four years to repair the President's Mansion, complete with a coat of white paint. There were many people who clamored to move the capital farther inland for safety, but Jemmy insisted on rebuilding Washington City as a point of honor. For the rest of his term, we lived in a borrowed house, and resumed all our duties, including hospitable entertainment, albeit on a smaller scale.

It was toward the end of Jemmy's second term that my troubles began, and I will commence words that would have never crossed my lips in my lifetime: My dearly beloved son caused great grief to me and to my husband. I must take full responsibility. Recalling the strictness of my own youth, I spoiled Payne terribly. He was both indulged and sheltered, and consequently never learned responsibility.[10] Jemmy tried to administer discipline, but it was a half-hearted effort, since he knew that

[10]**ELEANOR ROOSEVELT**
Spoiled children become spoiled adults. I have always believed that responsibility must be learned in childhood.

punishing him would sadden me. I should have been more willing to accept that momentary sadness.

When Payne proved to be a poor scholar and unresponsive to tutoring, Jemmy arranged for him to attend his old college in Princeton, New Jersey. He thought that a "peer environment" might be more to Payne's liking and would make him more receptive to learning. Unfortunately, it was very much to his liking, but all Payne learned was to acquire a taste for drink, gambling and wenching.

When Jemmy was President, he remembered the fine educational opportunities John Quincy Adams had experienced abroad. Young Mr. Adams was on his way to becoming one of the finest diplomatic representatives the country would ever have, and was well regarded by nearly everyone. So Jemmy sent Payne to serve secretary to one of our delegations, thinking the experience would be beneficial. But Europeans only understood monarchies and further indulged Payne's bad habits by extending him credit "suitable for an American Prince." Unbeknownst to me, Jemmy paid tens of thousands of dollars throughout his life to keep my son from debtors' prison—or worse. All efforts to find him gainful employment or a suitable marriage failed. Payne never reformed.[11] Little by little, our property was sold to cover Payne's excesses.

> [11]**SARAH POLK**
> *Poor Mrs. Madison! To her dying day, she struggled to try to help her son. He was such a wastrel!*

James Madison was eighty-five when he died, and his last twenty years were spent in scholarly retirement. Our entertaining was limited, which usually happens when old friends pass away. I cannot say those were happy years. He worked ceaselessly editing and annotating his papers on the Constitution, and I stepped into the role of secretary, my poor spelling and penmanship notwithstanding. When he died, I had little more than memories and a sworn trust to see that Mr. Madison's papers were preserved for all time.

I finally sold Montpelier. I could barely pay the taxes. I could no longer maintain the slaves who had become like family to me. It had become my own Elba in the middle of nowhere. After visiting friends in Washington, I realized how much I loved that city with its teeming activity. I took my few belongings, two elderly slaves who absolutely refused to leave me (and who had nowhere else to go) and moved there.[12]

> [12]**LOUISA ADAMS**
> *I cannot fathom why Congress did not leap at the chance to acquire such a prize. My husband said that Congress was never a body high in foresight.*

My efforts to convince Congress to purchase the Madison documents took years. When the purchase was finally effected, it was done in such a way as to grant me a modest annuity so that my son could not touch it. I suppose it was for the best.

Happily for me, Washingtonians remembered me with affection. I was invited everywhere.[13] And once again, I opened my doors to everyone, even though I was frequently dependent on others to help me provide the necessary hospitality. God was kind in my old age (and I lived to be past eighty), and provided me with the greatest of all blessings: passable health, a sound mind to the end, and the warmth and good will of my many dear friends.

[13]**LOUISA ADAMS**
We were close with Mrs. Madison in her elder years. She would come by regularly to play whist with us. My personal affection and regard for her is no surprise, but I was amazed (and somewhat envious) of the affection and regard John Quincy had for her. He delighted in her company!

ELIZABETH KORTRIGHT MONROE
1768-1830
First Lady: 1817-1825

I am the very first of the "forgettable" Ladies, probably because I was intensely disliked.[1] My predecessors are well known in the pantheon of American History. Following a popular or esteemed predecessor is a difficult task for both men and women. I had the fortune—or misfortune—to succeed Dolley Madison.[3] All the more reason that I leapt at the opportunity to write my own chapter.

> [1]**MARY LINCOLN**
> *I doubt any First Lady was as disliked as I was.*[2]

> [2]**ROSALYNN CARTER**
> *I don't think I would win any great popularity contests, either.*

I was born and raised in New York. My father was a British Officer who, following the French & Indian War, made his home in America. We became part of a prosperous, upper class society inclined toward the Tories, although we were never disloyal to the American cause. I was only a child then, so I had little personal recollection on the subject.

> [3]**BESS TRUMAN**
> *I succeeded Eleanor Roosevelt. I admired her enormously, but I was nothing like her, nor did I wish to be.*

When I met and married James Monroe after the Revolutionary War, I was barely seventeen. He had been a dashing lieutenant, serving with General Washington himself, and I was enchanted by his charm and reputation as a soldier and scout. He was enchanted by my education and social graces. I was also considered comely and handsomely dowered. Despite my father's reservations about Mr. Monroe's prospects, my new husband had some excellent recommendations in his favor: He had studied law at the College of William and Mary; he was an intimate friend of both Mr. Madison and Mr. Jefferson, and he had the esteem and affection of General, and soon-to-be President, George Washington. A successful political career was practically guaranteed.

It was President Washington who saw promise in young Congressman Monroe, and dispatched him to France as our Minister. It was an exciting and important position and a great honor for James to follow in the illustrious footsteps of Thomas Jefferson, who he revered as a father. Our tenure in France coincided with the perilous times of the French Revolution. They called it the Reign of Terror, and indeed it was terrible. Rule by mob.

Leaders one day, victims the next. Nobody was safe. Every day, hundreds of people—men *and* women *and* children were taken to the guillotine. Those were dangerous times for everyone.

Our dear friend, the Marquis deLafayette, had been captured and held prisoner in Austria. James and the Marquis were close in age. They had met during the Battle of Trenton and had become close and indeed, lifelong friends. The General...President Washington...was deeply concerned. He loved Lafayette like a son. Our diplomatic instructions were extremely delicate. President Washington could not invoke any pressure without incurring foreign enmities.

All we could do was pray for the Marquis' safety. Then his wife was arrested. She was stripped of everything but the clothes on her back and thrust into a damp, dank prison, on the list to be guillotined.

"Let me go to her," I said to James. "Surely the French people must know the Lafayette family is especially dear to American hearts." "It's much too dangerous," he said. "Besides, you're not well."[4] I had occasional "spells."

But I said no. I said we must try to do something. "Surely the French people would not harm the wife of the American Minister," I insisted. So James found a carriage for me. (Ours had been confiscated some time before by the mob.) He affixed the Great Seal of the United States of America on the door, so the rabble would not mistake me for French nobility.

I was petrified. The filthy and uncouth mob spat on my carriage and shouted French obscenities.

---

[4]BETTY FORD

Little is known about Elizabeth Monroe's health, except that she suffered from some "unknown" problems. So-called "women's problems" were common then, and became a catchall for a wide range of undiagnosed ailments, usually some form of depression. There was talk that she had epilepsy, like Ida McKinley, only not as severe. But then again, it was fashionable for a woman to be "unwell" in those days. It released them from having to do anything they didn't want to do.[5]

[5]ROSALYNN CARTER

Betty is right about the "fashion" of being an invalid in the 19th century. Elizabeth Barrett Browning became a role model for an entire generation. I don't think anyone today wants to "languish," but a hundred and fifty years ago, women loved to put on a wan smile and "suffer." What a waste.

My French was fluent. I understood every word. But I persevered despite my fear, and when I arrived at the prison, I announced that "the wife of the American Minister was there to visit Madame deLafayette." I believe the dear lady nearly fainted when *I* entered that putrid cell. She was certain she was being called to her execution. In a voice loud enough to be heard by the guards, I greeted her and said how glad we were—*and especially President Washington*—that she seemed in passable health. I also added *all* the American people—*and especially President Washington*—were praying for her safe deliverance. I brought her some clean clothing and fresh bread. As I took my leave, I said I would visit again the next day, and bring her some fruit.

Providence, or perhaps the need for American political friendship, prevailed. The following day Madame deLafayette was released. Perhaps I helped save her life.

It just so happens, I was eminently suitable to be the wife of the American Minister.[6] I was a Lady of Fashion, just like Mrs. Madison. I was also better looking. But I was more reserved by nature, and more suited to European manners. My upbringing was patrician; after all, my father had been a British officer. I easily adapted to the conventions of polite European society, which, I admit, appealed to me far more than the democratic lack of decorum of my fledgling country. I suppose there were many of my countrymen who disapproved of my "fashion."

> **[6]LOUISA ADAMS**
> *I was also eminently suitable, having been born and raised in Europe, speaking several languages and understanding protocol. But we weren't rich and European diplomats were all independently wealthy to the extreme.*

I was on the tall side, and slender. Like Mrs. Kennedy. I had a figure modern women admire. I wore the "empire" style gowns, with high waists and low bosoms, which flattered me. Unfortunately, matrons of my day tended toward plumpness. That style was, needless to say, less becoming to them. But then again, Mrs. Kennedy wore what became her and did not worry over her "plumper" sisters either.[7]

> **[7]JACQUELINE KENNEDY**
> *No. I never worried about what other people wore.*

I also rouged. You would not believe the talk! Cosmetics? Why only the French could have invented—or approved—of that! Only a woman of questionable character would stoop to wearing cosmetics, they said.[8] But in Paris, the loveliest and most admired ladies added that "certain touch."

> **[8]DOLLEY MADISON**
> *When the Monroes returned from Paris, Elizabeth taught me to use rouge. I didn't see anything wrong in a lady wishing to add a little blush to her cheek, especially as she grew older. I snuffed, too. It was a common practice. I kept two handkerchiefs with me. A delicate lace one for blotting, and a big, checkered gingham one for serious blowing. Snuff felt good!*

After all, is it a crime to try to maintain your youthful looks? Never! So I rouged. So did my daughters. Queen Hortense of Holland, (Napoleon's step-daughter and sister-in-law in that family of convoluted connexions) had been an intimate school friend of my daughters. She rouged.

> [9]**NANCY REAGAN**
> *Shows you how a little makeup and dim lighting can work wonders!*

One of the few compliments I heard during my reign as First Lady, was that "Mrs. Monroe looks very much younger than her years." By the time I became a First Lady, I was nearly fifty. Most women guessed my age to be more like thirty-five.[9] They were astounded to learn that I had grown daughters and a grandchild!

Following Mrs. Madison (whom I had known and liked for decades), I doubted that anyone could match her style and popularity. I had spent too many years in Europe. I had been surrounded by the social etiquette of a formal aristocracy. I enjoyed it. Democratic customs repelled me. I believed that the President of the United States was equal in status to European crowned heads. Thus I was equal in position to their consorts. I did not see my role as First Lady as democratically as Dolley, much as I liked her.

> [10]**LOU HOOVER**
> *I agree with Mrs. Monroe. I was not inclined, nor was Mr. Hoover, to pay calls. People came to us. We simply did not dine out.*

When I became First Lady, I believed it was unnecessary to return calls to women of lesser rank.[10] And as First Lady, *everyone* was of lesser rank. Because my health was not robust, I was able to plead infirmity, and dispatch my two daughters in my place. Needless to say, this did not please the fledgling Washington "Society." For some reason, people who lived permanently in the Capital City believed they had social equality with the President. They did not. Nor did Cabinet Wives. They enjoyed putting on their unwarranted airs. Succeeding Ladies also had their headaches with the "cave dwellers," which these society dames came to be called.

> **RACHEL JACKSON**
> *It was that la-di-da attitude of Washington City that so terrified and offended me. I visited there once during the Monroe years and vowed never to return. It was a heathen society through and through.*

> **DOLLEY MADISON**
> *Washington's "aristocratic" women made many cruel and condescending remarks about Rachel, albeit with some truth. She was poorly suited to society, and it was probably a blessing that she died when she did. She would have been eaten alive.*

My daughters had been raised in Paris since early childhood. They were on cordial terms with Kings and Queens, and, of course the Imperial Bonaparte family. They knew what was proper and what was improper for our position. Americans considered it monarchial. My girls were perceived as haughty. Since I would not return calls, no one called on me; and since they did not like my daughters, no one called on them, either. That was satisfactory to us. When my younger daughter was married in the White House, I kept the invitation list to a mere fifty close friends and family. If the "cave dwellers" thought they would be invited to a big social event they would be sadly disappointed. Why should they be invited when they treated us so disrespectfully?

They never forgave us. Presidential entertainment during the Monroe administration was a "man's affair." I was present on rare occasion, when it was absolutely demanded, and my daughters would occasionally do the honors, but there was no flurry of satin in the East Room.

LOUISA ADAMS
I was slender and attractive and the wife of the Secretary of State. I was also the daughter-in-law of a former President. Elizabeth Monroe's airs were unwarranted and intolerable. I didn't make as much fuss over it as did some of the other Matrons, but I had little sympathy for her. I also picked up a good deal of the slack during the social season. We entertained often.

MARGARET TAYLOR
I was a frontier wife for nigh forty years. I warn't about to change. I stayed in and let my daughter handle the fol-de-rol.

ABIGAIL FILLMORE
I wasn't about to be dissected by Washington's "elite" either, especially since we achieved our position by "default." Like Lady Washington, I seldom ventured out.

James was the last of an era that was quickly passing. He wore knee breeches and silk stockings long after men had turned to trousers. I suppose you could say that the Monroes "resisted change." But the Monroes also believed that nothing needed changing. We believed that good taste is always good taste. We believed that quality is always quality. We believed that if something is beautiful and fine in one year, it will be beautiful and fine the next. We also believed that Ladies ("First" or otherwise) had no business meddling with politics.

> **[11]LOUISA ADAMS**
> *It bears Monroe's name, but it has my husband's imprint all over it.*

I took little interest in affairs of state and can venture absolutely NO insight into the doctrine that bears my husband's name.[11] I am not proud of it. I am not ashamed of it. I like to think that I behaved in a manner appropriate to our position. If history votes me "nay," then sobeit.

We came to the President's Mansion in 1816, and the building still bore the scars from the War of 1812 when it was badly burned. We replaced the carpeting and draperies, and Mr. Madison had authorized the white paint exterior that forever gave the Mansion its name. But traditionally, the incoming President brought his own furniture—even for the public rooms. We ordered many fine pieces from France. Since it exceeded the amount Congress had authorized, we willingly paid it from our own purse.[12] We did not realize at the time that we would end our days in the same penury as Mr. Jefferson and Mr. Madison. The value of land fluctuated drastically from year to year, and most of our income was tied to our property. Our last years were impoverished and sorrowful.

> **[12]JACQUELINE KENNEDY**
> *One of the contributions of the Monroes was their excellent taste in furnishings. I discovered a few pieces when we restored the mansion in the early '60s. And there is a magnificent "Monroe" plateau centerpiece that has been used at White House dinners for nearly two hundred years!*

Historians named the Monroe Administration the "Era of Good Feeling," but whilst there may have been good feeling in general about the country and the direction in which it was going, there was little good feeling about the female Monroes in the White House.

LOUISA JOHNSON ADAMS
1775-1852
First Lady: 1825-1829

I remember exactly when I stopped trying to love my husband.[1] John Quincy Adams and I had been married for several years, and I did my best, my truly best, to be a good, dutiful and loving wife. And I loved him, difficult man that he was. But in 1809, the line was crossed.

> [1]**HILLARY RODHAM CLINTON**
> *Most women can pinpoint that moment exactly, if, of course, there is "that" moment.*

He came home one day and announced, "Madam, President Madison has just appointed me Minister Plenipotentiary to Russia." I was thrilled! A full and complete diplomatic pouch for a man who was without doubt the best suited and best qualified for the office! He continued, "We leave in a fortnight for St. Petersburg." I was astounded. A major change like that to be undertaken in only two weeks! "Sir," I protested, "it will require at least a month or more to prepare for such a monumental move!" Our third son was barely two, and only recently weaned. "It has already been arranged," he said. "George and Johnny will stay with the family in Braintree. You'll take the baby, of course. And your niece may accompany us as your companion and to and help with the lad." A small comfort.

"I cannot leave my boys with relatives," I said. "George is barely eleven. A child! And Johnny just two years younger. They need their mother." I pleaded with my husband on my knees. "I will stay behind with the children," I offered. "You can go on alone, and we will all join you in a few months." "You will accompany me with the baby," pronounced Mr. Adams. And, if you knew Mr. Adams, his pronouncements were inviolate.

It had all been arranged. We would sail in two weeks. Me, my niece, and the baby. The older boys would stay in Braintree with relatives. It did not matter that I cried; that I begged; that I grew ill over the prospect. None of it mattered. I begged my father-in-law, dear Mr. Adams Senior, to intercede. He consoled me, kind old gentleman that he was, but there was no intercession. I pleaded my case to my mother-in-law, Abigail. She insisted that my place was with my husband, and that she and Mr. Adams Senior would be keeping a close watch on the boys, and I shouldn't worry.

> **ABIGAIL ADAMS**
> *A woman's place is with her husband.*
> *I was separated from mine for so long.*
> *Truly, I would have given anything for*
> *some of those years back with my*
> *dear, dear John.*

What mother wouldn't worry about leaving two small boys with relatives! This was not for a week or two! This was leaving them for…it turned out to be five years till I next saw them. By then, they were half-grown men whom I barely recognized.

Mr. Adams cared little about me or my wishes.[2] He made all the decisions and I counted for naught. The day we sailed was the day I stopped trying to love my husband.

I went to St. Petersburg and tried my best to be a good wife to the Minister Plenipotentiary but my heart was stone. It was not easy to adjust. The Minister's salary, meager at best, was delayed by inevitably long transport, and the Adamses were not wealthy. Our means were strained. It was very difficult for us to maintain our numerous diplomatic social duties amongst the nobility of Europe with their deep pockets. There were even occasions I did not accompany my husband because I lacked the appropriate dress required by the Imperial Russian Court. My health began to fail, probably from my dozen miscarriages and stillborn children. Rheumatism set in from the harsh Russian weather.[3] And I have a baby daughter—our last child—who will forever lie beneath Russian soil.

It didn't start out like that. Dear me, no. My engagement to John Quincy Adams was a brilliant match, according to all who knew us. My father, a prosperous Maryland merchant, had married and lived in England for many years. I was born in London and educated in France. I played the harp and the harpsichord, spoke several languages, and wrote tolerable poetry. When I met young Mr. Adams, I was only seventeen. He, on the other hand, was an experienced diplomat, who had been given substantial responsibilities by President Washington. *And* he was the son of the Vice President of the United States, besides. Oh it was a brilliant match! I suppose I might have

> [2]**PAT NIXON**
> *I don't doubt that Dick had some regard for my wishes. But he probably decided that his wishes were more important than mine. This is "man." I doubt there is a Lady who didn't sublimate her own wishes to her husband's.*

> [3]**BETTY FORD**
> *Rheumatism, childbirths and lack of medical knowledge notwithstanding, several of our early Ladies used poor health as a crutch to support their depressed state. Repression usually causes depression.*

suspected that it would be less than ideal from the beginning, but I was so young and inexperienced. Our courtship...no, Mr. Adams' courtship...was lukewarm to say the least.[4] Oh, he had definitely proposed to me, and I, being very impressionable, was thrilled! Then he was dispatched to Holland, and I wrote nearly every day, as was the expected custom. He wrote occasionally, with uncommonly restrained affection.

> **[4]LUCRETIA GARFIELD**
> *It reminds me of the tepid courtship between James and me. Our "love letters" were weather and health reports. Nothing I could not share with the town newspaper.*

On our wedding day some two years later, my father confided to the new bridegroom that he had suffered serious financial reverses, and was desperately trying to avoid total ruin. The anticipated munificent dowry was non-existent. I did not learn of that matter for quite some time, but throughout our entire married life, I often wondered if I did not bear the brunt of Mr. Adams' disappointment in my father's changed status.[5]

> **[5]ABIGAIL ADAMS**
> *Nonsense. John Quincy was not raised to place undue importance on financial status. As a matter of fact, the Adams family did not become financially independent until my grandson Charles Francis married the daughter of a wealthy Boston businessman.*

It was not that my husband was without passion, to wit my many miscarriages, which seemed to affect him even more than they affected me. Every time I thought he was devoid of feeling, he would amaze me by the depth of his suffering every time we lost a baby. I suppose Mr. Adams did feel strongly about some things. Unfortunately, none of them pertained to me. Or our family. Unless, of course, they were contrary to *his* wishes.

As to my older boys, George and John: I could never forgive either Mr. Adams or myself for their eventual disappointing lives.[6] I have no doubt that had I been there during those crucial years, providing loving maternal guidance, they would have lived fruitful, and certainly longer, lives. My husband was a harsh, demanding father, who seemed to have inherited his mother's great talent for scolding, chiding, criticizing, setting impossible standards and general dissatisfaction with everything and

> **[6]ABIGAIL ADAMS**
> *Pish-tosh! I raised my children, buried a few myself, and had disappointments like everyone else. We do the best we can, blame only the capriciousness of fortune, and accept God's will. I always felt that my son Johnny deserved a strong New England wife, rather than a soft, foreign-born delicate thing.*

everyone. Oh yes, the boys would have fared far better under my tutelage,

41

[7]**ELLEN WILSON**
Men are not inclined to change. It is foolish to expect it.[8]

[8]**PAT NIXON**
Ellen is right. Dick Nixon never really changed either. Oh, he modified some of his views. He was certainly capable of growth. But he never grew or modified where I was concerned. I hated political life. I would have been far happier as a simple housewife and mother, with a regular bridge club—like Mrs. Truman.

[9]**NANCY REAGAN**
Louisa's adventure would make a terrific screenplay. I can think of a half-dozen actresses who would give their eye-teeth to play the role!

[10]**LOU HOOVER**
We were stranded in the middle of China during the Boxer Rebellion. But while everyone has heard of Napoleon, the Boxers have become a footnote to history.

had it been permitted. My George turned to drink, became ill and died by his own hand. My John also succumbed to the Demon Rum. And nothing, *absolutely nothing*, ever changed John Quincy Adams from the bitter, self-righteous, cantankerous, difficult man he was.[7] Nothing.

But I mustn't devote my chapter to complaint. I should take advantage of my turn to tell you of *my* Great Adventure.[9]

In 1815, whilst we were in St. Petersburg, Mr. Adams received word that he was to be Chief Negotiator for the treaty to conclude the War of 1812. This was an extremely important and prestigious assignment. He was instructed to leave immediately. "Pack up the household, sell whatever is not essential, and meet me in Paris," he told me. That was more responsibility than I had ever had! I purchased a carriage and engaged suitable (or at least what I thought was suitable) servants. The Tsar had taken a liking to our family, and was helpful. He even purchased a few of our personal items, "for souvenirs and affection," he claimed. Little Charles, who was six or seven by then, my niece, two servants, and I set out unescorted across war-torn Europe. It was a perilous journey during the best of times. These were not the best of times. The Napoleonic Wars had the entire continent aflame for a dozen or more years.[10]

My carriage was poorly constructed and broke down with depressing regularity (although it was the best to be had in all of Russia, according to the Tsar). The coachman was inordinately fond of his vodka, and eventually stranded us. A lad we hired to guide us along the way stole our horses and fled in the night. And the roads, where there were roads, were mired in mud from the spring thaw. Many nights we slept in the carriage, since we found no accommodations, suitable or not. Everyone in our small party looked to me for direction. I did the best I could, seeing as how I had never been trained to make a decision in my entire life other than to wear the blue silk or the green velvet.

I learned how crucial language was. I could speak some Russian. I was also reasonably fluent in German, and my French was as flawless as my English. I learned to read a map, to bargain with innkeepers and to bribe whoever could provide needed services. And I learned to mask my fears, no mean accomplishment, since I had many.

It was an astounding six-week trek until we finally reached the French border and learned that Napoleon had just escaped from Elba. He had started marching toward Paris with a handful of followers. Hundreds of soldiers joined him at each town along the way. Rumors abounded. A new army was being formed. The King of France had fled rather than submit to the vengeance of the Bonapartists. Every stranger was suspected of treason from one side or another. I could not even claim the weakness of my sex; French women had always been involved in politics.

Little Charles thought it was a great adventure! What seven-year-old wouldn't! My niece was frightened to death, as were the coachman and servants. My Russian-made carriage was an easy target for the mob, since Russia, at that time, was allied with England and Prussia as an enemy of France. "They will kill us!" my servants cried. They crossed themselves and muttered Russian phrases I did not understand. But thank God my French was fluent, and I bore a slight resemblance to one of the Emperor's nieces. I placed my little Charles' soldier's hat upon my own head and waved his toy sword out the window, shouting, "Vive L'Empereur! Vive L'Empereur!" Thus we were allowed to pass unharmed.

When Mr. Adams met us in Paris, he was totally amazed at my story. He believed me, of course, but I don't believe he *ever* realized the extent or the serious danger of our ordeal.

Not long thereafter, James Monroe was elected president, and appointed Mr. Adams Secretary of State. I doubt there was anyone more qualified or who distinguished himself more notably in that position. Those were mostly happy times for us. We lived in Washington City, which we both loved far better than New England. I was in a position to entertain, which I did often, since Mrs. Monroe declined to do the honors. And I had my two older sons back. George and John, however, were causing us anguish with their want of judgement and industry. Mr. Adams' harsh requirements for their behavior and accomplishments did not help. He was so much his mother's son.[10] If I had spent those crucial

> [10]**ABIGAIL ADAMS**
> *Stop blaming me for everything!*

years supervising their deportment, perhaps their tragic ends.....

My George, ill from the effects of constant drink, fell overboard on a boat carrying him to Washington City and drowned. I desperately wanted to believe it was an accident. His intemperance and despair, however, were remarked upon by many of the other passengers. I fear that George preferred death to his father's harsh disapproval. John was also showing the same signs of dissipation as his elder brother.[11] I know that my husband felt George's death deeply, although he was wont to show his emotions, but I firmly believe that his obvious disappointment hastened their decline. George's death only served to drive the wedge further and further between Mr. Adams and myself. And it also made him even more inward.

> [11]**ABIGAIL ADAMS**
> *It was in the blood. My sons Thomas and Charles succumbed to drink. As did my own brother.*

> [12]**BETTY FORD**
> *In today's vernacular, people would say that Louisa had a nervous breakdown. Between the deaths of her sons, her "cranky" husband and no real outlet for all her talents...plus her hormones playing games...it's no wonder. "That time of life" can be very difficult.*

> [13]**PAT NIXON**
> *John Quincy Adams' diaries have been edited and made public. In volume after volume, written in his very small handwriting, there is practically no mention whatsoever of Louisa, and they were married for more than fifty years! Dick Nixon mentioned me very little in all his writings. And we were married for more than forty years. Some wives just don't count.*

The Adams presidency was troubled, and my cranky husband became even crankier. I, on the other hand...let us say that it was the time in my life when great changes occur, and I suffered the consequences.[12] I found myself deeply depressed by George's death. There was a feeling of unutterable loneliness. Despite our usual retinue of relatives and long-term "houseguests," I had no one close to me. Not even in spirit. My husband's cantankerous behavior opened few vistas for friendships, and I was choked by his constraints on my activities. He shared nothing with me. Not his dreams, not his sorrows. Not even his daily activities. Whatever he had to share was confided only to his diary.[13]

So I kept to myself a great deal, nursing my numerous infirmities, with only my harp and harpsichord for consolation. I developed a fondness for French chocolates and my once slim figure grew stout. I wrote of my escapade in Napoleonic Europe, and made it into a little play called *The Adventures of a Nobody*. And I was indeed a nobody.

But fate sometimes takes a whimsical turn. After my husband's term and subsequent ignominious defeat by General Jackson, we returned to Braintree to pick up whatever was left of our old life. There was not much. We had moved from Massachusetts so many years before. Our ties there were strained, and neither of us cared for rural New England after so many years in the glamorous capitals of the world. Mr. Adams positively *dreaded* the thought of practicing law. He disliked it intensely. He planned to devote his remaining years to literary efforts—his first and only true love.

But some of the prominent men in Boston suggested that Mr. Adams represent them in Congress.[14] I was appalled! A former president holding a common seat in Congress? I insisted it would be beneath his dignity. But Mr. Adams (who never listened to me anyway) was indeed the wiser. "Madam," he said, "it is a singular honor to have the respect and trust of our neighbors. How could it ever be beneath anyone's dignity to represent his fellow citizens?"

> [14]**ELIZA JOHNSON**
> *The greatest honor of Andrew Johnson's life was his election to the Senate after his Presidency. I felt it was a complete vindication of all the turmoil durin' his term.*

So we took a house in Washington City again, and spent most of the year there. It was much livelier, and I had friends. John Quincy Adams served in Congress for sixteen years, and I even began to enjoy my advancing age. My husband became less cranky with me. Perhaps we finally grew together after fifty years of a tumultuous marriage. More likely it was just habit.

Actually, it was in my elder years that my husband finally found some use for me. Thousands of letters and petitions were sent to him; far more than he, with his failing vision, could catalogue. So I was dispatched to read them and sort them and prepare them for his reply. I was delighted to help. Even more, I was thrilled to play my very small part in the growing anti-slavery movement. While neither of us were true abolitionists (fanaticism was alien to both our natures), we both abhorred slavery and considered it a moral wrong. And we *both* maintained active correspondence with many of the leading figures in that vital movement. People actually wrote to *me*, and sought *my* views. Imagine.

John Quincy Adams died at his desk in Congress.[15] I was overwhelmed at the respect and devotion that the nation showered on him in death. It was far more than he

> [15]**BESS TRUMAN**
> *It is not unusual for history to give a dead President the recognition and respect he deserves. Harry was definitely NOT popular or respected while he served. It is only history that has judged him accurately.*

> [16]**ABIGAIL FILLMORE**
> *I remember the outpouring of affection and respect when Louisa Adams died. It was certainly more than they paid to me when I died scarcely a year later.*

had ever have achieved in life. And when I finally met my reward a few years later, I was astounded at the great show of respect and admiration that the people gave this "nobody."[16]

Oh, and one more thing. When my son Charles began to edit his grandmother's letters for publication, I began to find myself envious of Abigail. I had always respected her intelligence and insights. Now I found myself envious of the freedom of thought and expression that she was so fortunate to have had nurtured by her husband. It allowed her fine mind to soar. And of course, I always envied his undying affection for her.

Abigail Adams was never unkind to me, at least never *deliberately* unkind. But she was overbearing, opinionated to a fault, insistent on plying her grown children with unsolicited advice, meddlesome, demanding and generally unaffectionate. I always thought that much of my husband's critical and unforgiving behavior was due to his inability to please his mother. And so he became her instead.

> **ABIGAIL ADAMS**
> *Oh for heaven's sake,*
> *Louisa, enough is enough.*

It is my chapter. I can say whatever I please.

*RACHEL DONELSON ROBARDS JACKSON
1767-1828

If'n it were m'own choice, I would never lift pen to paper for this volume. I have no wish to be in public. But I know it would please the Gen'ral to have me included, thus I am loath to refuse.

When I was seventeen, I married a man named Lewis Robards. My widowed mother knew his kin, and

thought it would be a good match. But Lewis Robards was a violent, jealous and abusive man. If'n I so much as nodded to the parson, or bid the grocer good-day, he would accuse me of the most vile things. There warn't ever any cause. I was a Godfearin' woman all m'life. I tried to be a good wife, I did. But Lewis Robards brought me back to my mother's house in disgrace. Said he would no longer live with me.

My mother, a-course, took me in. She ran a boardin' house and needed the help anyways. My brothers and sisters—I had plenty of 'em—were very kind to me. The Donelsons (that's me) were well respected in western Tennessee. Poor, we were, but well respected. There warn't any blab about m'unhappy situation with Lewis Robards.

Then I met Andrew Jackson. He was a tall and lanky young lawyer who was boardin' with us. He was kind to me, and it would be sinful to deny that I found him agreeable company. But b'fore the Almighty, nothin' but the most proper friendship ever passed betwixt us. Then Lewis Robards had a change o'heart, and came to take me back. I was agreeable, since I was his lawful wife and my rightful place was with him. But he became enraged at what he thought were Mr. Jackson's "attentions." I swore that everythin' was proper. So did Mr. Jackson. Even my mother and brothers took an oath that our conduct was above reproach. But m'husband called me terrible names and rode off in anger. Mr. Jackson would-a challenged him then and there. He had a temper, too, y'know. But Lewis Robards vowed he would be done with me, and I never seen 'im again.

It was troublin' for me. In those days wives stayed with husbands no matter what. And b'lieve me, there was many a wife like me who suffered at the hands of a mean man. It was pitiful. Anyways, my mother suggested I go 'way for a spell, and let the talk die down. We had kin in Natchez, and my brother and some-a his friends offered to 'scort me down river. Mr. Jackson was in the 'scortin' party. His conduct was completely proper, like the true gentleman he always was. But by the time we reached Natchez, our friendship had begun to deepen. We read in some Tennessee newspapers there, that Lewis Robards had been granted a divorce from Rachel Donelson Robards for reasons-a desertion. Thus I was free. Andrew Jackson and I were married—a union I never regretted.

Three years later, we learned that the report about the divorce was wrong. Lewis Robards had only filed papers back then, declarin' his *intention* to divorce me. The actual divorce had not been granted at that time. I warn't smart enough to understand the legal words in those papers, and since divorces were so rare, 'specially in our neck o' the woods, even a lawyer like Mr. Jackson could easily miscalculate. The upshot was it appeared like Mr. Jackson and I had been livin' in a sinful way—even though we truly believed our marriage was legal and bindin'. A-course we were re-married at once.[1]

> [1]**FLORENCE HARDING**
> *Sex, sex, sex. That's the only thing people are interested in. I never saw a country so eager for scandals!*

Ida McKinley thinks she was the best beloved wife of all the Ladies,[2] but I daresay I was the only one whose husband was a-willin' to die for 'er. Gossip-mongers said terrible things and called me foul names. Mr. Jackson carried bullets in his body till his dyin' day from duels he fought defendin' m'honor. He even killed a man in a duel for slanderin' my reputation. He never told me about those things, a-course. But other people talk. I heard.

> [2]**IDA McKINLEY**
> *No one had a more devoted husband than I. No one.*

Maybe because of that, I kept to m'self. We warn't blessed with children, which caused me deep sorrow. I prayed and prayed for a child, and I s'pose my barren body was penance for not stayin' with Lewis Robards. But I had a large family and dozens of nieces and nephews. There was plenty of little Rachels and Andrews 'mongst the Donelson clan on account-a how they adored m'husband, who was becomin' an important man in Tennessee. When m'brother's wife had twin sons, times was hard for 'em, so they let us adopt one of the babies and I finally had m'Andrew Jackson Junior. Nothin' in the world gave me more pleasure than being 'mongst family, 'specially the li'l ones. Nothin' 'cept the solace I felt from m'prayers. I was always a Godfearin' woman.

Then Andrew Jackson went on to b'come *Gen'ral* Jackson, the hero of the Battle of New Orleans. He became a *very* important man, and not just in

Tennessee. Our finances improved with his reputation so he built me a big beautiful house on a thrivin' plantation. We called it the "Hermitage," since we could have a life t'ourselves. He even built me a small chapel for my daily devotions.

The Gen'ral was away a good deal, bein' an important man, so I had to manage the Hermitage best I could. The Lord provided for me, since m'brothers and their wives were nearby and I could lean on 'em when I needed. We also had near a hundred slaves who took care-a us, and we in turn took care-a them. They was part of our lives. I didn't think of 'em one way or t'other, 'cept as a part of our lives. Their young-uns ran in and out-a the house same as all the nieces and nephews, and ev'body played together. Come Christmas and Eastertime, they got gifts and treats and parties—same as family. I s'pose our overseer saw fit to whup a field hand sometimes, but it was never brought to my 'tention. The Gen'ral had strict orders that Miz Rachel was not to know 'bout those things. He knew I had a soft heart and would be upset. And I don't b'lieve the Gen'ral was inclined to sell slaves less'n it was absolutely nec'sary.[3] I s'pect I was sheltered 'bout a good many things.

> **[3]SARAH POLK**
> *We only sold slaves when absolutely necessary: when they were unruly, or when we needed to trade for other skills. I don't think our finances were ever so desperate that we were forced to sell slaves for money.*

I was lonely with the Gen'ral away so much. When he finally rode up that long pathway to the house I could barely contain m'joy! He'd be m'very own for a spell, and we could set together on our veranda, sippin' a cool drink and lookin' out over the flower garden. Heaven don't come much closer than that.

Once, some years after we was married, the Gen'ral took me to New Orleans. I didn't want to go but he insisted. So I went and hated ev'ry minute of it. If there was ever a sinful City, it was New Orleans. Then the Gen'ral took me to Wash'ton City. He said it would be "good for me to venture into society some." I think he was lonely too, bein' away from home so much and craved m'company. But I reckon I was as much cut out to be the wife of an "important man" as I was cut out to fly to the moon. All I ever wanted was to be "Aunt Rachel" in m'own house with m'family and m'friends and m'chapel and as many children 'round me as possible.

[4]SARAH POLK

Rachel is right. We were well acquainted with her of course, since the General was our "matchmaker." If we had been blessed with children, they would surely have been their godparents. People from our part of the country were much more devout than the Pagans in Washington. I was appalled the first time I went there, and while I grew to like it, I never became accustomed to its disregard of Christian practice.[5]

[5]JANE PIERCE

I was from New Hampshire, and I thought Washington City was just as Godless as Rachel did. I was miserable there, and urged my husband to abandon his political ambitions.

[6]ELIZABETH MONROE

I was never acquainted with Mrs. Jackson, but she bore the brunt of Washington Society's intimidation. They said dreadful things about her: that she was stout and unattractive, that she did not dress in style or behave with the sophistication they liked. It's probably a good thing she died, else they would have made her life miserable. Of course I doubt that she and I would have had much in common....

If I thought New Orleans was sinful, it was nothin' compared to Wash'ton City. I was truly shocked by the heathenism and total disregard of Sabbath worship.[4] I warn't comfortable 'mongst all those Godless Eastern women with their indecent low-bosomed gowns and jewels. Sippin' champagne and eatin' foreign soundin' foods. And talkin' 'bout subjects that warn't fittin' for a woman to *know* about, let alone *talk* about. Women in Wash'ton City talked about politics just like the men. They thrived on gossip about the private lives of the officials. They warn't interested in domestic things, and I warrant nary a one of 'em could make butter! I told m'husband I never wanted to go back there again! I was perfectly content a-settin' on our veranda, overlookin' God's good earth.

But Andrew Jackson was destined to be a great man.[6] The good people-a Tennessee saw fit to send 'im to the Senate, and then they wanted 'im to be President. He warn't inclined to ask *my* opinion on such matters, nor was it m'way to offer it. After all, *my* wishes were a heap less important than the wishes-a the whole country. But if he *had-a* asked me, and if I *had-a* offered, I would-a told him that it would-a been the cruelest punishment he could inflict upon me.

The election in 1828 was one of the nastiest. The gossip was at its worst! Gen'ral Jackson's enemies—and he had a bunch—dug up all the old stories 'bout our marriage. "A divorced woman in the President's House!" "A couple livin' in sin for years!" "An adulterer as President!" I thought the Gen'ral would-a had apoplexy! He warn't a forgivin' man. He could hate with the best of 'em. Maybe even better. Not that I approved. But the stories warn't just 'bout our marriage. I warn't a fancy, educated woman like Louisa Adams or Elizabeth Monroe. My learnin' was limited to readin' the Bible, and writin' a little, and doin' the usual cipherin' for the accounts. I didn't talk French. I could never be comfortable in society like Miz Madison. My youthful looks, what little I had, had long since been worn away by time and sorrow.[7] The Eastern women said I wouldn't know how to b'have. That my manners would be coarse. That I would bring shame and embarrassment to the President. A-course m'husband tried to keep those newspaper stories from reachin' me. But I heard the gossip.

> **[7]NANCY REAGAN**
> *Rachel Jackson was fat. Just plain fat. Not plump like Lady Washington, or buxom like Julia Grant. Susan Hayward played Rachel in an old movie about the Jacksons, but Rachel didn't look anything like Susan Hayward. The "eastern" women might have forgiven just about anything—except fat.*

I was in Nashville, bein' fitted for my 'naugural gown. It was white, and I thought it was lovely. For sure it cost a heap more'n any gown I ever had before. There was a newspaper at the dressmaker's shop, and I read some-a those hurtful, mean stories.[8] My heart had been po'ly for some time and it was Divine Providence that I fell ill and died. They buried me in what would-a been my 'naugural gown.

> **[8]LOUISA ADAMS**
> *I never met Rachel Jackson, but I did meet the General. He spoke of his wife with such warmth and affection that I was deeply moved. He obviously loved her dearly.*

Andrew Jackson went to Wash'ton City wearin' a mournin' band. He lived alone in that cold White House with my portrait by his bedstead. Many a time he must-a wished he was settin' with me on our veranda instead. But I would rather be a doorkeeper in the Temple of the Lord than to live in that big palace. I would never wish to cause anyone shame.

JULIA GARDINER TYLER
1820-1889
First Lady: 1844-1845

> [1]**JACQUELINE KENNEDY**
> *I suppose Julia is right. I had a desire to succeed, but I wouldn't call it "drive."*

"You can say whatever you like," Lucy said. Well then, I'll say whatever I like. Let's start by saying I was born 150 years too soon! I would put them *all* to shame today! I had every quality attributed to Mrs. Kennedy: good looks, plenty of money, excellent breeding, charm—plus one she sorely lacked: drive[1].

My father was David Gardiner of Long Island, a wealthy and prominent businessman. He gave me every advantage possible for my sex. I was educated liberally, although not so intellectually as to stunt my femininity. I had a carriage of my own and the most beautiful clothes, which showed off my handsome form. I was brilliantly introduced into society at lavish balls and was told I held court "like a queen." My name was frequently mentioned in the society pages of New York's newspapers, and all the eligible young men vied for the honor of filling my punch glass or fetching my cloak.

When I was 18 or 19, a Broadway mercantile establishment obtained a steel engraving of me and printed it on their handbills, stating that "Miss Julia Gardiner, The Rose of Long Island…." (I liked that phrase, "the Rose of Long Island")…"would purchase at Bogert and Macamly's. Their goods are beautiful and astonishingly cheap." I thought it was a great lark, and anticipated that Mr. Bogert and Mr. Macamly would be thrilled to supply me with the latest dress goods and ribbons and fans. I loved pretty clothes as much as Mrs. K. Maybe more.

> [2]**HILLARY RODHAM CLINTON**
> *It seems that no matter what talents or accomplishments a First Lady has, people always seem to make the biggest fuss about her clothes.*

My father took a dim view of the affair, however, and shipped my mother and me off to Europe for a year. "We must calm our daughter," he said, "otherwise she will be the scandal of us all!" Well Papa may not have realized the enticements of shopping in Paris and Rome. I returned with six more trunks than I took. I was not calmed, either.[2]

Anyway, when we returned from the Grand Tour, my father announced

LADIES: A CONJECTURE OF PERSONALITIES

that he had business in Washington City, and we would take up residence there for the "season." Quite naturally, as a member of fashionable society, we were presented at the White House, where I met President John Tyler. A word about him.

When we met, he was a middle-aged widower. Letitia, his first wife, had died two years earlier, after a long illness, which accounts for her non-participation in this endeavor.[3] He had six or seven grown children and a few grandchildren, most of whom loathed me. I could never imagine why, given the fact that I was always most cordial and generous to them.[4]

Mr. Tyler had assumed office following the sudden death of President William Henry Harrison, a mere month after his inauguration, which also accounts for the non-participation of Mrs. Harrison.[5]

> [3]**LETITIA TYLER**
> *I would have been a gracious and graceful First Lady, since I was a product of a traditional Virginia upbringing. But I had a stroke two years before John Tyler became President, and I was crippled and confined to a chair. My health declined steadily. I delegated all the official responsibilities to my daughter-in-law.*

> [4]**NANCY REAGAN**
> *It's the money, Julia. It's always the money. You just dissipated their inheritance.*

> [5]**ANNA HARRISON**
> *I would not mind saying a word or two. I was planning to come East in May—after the spring thaw. I was close to seventy at the time, and the journey was arduous—especially at my age and with my poor health. I was looking forward to my new "position," albeit not as an "active" Lady. I was far too old, and would have asked one of my daughters or daughters-in-law to do the honors.*
> *But I did wish to be with my dear husband of nearly fifty years. His death was a great blow to me. I expected to join him soon in the Hereafter, but I had to wait for twenty years, poor health and all. I lived to be ninety!*

Due to the peculiarities of politics at that time, Mr. Tyler, a lifelong Democrat, became, for all intents and purposes, a Whig President. He had his own interpretation of the Constitution, particularly regarding States' Rights,

[6]**EDITH WILSON** *What one man calls stubborn another calls steadfast.*[7]
[7]**ELLEN WILSON** *Ah'll bet if we took a poll-a all the Ladies, each one would vote a hearty "aye" on the stubbornness of her spouse! Maybe we could hold a contest. Which-a us had the most intransigent spouse!*[8]
[8]**LOUISA ADAMS** *I would win in a heartbeat. No one even comes close!*

and could be rather stubborn, which did not endear him to the political leaders of the day.[6] He was derided and called "His Accidency." His entire cabinet resigned. Needless to say, Congress and Mr. Tyler had four years of constant bickering. But that is another story best gleaned from far more learned sources than I. Besides, it's *MY* chapter.

When I met Mr. Tyler, all I knew was that he was President and a very important man. I knew little about the ins and outs of politics and cared less. Call me shallow if you will, but I was just twenty-three and only wanted to show off my gowns and jewels and the fact that I was "the Rose of Long Island"—the prettiest and most eligible young lady in the Capital.

My initial acquaintance with President Tyler was very proper. Our family was formally presented, and subsequently invited to any number of social levees, where he greeted me and always passed a few minutes in pleasant conversation. That was all. Since he was so many years my senior, I gave him little thought. Except that he *was* President of the United States and a very important man.

Then came that terrible, terrible day.

We had been invited, along with several dignitaries including the President, on cruise aboard the gunboat *Princeton*. A new and powerful cannon had been installed, and the President had been asked to witness a demonstration. It was a beautiful day, and everyone was in a party mood. My eyes still fill when I think of the events. The cannon misfired. There was a great explosion. My mother and I were below deck and spared, but several people were severely injured. A few were killed instantly. My beloved father among them.

My grief was intense. I was what modern people would call "a daddy's girl." He spoiled me terribly, and I loved him dearly for it.

It was not surprising when large bouquets of flowers arrived with President Tyler's card and condolences. We received many bouquets and letters of sympathy after such a horrible tragedy. My mother and I were distraught. My brother assured us that we would always be provided for, but that meant little in comparison to losing Papa. I adored him.

After an "appropriate time," my mother and I were invited to take luncheon with the President. Discreetly. Properly. No unbecoming gaiety.

Later came invitations to private suppers. President Tyler's attention toward me became that of a devoted friend and admirer. And my feelings toward him…well, he was a father figure, and I had just lost mine.

Our courtship was a secret. Convention demanded the utmost propriety. After all, is there *any* President who is permitted a personal life?[9] I've always thought that the national pastime of the country was gossiping. But I was thrilled at the thought of the President of the United States courting *me*. And despite being many years my senior, John Tyler was still a very attractive man. He was slim and athletic, a fine horseman and an *ardent* suitor.

> [9]**JACQUELINE KENNEDY** *Presidents are allowed a "personal" life only if they are dull enough not to have one.*

We eloped—at least from the Capital busybodies.[10]

We had a quiet family ceremony in Long Island, and I returned to Washington City as Mrs. President Tyler. The "Rose of Long Island" was now First Lady of the Land! There hadn't been one for nearly twenty years.[11] Both Presidents Jackson and Van Buren had been widowers. I would make up for my husband's political unpopularity with my own *personal* popularity!

> [10]**EDITH WILSON** *I was very hesitant about marrying Woodrow while he was still in office. It was less than two years since his first wife died. Many people considered it scandalous.*

I didn't have much time, since we married only a few months before the election of 1844, but I gave one of the grandest balls ever hosted at the White House. I planned every detail of the menu, the table arrangements, the flowers and even which tunes the band would play! I invited my sister and my cousins and a few close friends to be my "maids of honor." We co-ordinated the colors of our gowns and bouquets and where we would stand in the receiving line. We rehearsed our "tableau" for days!

> [11]**MARY LINCOLN** *I remember when I heard of President Tyler's wedding to the young bride. A girl two years younger than I was Mistress of the White House! And here I was, with a young baby, and still living in a boarding house.*

> **DOLLEY MADISON**
> *I was there. It was a lovely ball, except perhaps for the "tableau" part. I would have preferred Julia to mingle with her guests. Instead, a group of young women, including Julia, sat immobile on a platform, posed in some ridiculous "artistic" fashion.*

ELIZABETH MONROE
*Tableaus had been all the rage in Paris.
I was the one who introduced them
here. Ladies of status would become the
centerpiece for the whole affair. It was
a great honor to be invited to
participate in a tableau.*

**DOLLEY
MADISON**
Pooh.

All my effort was worth it! It was a gala affair! A triumph! The "Rose of Long Island" had conquered the heart of Washington City! There hadn't been such elegance since the days of Mrs. Madison. No one could have been prouder than I, except perhaps Mr. President Tyler, who claimed he had never attended a finer gathering, nor been accompanied by anyone so beautiful.

Lucy said to "speak my mind." Well my mind says this: I desperately wanted Mr. President Tyler to be re-elected. I didn't give a fig about politics (except for acquiring Texas, which I thought was very exciting), but I did enjoy those eight months as First Lady and wanted to continue my conquest of the nation's heart. The nation did not want its heart conquered. It wanted someone else as President. Anyone else. Mr. President Tyler had no party. There was no clamor for his nomination, let alone re-election. Mr. Clay was nominated by the Whigs. Again. But a Mr. Polk was nominated by the Democrats and elected. I had never heard of him before that time.

So Mr. ex-President Tyler and I retired to his Sherwood Forest plantation in Virginia. Despite the thirty-two-year difference in our ages, my husband was a *very* romantic man.[12] Raising a new generation of Tylers and being mistress of a large plantation was a happy time for me. I became a true companion to my husband, and took a more active interest in politics, especially States' Rights and the slavery issue.

> [12]**FRANCES CLEVELAND**
> *Grover Cleveland was nearly thirty years older than I was, and we had a fine marriage and five children.*

Bein' an adopted Daughter of Dixie suited me just fine. Within a year, I adapted to that slow and elegant way of life as if I'd-a been born to it. My New York way of speakin' softened to that dear familiar drawl surroundin' me. We had dozens of friends, and attended and gave balls and barbecues all the time. Needless to say, I loved it! Our active social life was interrupted only by my seven confinements. Like I said, Mr. Tyler was an *ardent* husband. Our "baby" was born when he was nearly seventy!

We remained involved in politics, 'specially durin' those tryin' years before the War. Mr. Tyler never completely lost hope that the Democrats would nominate him. "Available" candidates were very scarce, and my husband believed he might be selected as a compromise. After all, *somebody* had to be nominated. And, a-course, I dreamed of returnin' to the White House in triumph. I was told by very reliable sources that Miz Polk gave the dullest parties and receptions ever held there.[13] No food. No wine or brandy. No dancin'. How could you tell it was a party?

> [13]**DOLLEY MADISON**
> *I was always fond of Sarah Polk, but I admit, her parties lacked gaiety. By that time, I was nearly eighty and fashions change. Mingling with guests gave way to "tableaus." Then to austere hospitality. It would be another ten years before there was gracious entertaining in the White House again.*

Those "retirement" years were difficult in the South. The slavery issue would not die down, despite this compromise and that compromise. The Northern abolitionists just kept meddlin'. That's what it was. Pure meddlin'. If those damnyankee abolitionists had only come down to our Sherwood Forest, they would-a seen how much better our darkies had it than all those new Irish and German immigrants floodin' the cities every month. We took fine care-a our people. They were well fed and clothed. We didn't flog anyone. And we made it a point-a honor not to separate families. We never overworked them, exceptin' maybe harvest time, but everybody worked hard then. They had it a heap better than those Northern factory laborers. My babies were all Mammy-raised. What better proof can there be of true affection and regard than to entrust your *own babies* to a darky? Meddlin'. That's what it was. I was deeply ashamed of my Northern roots.[14]

> [14]**JANE PIERCE**
> *We New Englanders did not hold with slavery, but we knew many Southerners who were responsible and kind slave owners. Some of them were far more responsible and kind than our New Hampshire neighbors. We believed slavery to be peculiar institution to the South, and that we had no right to impose our will.*

Most-a our friends and neighbors believed as Mr. Tyler. That slavery would die out on its own, just leave it be. "It wasn't economical," he said. "Figure the cost of feedin', clothin', shelterin', and doctorin' a hundred slaves.... Why all you need is a couple-a spells-a bad weather, and you'd be ruined."

Now for all Mr. ex-President Tyler's inclinations toward slavery, he did *not* support Senator Calhoun, who we both thought was a hothead and as much a trouble-maker as the abolitionists. After all, Mr. Tyler *was* an ex-President of the *United States*, and while he was steadfast about states' rights, he loved the entire country deeply. When talk-a secession crept more and more into daily conversation, he was distraught. "Disunion," he declared, "never! Never!"

But like Robert E. Lee, we were Virginians, and when our State reluctantly followed her Southern sisters out of the Union, ex-President Tyler won a seat in the new Confederate Congress, despite his advanced years. Then a Peace Commission was formed to make one final effort to stave off the terrible War that loomed and my dear husband leapt at the chance to do both his "countries" one last service. He was appointed President of that Commission. "Surely the only livin' Southern-born President can help keep the country from tearin' apart," he said.

Alas, it was not to be. The Peace Commission failed, and my beloved husband died suddenly in a stroke of apoplexy. I had had a strange premonition of his death, and he *was* past seventy, but I was still unprepared for widowhood on the eve of War.

Nearly all we owned went to the Cause. I filled wagons with food and supplies. I gave horses and livestock. I donated our prized possessions for auctions and fund-raisin' events as the War dragged on and on. My eldest son fought for the South. The fightin' came up the Tidewater, close to my beloved home. Many a straggler or wounded soldier made his way to the house. I never turned anyone away—not even the occasional Yankee—if he minded his manners. We shared what little we had left, nursed their wounds as best we could, and sent them on their way with flour biscuits and whatever we could spare.

Finally it became truly perilous. The Yankees were in Yorktown, less than 50 miles from my house. My friends pleaded with me to go North, which I finally did, mainly for my children. The baby was only three. I was certain I would never see my beloved Sherwood Forest again.

My brother took us in a-course, and urged me to stay in New York permanently. And, like my dear departed father, he tempted me with the fine clothes and parties that I had always loved. But I had changed. I was no longer a New Yorker, let alone the "Rose of Long Island." And, too, my brother's friends were less than cordial to Mrs. ex-President Tyler, the outspoken and unrepentant Confederate. I found it hard to dance and be the "merry widow" when all my friends and neighbors were mournin' their menfolk. My once-dear brother and I became estranged.

After the War, my children and I returned to Sherwood Forest, which had been spared from total ruin. But the War had taken its toll. The crops had gone to seed, and the house needed extensive repair. Our slaves were gone, 'ceptin' a few old retainers who had nowhere else to go. So they stayed on, and I was grateful for their loyalty and help. It was a lonely time in the South.[15] People were either mournin' or ailin' or bein' ashamed of their reduced means. People who once lived in lovely homes with lovely things; who once gave dinners and dances in elegant rooms; now all they could offer was chicory-ground coffee and hard biscuits in a desolate room with broken furniture and torn draperies. If they even had that.[16] My own finances were such that I was once again dependent on the generosity of any-a my kin still speakin' to me. I hired some-a my former slaves for whatever small wages I could give 'em, and began slowly, very slowly, rebuildin' my home and my life.

> [15]**ELLEN WILSON**
> *Ah was a small child when the War ended. We were Georgians, and our State was ravaged. Mah father was a minister, and thus dependent on the parish for support. People barely had enough for themselves, let alone supportin' a minister's family. We did the best we could. It was not easy.*

> [16]**EDITH WILSON**
> *I was born in Virginia a dozen years after the War. My family was still feeling the effects of those terrible times.*

I was well into my middle years then. Mary Lincoln and I were the same age. But I still had my good complexion and graceful figure, and my New York elegance was now heavily laced with Southern charm.[17] Thus I embarked on my own personal "Great Cause." I believed it was an embarrassment to the country for a President's widow to live in want. There were only three of us at the time: Myself, Sarah Polk, who was financially more fortunate, and poor Miz Lincoln, who was in sorry straits. Later Miz Andrew Johnson would join our ranks for a short time, poor, and in frail health. When I was a young girl, I remember readin' how Dolley Madison had to plead and petition Congress to purchase her husband's papers so she could live decently in her declinin' years. Congress was *very* slow to respond to her, and they *loved* her. They did *not* love me. They were even slower to respond.

> [17]**JACQUELINE KENNEDY**
> *Julia Tyler was a beauty till the day she died.*

JULIA GRANT
Julia Tyler chose the wrong side and wanted to be paid for it! She was a pain in the derriere!

LUCY HAYES
I was sympathetic to widows of Presidents, however we had to remember that HER husband, also served as a Congressman to the Confederacy. Julia Tyler was always unrepentant in her Rebel sympathies. There were a good many people who were angered at the thought of supporting a traitor.

JULIA GRANT
We were constantly besieged with letters from her demanding financial support. Personally, I thought it was beneath her dignity to beg for public assistance when she had seven children to care for her.

[18]MARY LINCOLN
I barely had enough to live on. I, the widow of our great martyred President who gave his life for his Country.[19]

[19]JULIA GRANT
Hah! Mary Lincoln had $30,000 in bonds sewn into her petticoats. She was never quite right in the head.

I wrote to every Congressman I knew and even those who were strangers. "There should be an annual pension for widows of ex-Presidents," I said. "It is offensive to the memory of our dear husbands, who served their country in its highest office, for their widows to be reduced to family charity."[18]

My request was finally granted after fifteen years of persistence. After the assassination of President Garfield, Congress finally awarded us a small pension so we could live respectably.

I was told to speak my piece, and I say this: I consider the Presidential Widow's Pension my own personal contribution to the country. And I am damn proud of it!

IDA MCKINLEY
I had no one to care for me after my husband was assassinated. My children had died in infancy. My health was very frail, and the Major had never been a wealthy man. I will always be grateful for Julia Tyler's persistence.

SARAH CHILDRESS POLK
1803-1891
First Lady: 1845-1849

I was the daughter of a successful businessman-planter in Tennessee in the early part of the 19th century. My father believed in educating his children, including his daughters, and like Abigail Adams, I memorized and interpreted much Scripture, read copious amounts of fine literature, and participated in lively family discussions, frequently about the political issues of the day. In our part of the country, politics was as popular a diversion as a sporting event.

Quite naturally, our family was acquainted with Tennessee's Favorite Son, General Andrew Jackson. We also had a passing acquaintance with a young Clerk of the State Legislature named James Knox Polk who had ambitions for higher office. Mr. Polk was, by that time, in his late twenties, and desirous of matrimony. He was a protégé of the illustrious General, and sought his advice about the qualities he should seek in a spouse. "Look no further than Miss Sarah Childress," he told Mr. Polk, "for she has every attribute a man of your temperament would find desirable in a wife."[1] Mr. Polk took Andrew Jackson's kind recommendation to heart and began courting me in earnest. In due course, we married.

It was a fortuitous match, and I believe General Jackson took pride in his success drawing Cupid's bow.[2] Mr. Polk and I were more than spouses: we were companions. I was his confidante; his dearest and truest friend. He was the reason for my being.

I believe there were two reasons for this felicitous situation.

First and foremost, we were not blessed with children. My husband had undergone a serious operation in his early manhood, which left him unable to sire a child.[3] Secondly, we were of similar character and disposition, which contributed in no small part to the

> [1]**LADY BIRD JOHNSON**
> *It is interestin' to note how many of our Presidents "married up" as they say. They married intelligent women from better families than their own.*

> [2]**DOLLEY MADISON**
> *Andrew Jackson was an expert marksman. I don't suppose that his aim with Cupid's bow would be far off the target.*

> [3]**NANCY REAGAN**
> *James Knox Polk had a stone removed from his bladder. You can imagine the "delicacy" of that operation in the early nineteenth century! With no anesthesia, either!*

complete lack of friction between us. I cannot remember having a cross word with James in nearly twenty-five years as man and wife. We both had numerous young nieces and nephews on whom to bestow our affection, but our want of progeny left my time unoccupied and free from those conditions of health which took a severe toll on so many of my female acquaintances. I was thus free to be that companion which James needed and craved so deeply.[4]

> **[4]IDA McKINLEY**
> *Couples with no children tend to draw closer together. My Major and I were inseparable.*

Our detractors (and there were many) would call us descendants of those "dour Scots." It is true that neither of us were frivolous or given to exuberance. We were both deeply religious and scrupulously followed the observances of the Presbyterian Church. I always believed that we were put on God's earth to further His purpose. A life of merriment and want of industry was sinful. Both James and I devoted every day of our lives to hard work and purposeful habits.

> **[5]BETTY FORD**
> *James Polk was the first and only Speaker ever elected to the Presidency. Jerry always wanted to be Speaker, but I guess you could say that "he was skipped."*

James was elected to Congress shortly after our marriage. He served for fourteen years, and eventually became Speaker of the House.[5] I went with him to Washington since I had no obligations in Tennessee, and James desired my company. Those were the heady days when "General" Jackson was "President" Jackson. Since James was a Tennessean as well as his loyal supporter and protégé, he became an important person in the Capital City. And since Andrew Jackson was a widower after his dear Rachel passed on, the wife of the Speaker became an important social figure.

> **[6]RACHEL JACKSON**
> *I never knew Peggy Eaton, but it would not surprise me if she were very beautiful. "Society" women are a jealous sort and would find any reason at all to snub her.*

During much of the Jackson Administration there was an enormous social hue and cry over the outspoken and scandalous Peggy Eaton. She was the wife of a Cabinet member, but none of the other ladies in Washington deigned to recognize her.[6] Her first husband had died under questionable circumstances, and her subsequent courtship and remarriage was far too soon and far too public to suit polite society. President Jackson championed Mrs. Eaton steadfastly, and since the Cabinet wives and daughters refused to be in her society, they were seldom invited to the President's Mansion.

"We will not be involved in the gossip about Mrs. Eaton," cautioned James. "The President feels so strongly in her favor that it would be foolhardy not to abide by his wishes." I expect President Jackson had been pained by scandals and social ostracism because of his beloved Rachel, and would not suffer any other woman to be exposed to such ignominious treatment. For myself, however, there were enough suspicions about Mrs. Eaton's character to keep me at a very respectable distance.[7] I nodded to her when courtesy demanded, and pursued the matter no further. We stayed within President Jackson's good graces.[8]

We always boarded whilst in Washington and our boarding house was always full of congressmen, senators and other dignitaries. I usually did the honors at dinner since I was the only lady present. The few women who lived in town frequently came to call, and my days were filled entertaining, returning social obligations and attending the customary functions during the season.[9] I enjoyed it, and why not? I was young and comely. I never inclined toward housewifery, and besides, I liked politics. I found it much more to my intellectual taste than woman-talk of babies and recipes. Of course I never ventured my opinion to anyone other than my husband; and that was always in private.

All was not roses in our lives, however. After fourteen years in Congress, James was elected Governor and we returned to Tennessee. Then politics and a severe financial "panic" played havoc with our fortunes, and James lost two separate bids for re-election. A lesser man might have retired to practice law and tend to his property. I encouraged him to do so. "Husband," I said, "you still have a profession and we have our two plantations to sustain us. Why pursue politics and exhaust your health traveling throughout the state?" But James did not enjoy the practice of law nearly as much as the practice of politics, and he positively thrived on oratory. For a man of modest physical stature, James was a powerful speaker.

> [7]**JANE PIERCE**
> *We spent a brief period of time in Washington during the Jackson Administration, but I did not mingle with Mrs. Eaton. I would have been mortified. She was not the type of person with whom I wished to associate.*

> [8]**GRACE COOLIDGE**
> *James Polk was a lot like Calvin. Hard-working and extremely astute regarding the political tenor of the times. He always knew who his mentors were.*

> [9]**JANE PIERCE**
> *I don't remember meeting Mrs. Polk. Washington during the 1830's was still a marsh and sink-hole of pestilence and disease. My lungs were always weak, and I believe the foul climate of the Capital did irreparable damage to my health.*

He could enthrall a crowd for two hours or more without stopping, and like I said before, in Tennessee, politics was as much a diversion as a sporting event.

LOUISA ADAMS	ELEANOR ROOSEVELT	NELLIE TAFT
My husband hated the practice of law, and often regretted that he allowed himself to be "talked into" becoming a lawyer. But he was an excellent lawyer.	*Uncle Theodore studied law and so did Franklin. But the political bug bit them early on, and practicing law held no challenge or appeal to either of them.*	*Will was just the opposite. He adored the law, particularly the bench. I hated the court! It was full of old fuddy-duddies. But it was an excellent stepping stone for his future. I would have loved to live a century later when I could have been a lawyer myself!*

The Democratic convention in 1844 was a convulsion of partisanship and enmities. The Whigs, for the *third* time, turned to their old warhorse, Henry Clay. After the turmoil of the divisive Tyler "Accidency," most people assumed that Mr. Clay would finally achieve his dream. It was obvious that Mr. Tyler would not be nominated by *any* party, and former President Martin Van Buren had become associated with the anti-slavery movement. *That* was becoming a very serious problem. There were a dozen or so lesser candidates. Mr. Polk lacked support for the major office, but he sought to become the Vice Presidential candidate for whoever would be nominated. "After all, Wife," he said, "we both love the excitement of Washington, and our home ties have grown slack."

Few people outside of Tennessee had heard of James Knox Polk. It had been several years since his Speakership. He was no longer a national figure, and as an ardent Jacksonian with politics that were becoming out-dated, he had lost much support even in his own state. And his "dour Scot" nature did not inspire warm friendship and party enthusiasm.

[10]**LOUISA ADAMS**
Neither my husband nor I cared for Mr. Polk, although we admired his industrious character.

But politics can be capricious, and somehow James Knox Polk became the Democratic nominee, and even more surprisingly, managed to defeat Henry Clay. We were both amazed.[10] But since God had obviously ordained this great honor, there was no doubt that James would honor this obligation to the very best of his ability.

There are some who believe that Mr. Polk did not win the election so much as Mr. Clay lost it.[11] After all, everyone knew of Mr. Clay. No one knew of Mr. Polk. But James remained steadfast in all his political beliefs: about banking, about States' rights, about slavery, and mostly about our Manifest Destiny to rule the continent from sea to shining sea. Mr. Clay, however, waffled according to his audience.

> [11]**MARY LINCOLN**
> *As a Kentuckian, Henry Clay was a hero to our whole family—Todds and Lincolns. We were heartbroken in 1844 when he lost. Clay "kinder shot himself in the foot," my husband said. "He did everything wrong."*

So there we were. President and First Lady Polk. Mr. Tyler and his second wife had left Washington in a blaze of social (if not political) glory. We felt, however, a solemn obligation of office descend upon us. I became James' private secretary. He required someone who he could trust implicitly; someone whose discretion would never cause embarrassment; someone who would unfailingly support every decision. Who else could qualify so well? I arranged his office in proper order to find whatever we needed quickly. I had access to all his confidential papers. I made his copies in my clear round hand, and wrote letters for his elegant signature. And many a time he would say, "Sarah, I wish you to read such-and-such letter, or such-and-such newspaper and let me have your comments." Or "Sarah, would you please summarize the contents of such-and-such report." We frequently had lively discussions about the affairs of the day and I like to think that I helped him develop his ideas.

LADY BIRD JOHNSON	**EDITH WILSON**	**ROSALYNN CARTER**
I always worked actively with Lyndon. I loved politics and had a real knack for it.	*It's interesting that no one ever accused Sarah Polk of influencing or interfering with politics. I participated far less, and my reputation has forever been tainted by the accusation of a "Petticoat Government."*	*It's the nature of the times, Edith. No one thought a woman could possibly have any political influence in Sarah's day. Ironically, I was accused of having too much influence with Jimmy—and now a woman as President is a very real possibility.*

I do not believe any President labored as hard as James. In our four years, we never took a "vacation" of more than two or three days. My only condition was that we *never* worked or entertained on Sunday. Political discussion was absolutely forbidden on the Sabbath. If someone stopped by on the Lord's Day, we invited him to accompany us to Church, but that was the extent of our hospitality. Most declined and offered to pay their respects at another time. No matter. Our purpose was to fulfill the great office with honor, dignity and accomplishment.

Thus it pained James to hear the War with Mexico called "Mr. Polk's War." My husband was the least warlike person imaginable.[12] He believed that it was important for the country's future, however, and acted accordingly. He had the unflagging conviction that the United States should span the continent and set out to accomplish the deed. Every President is deeply troubled to send young men to die in battle. But war was different then. Soldiers paraded in the streets and the bands played. Pretty girls threw flowers. Wives and mothers took great pride in sending their husbands and sons to war, and were comforted knowing that they died bravely. It was considered noble.[14]

It was not easy for James to be Commander-in-Chief. He was unschooled in the science of war. It did not suit his temperament. He knew little of military strategy, supplies or weaponry. But he learned what he needed to know, and spared himself no detail. He rose early and retired long after midnight in an effort to supervise the progress of the war and the peace initiatives that followed. He cared little for his generals or his diplomatic advisors. He believed them to be vainglorious and quarrelsome. They quarreled with each other, with the Secretary of War, the Secretary of State and with their Commander-in-Chief.

[12]DOLLEY MADISON
The War of 1812 was known as Mr. Madison's War. Imagine my Jemmy having his own War! The least likely person in the country! Yet he took the field as Commander-in-Chief. A foolhardy undertaking to be sure, but no one could ever say that he lacked courage.[13]

[13]IDA McKINLEY
I always resented the fact that the Spanish-American War was called "Mr. McKinley's War." He was opposed to it from the beginning and believed it was ill-conceived and not in our best interest. It should have been called "Mr. Theodore Roosevelt's War." He was the one who was relentless in his quest for martial glory.

[14]MAMIE EISENHOWER
That is probably because they didn't see how brutal and bloody and terrible a death it can be.

A hundred and fifty years after "Mr. Polk's War," history accuses us of behaving treacherously in Mexico, imperialistically in Cuba and recklessly in Viet Nam. There may well be truth to it, but progress demands action. Sometimes action is harsh. And progress, like us Ladies, must be judged according to our own times. James believed that the United States should extend from ocean to ocean. It was the major goal of his Presidency, and he achieved it. When he left office, the United States spanned the continent. It was, to be sure, equal to the Louisiana Purchase in scope. Sometimes we must acknowledge that the end indeed may justify the means.

History is always wisest in retrospect, but sometimes, like Mr. Henry Clay, history waffles.

Our entertainments in the White House were modest. We were certainly financially comfortable, but we were not wealthy like the Tylers. Since we were obliged to pay for our own living and entertaining expenses, we frowned upon profligate waste.[15] Neither my husband nor I took spirits, thus we believed it unnecessary to offer them to others. The Temperance Movement was not yet a political force; those preferences were personal. And unless it were one of the prescribed state dinners that were expected from time to time, we saw no reason to have fruits or sweets at informal gatherings. In the summer (if anyone stayed in the sweltering capital), we would always provide guests with ice water.[17] Suffice it to say that our greatest pleasure was knowing that we were doing the very best possible job we could do with the least expense to the government.

James frequently worked fifteen or sixteen hours a day, and was plagued by chronic indigestion. Between the indigestion and the exhaustion, his life was shortened immeasurably. He died within three months of leaving office.

> [15]**GRACE COOLIDGE**
> *We Coolidges were a thrifty pair heaven knows, but the Polks were just about the tightest couple to ever live in the White House. They served no wines (we didn't either because of Prohibition), served no refreshments (we did), and allowed no dancing. I cannot imagine how anyone could have had a good time.[16]*

> [16]**JULIA TYLER**
> *I had tried so hard to bring back gaiety in the White House. Sarah Polk turned it into an ice-box. An empty icebox.*

> [17]**JULIA TYLER**
> *I hope Sarah didn't strain herself too much carrying the pitcher. There was not one ounce of gaiety in this woman![18]*

> [18]**NANCY REAGAN**
> *Agreed. She was as dry as yesterday's toast. Yesterday's rye toast.*

He was 52; I was only 45. I was destined to live until I was nearly ninety.

When Mrs. Hayes and Mrs. Harrison invited me to participate, they said I could discuss whatever I wanted. I have just given a sketch of my life up until my retirement from the public. After that, I spent my years in total inactivity. I behaved as I was expected to behave. I led a quiet, pious life, surrounded by nieces and nephews and a few close friends. My minister was a frequent visitor, and any dignitary passing through our part of Tennessee considered it a point of honor and privilege to take tea with Mrs. President Polk.[19] Then, when I was nearing the end of my life, a nice local couple endeavored to write my memoirs. I was pleased to meet with them and tell them of the events in my life. In doing so, it occurred to me how truly commonplace I was. How commonplace were my own thoughts! I did only what was expected of a well-brought-up lady of the time. I strictly obeyed the standards set by society. I did nothing outstanding. I had no outstanding thoughts.

[19]**JULIA TYLER**
Nice of her to finally serve refreshments.

History has treated me kindly, perhaps with some reflected luster of Abigail Adams' brilliance. It has come to appreciate intelligent women. History has even treated my husband kindly; certainly more kindly than his contemporaries. But it is obscure history, not the glorious kind. Not the merited kind.

When I was First Lady, there was a group of women in upstate New York who caused a commotion because they wanted the ballot. I was educated and intelligent. I was *extremely* well informed about the issues of the day. But I was shocked at the thought of women voting. My husband was relieved when I expressed my disdain for such unladylike activity. Perhaps it was the admonitions of my religion. God created woman from Adam's rib; thus women were subservient creatures. We did as we were expected to do. We obeyed our fathers, and then our husbands. It was in the Bible.

As I recollected my life for my neighbors, I realized that I sat for more than forty years. I never left my house save for Church. I sat through a country convulsed by slavery (I supported it, since I had large slave properties), and through a tumultuous War that took hundreds of thousands of lives. No one asked me at the time, but I was deeply torn by my fierce loyalty to the Union that my husband helped expand, and to my beloved Tennessee and our way of life. I have great empathy for Julia Tyler and her divided loyalty, but unlike her courage in taking a stand, I kept quiet so I could continue to enjoy the respect of both sides.

Great care was taken by both the North and the South to keep my home from harm. I did not feel the pangs of want. I did not feel the suffering of the mourner. Because it did not affect me intimately, I chose to leave the War on the outskirts of my life and immerse myself in the security of daily routine. Had I been an ardent Confederate, at least I would have been something! Had I freed my slaves willingly…had I sheltered soldiers of either side…had I lent whatever small prestige might have still been associated with my name for some worthwhile cause…had I spoken out even once and supported Senator Andrew Johnson in his lonely stand for Union, I might deserve to be remembered with honor today.

But I sat.

I sat and I served tea to visiting dignitaries who came to pay respects. And I read a bit and I sewed a bit and gave children's parties for the orphans. And I arranged and re-arranged and sorted and re-sorted my husband's papers and diaries. And I defended his policies and actions to anyone who sought to do him discredit. I did that for over forty years. By that time, Mr. Polk was nearly forgotten.

I know other Ladies beg to be judged according to their own times, but I had a chance to do more, and I let it slip by. What a waste I was. What a waste of all those years, when perhaps some remembrance attached to my name might have allowed me to be useful. There are those today who praise me as an "important" First Lady. They are wrong. I could have been truly important, but forgive me, I just sat. And I am ashamed.

HILLARY RODHAM CLINTON
We desperately seek signs of accomplishment in our past "Ladies." We know they were all intelligent—some more so than others. But there is so little documentation, that when we find even a few shreds, we cling to them!

LUCY HAYES
And that is exactly WHY we have endeavored to write this little book of ours!

MARGARET SMITH TAYLOR
1788-1852
First Lady: 1849-1850

> **[1]HILLARY RODHAM CLINTON**
> *There is practically nothing remaining about Peggy Taylor. Not even a portrait or tintype. All the more reason she should come forward.*

So they finally got me involved, eh. I spent my entire life and most-a eternity trying *not* to be involved, but this time the other Ladies prevailed.[1] Well, I s'pose, I might as well say a few words. Miz Clinton is right. There ain't much around 'bout me. Nobody was ever hired to paint my portrait. I think a tintype was made once, but we lost it. No matter, I warn't much to look at. Short, and when I got old, I tended towards stout. I had dark hair and dark eyes. When I got old, the hair got gray. Eyes stayed the same.

I was married to Zachary Taylor—'nother one of those presidents nobody remembers or cares about. Good. That's the way I like it. I din't want him to be president; I din't want to be First Lady; I din't want to live in Washin'ton. I reckoned it shortened both our lives.

> **[2]CAROLINE HARRISON**
> *In the late 1700's, when Margaret Taylor was born, if you came from an old "eastern" family you were probably connected in some way to the FFV's.*

I came from a good Maryland family, connected to some of the First Families in Virginia.[2] We warn't rich. We warn't poor. We was just fine. Then I met and married Zachary Taylor. He was a soldier, so I became a soldier's wife in every sense of the word. If you're looking for a "Lady" who was a frontier woman, you got 'er. I was the one.

> **[3]MAMIE EISENHOWER**
> *I think Ike and I moved twenty times in twenty years. We didn't buy our first home until he was President. And then I never wanted to leave it!*

Where Zach went, I went. And I raised our chil'en from pillar to post, like most army wives, buryin' a couple 'long the way. I lived in tents, in barracks, in lean-to's, in cabins—name it. It warn't the lap of luxury. Soldierin' never is. Matter-a fact, it warn't till I was past fifty that we even had a real home.[3] We bought a nice plantation in Baton Rouge.

It warn't so bad bringin' up the young'uns in an army camp. When they was babies, they played. When they got schoolin' age, we sent 'em East to the family, like everybody did. They all grew up fine and strong. But I stayed with my husband.[4]

I remember when they was a-growin' up, that Andrew Jackson, 'nother soldier, was bein' talked of for President. The gossip about Miz Jackson was pitiful. I felt bad for her, 'cause they accused her, 'mong other things, of bein' fat, and "backwoods." I tended toward stout myself,[5] and even though I was raised in Maryland, most people would think of me as bein' "backwoods" after all my years as an army wife. But then again, I had no thoughts of bein' anythin' else but an army wife.

Zach loved soldierin' more'n anythin'. He could eat anythin', sleep anywhere and spend days in the saddle. He was a tough 'un. I din't mind it so much either, 'cept it was mighty hard on m'health. But when our daughter Sarah wanted to marry a soldier, Zach was furious! It din't even matter that her young man come from a good family and was West Point trained. Zach was so agin' it, that our Sarah run off and eloped. Broke m'heart, it did. I fancied havin' a nice weddin'. There warn't many occasions for partyin' on the frontier and it would-a been nice to use some of the pretty plates and linens I kep' in the trunk for special times. But she run off. In a month, she was dead from malaria. Like I said, soldierin' is mighty hard on the health. Her widowed husband remarried some years later. Durin' the War with Mexico, his valor come to the 'tention of his commander, my husband, who, by that time, was "the famous Gen'ral Zachary Taylor." Our former son-in-law Jefferson Davis and his new wife Varina were embraced by both-a us, and became a part-a our family. Varina was a nice gal. I liked 'er. My Sarah would-a liked her too. Funny, both m'other daughters married soldiers. And my son Richard later served as a General in the Confederacy.

Durin' the War with Mexico, Zach and President Polk never saw eye to eye. "Blast it, Peggy, it's hard to follow orders from a confounded imbecile," he would tell me. "He don't know nothin' 'bout military matters or the

> [4] **ABIGAIL ADAMS**
> *See? She sent her children away for schooling and stayed with her husband. And everyone turned out fine!*

> [5] **BARBARA BUSH**
> *I've been a size 14 all my life and will probably die a size 14. When George was elected, I told everyone I had no intention of dyeing my hair or losing weight. And I think people respected me for it.*[6]

> [6] **LADY BIRD JOHNSON**
> *Barbara Bush is the luckiest of all the modern Ladies. She is what she is, she knows it and likes it. Hooray for her!*

problems we face. But he's the one tellin' everybody what to do. Politics! Bah!"

> **SARAH POLK**
> *Which is correct? Being Commander-in-Chief has nothing to do with politics, or being Commander-in-Chief has everything to do with politics?*

> **MAMIE EISENHOWER**
> *Depends on the Commander-in-Chief, I would think. And also whether or not there was a war on.*

> **BESS TRUMAN**
> *I think it must be incredibly difficult to be a Commander-in-Chief when you have limited military experience. War or no war.*

For a long time I b'lieved the President of the United States was a half-wit whose one goal seemed to be discreditin' my husband's reputation. But Zach won the battles and became a popular hero. We din't care much for the hero business 'cause ev'body knows it's the soldiers who do the fightin' and the dyin' who are the heroes. But then there was General Winfield Scott. He won battles too and liked the hero business. He liked the hero business a heap! General Scott towered over my husband physically. He was also full-a military spit and polish. Zach warn't tall. He warn't a tidy man either. As you might-a figured, they din't get on too well.

But after the War, my "hero" husband was talked about as a presidential candidate. Din't matter that he knew nothin' about politics and prob'ly never cast a ballot. He din't even know if he was a Democrat or a Whig or anythin' else. I reckon he went to the Whigs because he hated Polk so much. I prayed on my knees every night for six months that Henry Clay would be nominated and they'd leave us alone. Seemed to me that after so many years a-tryin', Clay ought-a finally get the prize. He was an old man by then, but Zach Taylor was past sixty, too. He had rheumatism. Bein' president would destroy his health. I had bad rheumatism m'self. And a few other ailments

> **[7]MAMIE EISENHOWER**
> *I had a dining room set that went around the world! Literally.*

besides. I'd-a been so happy in Baton Rouge. I had real furniture. Those pretty things I got for weddin' presents were finally taken out-a the trunk and put on the table.[7] The warm weather was good for m'rheumatism, too. I

72

'spected to pass our last years in Baton Rouge, surrounded by our chil'en and grand-chil'en.

The Whig Party din't want-a spoil their chances by lettin' Zach say anythin' important, not that he had much to say anyways. He warn't a talker. But talkin' or not, fate decided otherwise, and there we were in Washin'ton. I declined to participate in the fluff and fanfare and listen to ev'body gossip 'bout how stout I was. I was near twenty years older than Sarah Polk, and I looked it. Hard livin' takes its toll and leaves its mark. People said I din't want-a be sociable 'cause I smoked a pipe. They said that about Miz Jackson, too. My husband denied it, and so did Varina Davis, and a few other people who knew us. Truth is, I did take a pipe every now'n again. I reckon Miz Jackson did too.[8] Settin' outside an army tent with your husband on a balmy evenin', havin' a cup-a coffee and a pipe seems natural. If that's the worst thing I ever done, I'll be content. When we lived in the White House, I let my daughter Betty be the *official* hostess for the *official* rig-marole. She was young and pretty and ev'one seemed to like her fine. I presided over the family table. I liked that fine.

> [8]**RACHEL JACKSON**
> *Miz Taylor did the right thing keepin' to herself. Those evil tongues would have made her life a misery. She was lucky to have a daughter to look after the social affairs.*

Bein' president killed my husband. Too much stress and strain about things he warn't able to fix. Too many headaches for a sixty-some-year-old man with rheumatism. I din't survive much longer. I think both-a us might-a had another ten years together, if the Whig party din't interfere. An' I don't have anythin' else to say. Thank you for lettin' me do my piece.

ABIGAIL POWERS FILLMORE
1798-1853
First Lady: 1850-53

I am the "other" Abigail. Hmmpf. Nobody even knows there *was* another Abigail, so thanks to dear Lucy Hayes, here commences the secret life and thoughts of Abigail Powers Fillmore.

I was the first "Lady" to be gainfully employed outside the home. I taught school. My father was dead, and my family needed the extra wages. I could read and write and knew figures. It was a natural and respectable occupation.

So there I was, sixteen years old, teaching basic learning to the children in upstate New York. They paid me less than a dollar a week, but sometimes a grateful parent would supplement that pittance with some eggs or apples or a bushel of potatoes. Sometimes they invited me to take supper with them.

One of my students was a bright young farm boy near my own age. He was a big strapping fellow who was eager to learn. Sometimes he stayed late for extra lessons. As his learning grew, so did our affection for each other. Millard Fillmore and I agreed to marry—but it would be a long engagement.[1] We were both very young and terribly poor, and Mill had to be one of the proudest boys alive. He refused to marry till he could properly support a wife. "I don't want my wife to struggle and make do with scraps," he said. "I want her to hold her head high in the community."

> [1]**LUCRETIA GARFIELD**
> *Mine was a long engagement too. Four years long.*[2]
>
> [2]**BESS TRUMAN**
> *Nobody's courtship was longer than mine. Harry was my beau from the time I was five or six, and we didn't marry till I was well past thirty!*

So he continued his education, eventually reading law with a barrister in Buffalo, and I continued to educate others. I loved being a teacher, but once Mill and I were married, my teaching days were over. It was unseemly for a married woman to work, especially the wife of an attorney with a growing reputation. My working would reflect poorly on my husband's ability to provide, and from the start, he was a good provider.

So I maintained our home, raised two children and bought a piano and took lessons. I also read every book I could lay my hands on, and became one of the founding members of our "Library Society." I read poetry and philosophy, the racy novels by Henry Fielding, and even Mr. Fenimore Cooper's Indian stories. I had a fondness for them since they supposedly took place not far from where we lived. And I'll tell you a secret! I read some of Mr. Poe's stories and poems as well. Many people said they weren't suitable for a lady, but I read them anyway.

As Mill became more and more active in politics, I continued to be active in the domestic and social world around Buffalo. The Library, of course, was my first love, but I also helped at our Church and with local charities: the usual things that were acceptable to occupy a woman's time. We Fillmores were a solid family.

But even though Mill was becoming well known in local political circles, he was always aware of his limitations and haphazard education. Thurlow Weed and young Billy Seward were the rising political men in New York, and to be sure, either one of them could run rings around Mill in both style and leadership, not to mention in intellect and oratory. Mill was not a gifted speaker.

Nothing against my husband. He was a fine, decent man. He was first elected to office on the "Anti-Masonic" Party ticket, of all things. There had been a scandalous murder involving the secret Masonic Society, and it created an enormous hue and cry in our area. I thought a whole political party devoted to being against the Masons was strange and trivial, but then again, no less a personage than former President John Quincy Adams was associated with that bunch, so I suppose it must've been all right. [3]

Anyway, Mill's greatest quality was his doggedness. If he took on a job, you could rest assured it would be done well and brought to completion. His political allies found it admirable. So did I. It was one of the things that attracted me. When he wanted to learn, nothing stood in his way, no matter how long it took! He was solid as a rock. And in those days, a solid-as-a-rock husband was like gold.

Mill served diligently in the State Legislature so they elected him to Congress. He dreamed that someday the legislature might send him to the Senate. (The State legislature appointed Senators then; they weren't elected directly.) That was the height of his ambition. He had already come further than he had ever expected. As for me, since a Congressman's term was only two years, it made little sense to pack up bag and baggage to live in a boarding house with two small children. After all,

> [3]**LOUISA ADAMS**
> *My husband did espouse the Anti-Masonic party—at least on paper. The two-party system was very weak during the 1830's, and it was merely a vehicle for Mr. A. to become re-involved. The Anti-Masons later became the Whigs. I don't think Mr. Adams gave any thought to the Masonic organization at all. As a matter of fact, he had great respect and affection for George Washington, who had long been an active Mason.*

[4]**JULIA GRANT**
*Ulys said he would like to be
Mayor of Galena so's we could
have a sidewalk built in front of
the house. That was the height of
his political ambitions.*

I had a nice six-room house, my piano, many friends and all my books. Why should I leave?[4]

Mill wrote me nearly every day, and I responded to every letter. He was always sending me packages with sheets of music or books for my own pleasure. Since he passed through New York City and Philadelphia where books were plentiful, I gave him the purchase lists from our Library Society. By the time Mill served a couple of terms in Congress, that little lyceum had grown into a thriving enterprise!

Mill would frequently discuss politics with *me*. Never in company, of course, only in private. He was very unsure of himself, and never inclined to take a firm stand about anything without knowing that others would be in agreement. We talked about all the great men and the great issues. Mr. Clay…Mill liked him. Mr. Webster…we both admired him above all others. Slavery. We were both against slavery, but we were also opposed to the abolition societies. Most of the abolitionists we knew or heard about were rabble-rousers and trouble-makers. No doubt they meant well and their hearts were in the right place, but they were a loud and disagreeable bunch. Mill and I understood that slavery was necessary to the Southern economy, and as long as slave owners were humane in their treatment of their "legal property," we believed we should mind our business and let it lie where it was. Unfortunately, since the country was expanding rapidly, slavery refused to lie where it was.

But I will leave that to other Ladies with much keener insights than I. I want to talk about my two secrets.

The first is this: Some women held a meeting in Seneca Falls (not too far

[5]**ABIGAIL ADAMS**
Of course this was all before my time, but I would have been in total support! I especially cared about a woman's right to obtain and manage her own property. So many women were impoverished because of mismanagement by their husbands or brothers or sons.

from us) to discuss women's rights, including the right to vote. Notices for the meeting were buried in the back pages of the local newspapers, but there were a few handbills posted in town. It was the subject of great ridicule, and of course, as the wife of a Congressman, it would have been scandalous for me to attend this convention! But I was interested, and made it a point to discreetly learn the outcome.[5]

I figured thus: I definitely favored women being able to inherit property and maintain an income. I also favored higher education and employment opportunities for women. After all, I had been a school teacher and was well aware of how much I did *not* know. I realized that not *all* women were capable of understanding the complexities of politics and government, but then again, neither were all men.[6] There was many an illiterate laborer or naturalized immigrant totally incapable of a reasoned vote, yet they were allowed that privilege. I did *not* favor granting suffrage to *all* women, merely the ones who were educated; those who could read, write and understand the subject. I had read some of the recently published letters of the "first" Abigail. They were wondrously intelligent. Surely she could have been trusted to cast a reasonable vote.

> [6]**ELEANOR ROOSEVELT**
> *In my youth, I was opposed to women's suffrage. That was the "politically correct" way to behave. As time went on, I changed my mind and I became active in the League of Women Voters. I believe if you have the right to vote, you also have the responsibility to cast an intelligent ballot.*

But I was not a daring woman. I had neither the intellect nor stomach to defy convention nor harm my husband's prominent career. So I kept my thoughts to myself. Till now. This is one of those thoughts: When did women stop being help-meets and become help-less, like those frail, pining sorts who had vapors and looked like they were too weak to lift anything heavier than the teapot? I believe it happened when we stopped being "colonies" and started being a "country." As the nation prospered and men became wealthy, they showered their women with fancy clothes and gewgaws from Paris and London. Elegant wives and daughters always reflect on how men are perceived. Always the men! But with steam engines and other new inventions, traditional "women's work" like weaving and making candles and soap was being done in manufactories instead of in the home. An immigrant population flooded our shores and provided a large and cheap servant class. Women had less and less to do. So they socialized and gossiped, and found little outlets or opportunities for their talents and abilities. Frailness became fashionable, and a frustrated woman of intelligence could simply "take to her bed" as her own form of rebellion. At least she could read in bed. That's my theory.[7]

> [7]**ROSALYNN CARTER**
> *Not a bad theory, Abigail. I can just see one of the modern Ladies "taking to her bed" for anything other than a very serious illness! Most of the time we work on, sick or well! We have too many people counting on our presence. Frankly I would not have minded taking a few days off to stay in bed and read every so often!*

My second secret happened when Mill was in the White House. He had been elected as a "compromise"

Northerner to run as Vice President with General Zachary Taylor, who was from the South. They needed balance, and Mill was safe. He offended no one with his principles. He had a genial nature. Vice President! Who would have dreamed such a dream! Of course I came to Washington then! The children were nearly grown and the Library would just have to struggle on without me! I met whomever I needed to meet, and we socialized pleasantly with everyone. It was a very easy life being the wife of the Vice President.[8] Mill loved it! I loved it! It was a lively time because of California and the gold. And slavery. But other than the controversial issues, life was pleasant!

> [8]**GRACE COOLIDGE**
> *I enjoyed myself immensely when Calvin was Vice President. We were invited everywhere and went everywhere. We had few real responsibilities or obligations.*[9]

> [9]**BESS TRUMAN**
> *Grace is right! You get invited out all the time when you are Vice President! Too bad we only had a few weeks of those good times!*

Then President Taylor died suddenly, and there we were: President and Mrs. Fillmore. It was practically inconceivable! We moved to the White House.

There wasn't a book in the entire place—not even a Bible! Julia Tyler takes credit for the Presidential Widow's Pension; I am responsible for the White House Library. Congress authorized the funds and I helped prepare the requisition list. When the books arrived, I lovingly inspected each one, and placed it on its assigned shelf. I spent a good deal of my time in that little Library. It was my favorite place.

I did very little socializing while in the House. It bored me. It was different than the more intimate gatherings we attended when Mill was Vice President. Presidential entertaining is more formal. Bigger. Elaborate and pretentious. I did not wish to spend my time amongst simpering ladies waving fans and talking about silly things. I had better things to do than worry over who sat where and which flowers should be on the table, or what color cloth to use. Besides, I had a broken ankle that never healed properly, so standing in reception lines was painful.

But back to my secret! I was Millard Fillmore's greatest and most loyal confidante, just like Sarah was to James Polk. We had established a pattern of discussing the affairs of the day, which continued till I died. He often came to me care-worn and confused by the great issues: States rights and slavery. Who wouldn't be confused? It was tearing the country apart, and it was tearing him apart. Mill was all too aware of his lack of genius or preparation for the office he held by default. "Oh why could not Mr. Webster be twenty-five years younger," he said, "or Mr. Seward twenty years older!

78

Either one is far more qualified than I!" "You must do the very best you can for all concerned," I advised. "Since you were not truly elected as President, no one could fault you for trying to steer an even course."[10]

Neither of us wanted Millard Fillmore to be the President responsible for fracturing the country, so we chose the path of least resistance. We placated and patched and compromised and bargained trying to hold everyone together as best we could until someone better equipped could resolve the problems.

Of course I couldn't tell anyone that Mill confided his deepest concerns to me, a lowly woman. He wouldn't even permit me keep a diary.[11] Mill would have been horrified if it ever became public that he asked *my* advice on issues of the day, and sometimes actually took it! Men have such fragile egos! But I was the one who pleaded with him to take the most "middle ground" possible. "You are not the man for this job, my dear," I said. "You are a fine and wonderful husband, father and Vice President, but these great concerns are best left to greater minds."

I believe Millard Fillmore did a fair job, considering his limitations. He had no pretensions or illusions about his abilities and he bought ten years of peace.

The day Mr. Pierce was inaugurated, I fell ill with pneumonia and died in a Washington hotel within a week. I never saw my little house and piano again. If I hadn't died then, I would have tried very hard to dissuade Mill from being involved with that foolish "American Party." Politics during the 1850s was increasingly troubled, and third and fourth parties were cropping up all over. The American Party was like the "Anti-Masons." It was an "against" party. Against foreigners, against Catholics, against everything. I figure you probably have a much better chance being elected if you're *for* something rather than *against* it. It was apt that they were nicknamed the "Know-Nothings," since a man couldn't know too much if he joined that bunch of fools. They used my husband very badly. I'm sorry I wasn't alive to tell him

> [10]**GRACE COOLIDGE**
> *History doesn't always take into account the difficulties Presidents go through deciding what is best for the country at the time, and what will be best for the country in the future. The Fillmores, like the Coolidges, tried to do what was best at the time.*

> [11]**LADY BIRD JOHNSON**
> *I think all Ladies keep diaries today. If they don't, they should. Future generations demand it.* [12]

> [12]**HILLARY RODHAM CLINTON**
> *A public diary, of course—of the events. I doubt if any Lady would wish to keep a "private" one unless they could be sure it wouldn't come to light till 50 years after both their deaths.*

so. Mill was conservative, yes. He was unimaginative, yes. But he was really not as bigoted as people make him out to be.

If I hadn't died when I did, I also would have followed the careers of Mrs. Stanton and those other ladies who met at Seneca Falls. I never would have joined them; I didn't have that kind of gumption. But I did sympathize. I did sympathize.

JANE APPLETON PIERCE
1806-1863
First Lady: 1853-1857

Lucy Hayes has entreated me to talk a bit about myself. She said history has been unkind to me, and I might rectify it with a few words on my own behalf. Since I am unaccustomed to such activity, I must plead for the reader's indulgence and trust to a kind Providence to ensure that only true and honest words flow from my pen.[1]

I know not where or how to begin, save that I was a New Englander, not given to the effusive emotions of those born in a warmer clime. Besides, it is unseemly for a woman to be so forward. I was frail and very reserved. Alas, I suffered a touch of consumption as a child, and I fear I was never fully restored to health.

My father was a minister and president of Bowdoin College in Maine, thus I was brought up in strict accordance with a God-fearing and moral society. "Social" obligations were an effort for me.[2] My education centered around the Bible, and Shakespeare and some selected poetry. Novels, even the works of Sir Walter Scott or Washington Irving, were not permitted in our house. I once defied father, however, and read an interesting book by an English lady, a Miss Austen. It was called *Pride and Prejudice*. I saw no moral harm in it, but I felt so ashamed for defying my father, that it gave me no pleasure.

When I met Franklin Pierce, I do not deny that I found him most attractive, as did every eligible young lady in town. I am not at all certain why Mr. Pierce favored me. He was my opposite in every way. He was outgoing and convivial; I was shy and retiring. He loved social companionship; I preferred my solitude and my Bible, and my family. He enjoyed discussing the events of the day; I chose to converse mainly about things suitable to my sex: children, housekeeping, and the pleasantries of the neighborhood.

> [1] **BARBARA BUSH**
> *I am also a "Pierce." Since I can trace my own family tree to a distant relationship with Franklin Pierce, I suppose I ought to do the apologia on Jane. She needs one.*

> [2] **BARBARA BUSH**
> *Living was an effort for her! Jane was pretty and had a small frame and slim figure. And had she ever smiled, she would have been very pretty. But from all information existing about Jane Pierce, smiling wasn't in the picture. Some people just don't want to be happy.*

My father was very strict about who was permitted to call. Had he know Mr. Pierce better, I doubt he would have allowed him to cross the threshold. But I was nearly twenty-eight then, and my choices were few. I would either marry Mr. Pierce or remain a spinster. I imagine my father thought that Mr. Pierce was God's answer to his prayers to find a husband for "poor Jane." In some ways, I think I might have preferred spinsterhood.[3] But an unmarried woman in the 1830s was a burden to an entire family. Someone had to be prevailed upon to support the "maiden aunt," since it was unthinkable for her to be employed. She usually ended up living under the protection of some male relative, caring for someone else's children, and trying to make herself more useful and less inconvenient.

> **[3]ELEANOR ROOSEVELT**
> *When I was eighteen, I expected to remain a spinster. I was plain and shy, my family fortune was limited, so I was certain no one would ever want to marry me.[4]*

> **[4]HILLARY RODHAM CLINTON**
> *Women have so many more options these days. The term "Old Maid" is only used in the children's card game.*

Mr. Pierce was an attorney from a distinguished New Hampshire family. His father had been a General in the late Revolution, and had even served a term as Governor. Shortly after our marriage, my husband was elected to Congress. I accompanied him to Washington for a short time. The pestilential climate was not agreeable to me, nor were its inhabitants, I fear. Most of the people there were casual in their Christian observances; the Sabbath virtually ignored. The few women of my acquaintance cared for nothing save position and fashion and jewels and, of all things, politics. I was shocked at how unseemly Washington women were![5]

> **[5]SARAH POLK**
> *I recall meeting Jane once or twice. My husband thought well of Mr. Pierce. I can't imagine how she possibly could think I was "casual" in my religious observance. No one was more devout! But I was definitely interested in politics.*

Mr. Pierce was a very amiable and popular Congressman, especially for a New Englander. We Yankees were usually perceived as either "staid" or else rabid abolitionists. He was neither.[6] At a time when the slavery issue was becoming increasingly strident, Mr. Pierce

> **[6]BARBARA BUSH**
> *Franklin Pierce was a charmer who drank to excess. He discovered that many Southerners had similar styles.*

was Democrat from the "right part of the country" and seemed to balance the

Southern influences. He was considered a jolly good fellow, sympathetic to the Southern viewpoints. Naturally we neither espoused nor condoned the practice of slavery, but we did acknowledge it to be a peculiar institution of our Southern brethren. Mr. Pierce believed it was none of our concern so long as it remained contained and humane. Mr. Pierce's Southern colleagues, of course, were humane masters.

As I said, my health had always been far from robust, and child-bearing was not easy, particularly since I was older than most new mothers. When God, in his infinite wisdom, saw fit to take my first two sons in infancy, it affected me deeply, just as it affected dear Ida McKinley many years hence.[7] I suffered grievously, believing that only the promise of Heaven could compensate me for the pain of living. When I finally was given one last chance with a third baby, I vowed that if God should give me the strength, I would devote every moment of my life to raising that child.

I pressed my husband to "retire" from Congress and limit his political activity to our State. "There are more than sufficient issues in New Hampshire to keep you occupied," I said. I wanted to be near the people I knew; where all was familiar and comfortable. We returned home to Concord, he to practice the law, and I to devote myself to domestic life.

When James Polk became President in 1845, he remembered Mr. Pierce from his Congressional days and tendered him the office of Attorney General. My husband was thrilled! He had always enjoyed Washington—choleric and Godless though it was. He still maintained his many friends there. I, on the other hand, was adamant. I absolutely refused to go. I would remain in Concord, and devote myself entirely to our last son, our beloved Bennie, who was a small boy, and all I had. I was near forty, and it was my last chance at motherhood. I convinced Mr. Pierce that his true place, his Christian place, was at home with Bennie and me, and not gallivanting to parties and socials and levees in that heathen city.

Mr. Pierce bowed to my wishes. He declined the appointment.

I believe that while he was always solicitous and considerate of me, it was a turning point in our private affairs. Mr. Pierce, who had always enjoyed a glass of Madeira or bourbon, turned to more copious consumption; I turned

> [7]**IDA McKINLEY**
> *I feel very deeply for Jane, since we had much in common. But Jane never wanted to be a part of her husband's life, and I wanted nothing more than to be part of the Major's world.*[8]

> [8]**BARBARA BUSH**
> *We lost our little girl to leukemia when she was only three. I believe most of our "Ladies" lost a child. I cannot imagine a greater pain.*

from him, and turned more and more toward Bennie. And God. My prayer-book was never far from my reach. Not long thereafter, our country was embroiled in a war with Mexico, and so eager was Mr. Pierce to be involved, that he enlisted as an ordinary private! Franklin Pierce, college educated, a former Congressman, grandson of a Revolutionary War general, a lowly private! [9]

[9]JULIA GRANT *He probably just wanted to get away from her.*[10]	[11]**BARBARA BUSH** *I can say those things, Nancy, but you can't. She was MY distant relative. Actually it was her husband who was my relative, but blood—and I suppose marriage—is thicker than water. But Jane was a pill. And Prozac might have helped.*
[10]**NANCY REAGAN** *I can understand that. Jane Pierce was a pill. Probably needed to be on Prozac.*[11]	

[12]JULIA GRANT
Franklin Pierce was a "political" general. He was a poor soldier and there was considerable speculation amongst the other generals that he was a coward. He had either been shot or fell from his horse. The wound was minor. He did not remount or take the field.

Of course, his innate leadership qualities quickly were recognized, and by the end of the conflict, he was Brigadier General Franklin Pierce.[12] I abhorred war, but I was proud of my husband. Say what they would about his lack of military genius, he was not a coward. He was perhaps not the bravest of warriors, but he was not a coward.

[13]**NANCY REAGAN** *Being married to Jane, it is not hard to understand her husband's "lapses."*

After the War, he returned to New Hampshire, and the practice of law. He even took the pledge and became president of our local Temperance Society. I, of course, was overjoyed and we both sought to renew the bonds of our affection. I fear, however, that his good intentions could not overcome his weak moral fiber, and he lapsed from time to time.[13]

By 1852, the country was in turmoil. The slavery issue, which had ebbed and flowed during the War with Mexico, had arisen once again causing an even greater rift. The outgoing Whig party was badly splintered and weak, and their candidate, General Winfield Scott, offered little political leadership. The Democratic Party, my husband's party, was even weaker and more splintered. I say this, not from any interest in politics or government on my part. (I was totally absorbed in my rightful duties raising our darling little Bennie and I would never have dreamed of interfering in such unwomanly pursuits.) But I say it because Mr. Pierce remarked casually one evening, that even *he* might be considered for President.

"But Husband," I cried, "you haven't been involved politically outside our State for more than a decade! Certainly you have been forgotten." I prayed he had been forgotten! Mr. Pierce agreed that he probably *had* been forgotten, but the Democrats needed a candidate acceptable to the South and they would never be able to elect a Southerner. "The only available candidate must be from the North," he insisted. "Western states like Ohio or Illinois are too sparse in population and don't understand the needs of the Country as a whole."

This was much too confusing for my simple female brain. I longed for nothing more than tending to my knitting while I listened to my dear son recite his Bible lessons. "Promise me that you will not become involved," I pleaded. "Why Jane," he comforted, "my only involvement will be to support the Democratic candidate, just as I have always done in the past. I'll write the usual letters to my old friends, and maybe give a speech or two, but I'll be staying right here with you in Concord." I was relieved.

"As a matter of fact," he continued, "my hope would be for the Democrats to nominate Jefferson Davis. He is a fine, competent man. A West Pointer. I knew him in Congress, and renewed the friendship during the late War. I would be proud to support him, but alas, he will never be nominated. He's a Mississippian. Too strongly identified with slavery."

The nominating convention cast more than a hundred ballots that year, and to everyone's amazement, Franklin Pierce was nominated. I do not believe my husband actively sought the honor; he would not have blatantly deceived me. I do believe, however, that he could have made far stronger objections. When I was told the news, I fainted dead away. My quiet, tranquil life was about to change. I would be expected to manage a large house and servants, to entertain frequently and lavishly, and take my place as a social leader in a Godless society. I was not a leader, social or otherwise, nor did I wish it. I cringed at the thought.

But the Lord had obviously intended for Mr. Pierce to be elected, and thus my wishes were insignificant in that light. I began to accept these new responsibilities as God's will and I feared no evil. I vowed to try my best to be a credit to my husband and to our exalted position. We packed our belongings, and boarded the train that would take us to Washington in triumph.

But the Lord raiseth up with one Hand and casteth down with the Other.

There was a horrific, unspeakable accident. The train cars derailed, and our best and dearest little boy, the light of my life, the only child left to my bosom…. It is unbearable to put pen to these words. My Bennie was thrown between the cars and crushed. He was only eleven. When they broke the news to me I collapsed, never to be the same again. I was crushed as surely as if my own body had fallen onto the tracks.

> **MARY LINCOLN**
> *I ached for Jane Pierce when we read about the accident in the newspapers. One cannot ever understand a mother's grief, unless you have lost a beloved child. I had recently lost my little Eddy, and I hugged my baby Willie even closer that night.*

> **JULIA TYLER**
> *Of course Jane was in shock at such an event! I remember my father's terrible accident! It is devastating!*

Mr. Pierce's Presidency was cursed by God. I had no doubt of that. There was no joy in the Capital on Inauguration Day, 1853. It was a hushed, strained affair. There were no parades or balls. We were in deep, deep mourning. Black crepe hung in the White House instead of red, white and blue bunting. I could never rise to the demands of social protocol. At my best, it would have been an extreme effort because of my frail health and retiring disposition. But with my intense grief, any attempt whatsoever would be impossible.[14] I sent for my aunt, who was close to my own age, and through her kindness, and that of some sympathetic friends, there was some semblance of society once the official mourning was lifted. But I attended no parties save once or twice, and it was such an ordeal that I retired to my rooms as soon as I could escape. Even the large fir tree that Mr. Pierce had brought into the East Room that Christmas could not lift my spirits. It was a new diversion that had gained popularity in England—a tree aglow with candles and ribbons and gingerbread. It looked so festive. Bennie would have clapped his hands for joy. My eyes filled with tears at the sight.

> [14]**ABIGAIL FILLMORE**
> *Within two weeks of the Pierce's inauguration, I had died too. The new Vice President, William King died as well. Margaret Taylor and Louisa Adams died that year. There was much crepe in Washington.*

Mrs. Jefferson Davis, whose husband had been appointed Secretary of War when Mr. Pierce took office, became my closest friend despite an age difference of nearly twenty years. I don't know how I could have borne that terrible ordeal were it not for Varina. She had a little boy of her own, and I doted on him, pouring into him all the love I would have given my Bennie. Varina Davis helped my aunt choose the menus and flowers, and hosted most of the teas and luncheons that usually lay in the realm of the First Lady obligations. She was charming and well suited to it. When she became First Lady in her own "country," it was no wonder that she acquitted herself with grace and dignity. She was as dear as a sister to me, and I am happy to have these few pages to express my admiration and affection.[15]

[15]**MARGARET TAYLOR**
Like I said, Varina was a nice gal. We all liked her.

I found it nigh unto impossible to do anything except read the Scriptures for hours, seeking answers that never came.[16] I wrote volumes of letters and poems to my dear dead Bennie. I poured my soul into those letters. I was sure he was in Heaven, and I implored him to look down upon his poor, devoted, woebegone mother, and lift her from her sorrow. I looked everywhere for signs that he was with God, so I might find some small comfort. Obviously I had failed in some way as a mother, or God would never have taken the child from my bosom.[17]

[16]**MARTHA WASHINGTON**
Of course we grieve. I lost all four of my children. But life is meant to be lived. Somehow we find the strength to survive.

[17]**BETTY FORD**
It would seem that Jane Pierce, like many women of her time, suffered from chronic depression. This is often "anger turned inward." And since any expression of a woman's anger was unheard of in the 1800's, it became "martyrdom."

I prayed for hours to be forgiven for all my sins. And I prayed even harder for my husband to be forgiven for his. Perhaps the punishment was his and not mine. But then, why was it *I* who suffered so? Perhaps God wanted Mr. Pierce to have no distractions in his exalted work. Try as I did, I found no answers.

I do not know how my husband managed to express his grief in losing our son. Rumors abounded that he had lapsed from his pledge.[18] If so, I would find it in my heart to understand

[18]**JULIA GRANT**
Word was that President Pierce went on a monumental bender.

and forgive him. He had been a devoted father. But Bennie was the son of my soul. We were much closer. I had instilled in him all the qualities and morals for a profound and pious life. A life cut so pitifully short…. Alas, I would that it had been mine.

> **EDITH ROOSEVELT**
> *Bennie Pierce was a little prig. Joyless and humorless just like Jane. A month at Sagamore Hill with Theodore and our children would have done him a world of good!*

> **BARBARA BUSH**
> *You are probably right, Edith, but Bennie was a great-great-great cousin or uncle or something of mine. Only I can say those things.*

When we retired to New Hampshire after Mr. Pierce's term, I suffered anew. Every room bespoke my absent child. His clothes, his books, his toys....

Those years remaining to me were a blur. My frail health declined further. I read my Bible. I sat with our Minister. I kept a steady and affectionate correspondence with Varina Davis until it became imprudent, nay dangerous to do so. We both mourned the loss of our contact with the Davises when the War finally came. It had been a close and sustaining friendship. My husband's outspoken and stalwart support of States' Rights had made him very unpopular in New England. He opposed disunion, of course, but he found it hard to support President Lincoln when he so admired "President" Davis. He even started considering that a separation of "countries" might be for the best. Old friends and neighbors stayed away.

So we went to Europe for a while. But even the glories and grandeurs of their great capitals held no thrall for me. I could not enjoy it, and begged to come home.

When death finally came to me, I greeted it with open arms and a glad heart. I knew that Heaven held far more riches for me than life ever did. I would be with my children again.

> **BARBARA BUSH**
> *Franklin Pierce lived for five or six years after Jane died. His old friends avoided him because of his obnoxious politics, and they say he was never sober for a day after his wife died.*

MARY TODD LINCOLN
1818-1882
First Lady: 1861-1865

I have no secrets. How could I? Every moment of my life has been analyzed, scrutinized and criticized. More has been written about me than any First Lady except Eleanor Roosevelt. And now that Mrs. Kennedy is with us in eternity, I suppose history will have its way with her, too, poor thing. When you have a strong personality instead of a submissive, compliant one, you are bound to make enemies, and further bound to have people slant information the wrong way. There are dozens of books purporting to define my life. All of them are correct, and all of them are wrong. Like the Blind Men and the Elephant. But I thank Lucy Hayes and Caroline Harrison for this opportunity to set the record straight on several issues.

I was born into a prominent Kentucky family in December, 1818. The Todds were well known throughout the State, and counted no less a figure than Henry Clay as a close personal friend. I was a Kentucky belle, educated at a fine finishing school. When I was twenty, I paid an extended visit to my sister in Springfield, Illinois, where I met Abraham Lincoln, among other suitors. We married in 1841, had four sons, one died as a babe. We prospered. Mr. Lincoln was elected President. We moved to the White House, fought and won a terrible War, and he was assassinated. I fell apart. Those are the *true* facts of my life.

Now, to correct the fallacies, the lies, the rumors and the gossip. First: I was not nearly as "plump" as people think. I had a round face and a short neck, and with those enormous hoop skirts of the 1860s, I probably looked like a bubble. I was five-foot-three inches tall, and at my *very* heaviest, four children notwithstanding, weighed maybe 130 pounds. *Maybe.* I was short-waisted, but I had slim hips and long legs for my height. People today would say I was an "apple" rather than a "pear." Julia Grant outdid me by at least forty or fifty pounds.

> **LUCY HAYES**
> *I was a pear. I was also 5'3",
> and weighed 128
> pounds—before my eight
> children. Then I fear I added on
> some matronly weight. But I
> looked a lot different than Mary.*

> **JULIA GRANT**
> *Let us not forget that being
> buxom was a considered a
> great attribute. Men
> preferred a soft, full,
> feminine figure, with
> rounded curves and flesh.*

> **FRANCES
> CLEVELAND**
> *Good point! I remember
> how popular Lillian
> Russell was in my
> day—and she tipped the
> scales at over 160
> pounds!*

> **LUCRETIA GARFIELD**
> *Don't forget that we were
> weighed with all our clothes
> on. I imagine all the crinolines
> and yards and yards of fabric
> probably added ten or fifteen
> pounds.*

Second: I suffered from migraine headaches. I don't remember when they started. I believe I had one when I was still fairly young in Kentucky. With each child, they became more frequent. I also *loved* chocolate. Today they say it can trigger migraine, but people didn't know it then. Staying in bed in a quiet, darkened room with a cold cloth on my forehead was as much treatment as could be given. Sometimes my headaches lasted for days. Mr. Lincoln was always concerned when I got "the" headache, since he knew how I suffered. My face became ashen and pinched. I had nausea and vomiting, and usually lost five pounds or more during an episode. Obviously, I was not *inventing* these headaches. I lived in fear of them, since they were truly incapacitating. *Anyone* who suffers from migraine can understand.

Third: I *did* have a temper. Everyone has a temper. There are some people who control their tempers well, and others who let their emotions run away with their better judgement. Mr. Lincoln was given to better judgement. I was more emotional. But I usually had good reason to lose my temper. I adored my wonderful husband, of course, but he was completely oblivious to domestic concerns. He took little interest in our house or its furnishings. He was indifferent to meals, careless in his dress and social graces, and was a poor disciplinarian to our sons. Not that they needed much discipline. They were good boys, all of them, and I firmly believed that they should have as much freedom as possible. But *when* discipline was needed, Mr. Lincoln was usually *nowhere* to be found.

> **EDITH ROOSEVELT**
> *I was always the disciplinarian in our family. Theodore was usually off politicking or hunting during the family "crises."*

> **JULIA GRANT**
> *The Lincoln boys were decent enough and well behaved, but I suspect the youngest, Tad, was a little "backward." Of course nobody mentioned it in public.*

> **BARBARA BUSH**
> *Tad Lincoln had a cleft palate, and may have been mildly dyslectic. But he was definitely not "backwards."*

Since I was brought up (like most women of my time) to place a high value on all of the above, I felt very much *alone* in providing a home life suitable to growing stature. It was frustration rather than anger which led to the outbursts. And once I gave way to an outburst, I found it hard to stop. I know I vexed Mr. Lincoln from time to time, but he loved me dearly and always forgave me.

Fourth: I admit to the shopping. I suppose we all have our reasons for our little "vices." I think Mrs. Kennedy "shopped" because she was allowed little outlet for her talents. I "shopped" because I had to show that I was *not* the "Western woman of low tastes" that my critics assumed. I was a Kentucky belle. I was educated. I spoke fluent French. I was certainly more cultured than upstart Julia Grant. She didn't speak French. I was certainly better looking! My clothes were the latest fashion from Paris.[1] Perhaps the style was somewhat ornate, but then isn't haute couture always extreme?[2] At least I wasn't frumpy and dumpy like Julia Grant. She always looked like she was mad at somebody!

> [1] **JULIA GRANT**
> *Mary Lincoln had the worst taste in clothes of anyone! She decked herself out with all those flowers and flounces. It was totally unbecoming.*

> [2] **JACQUELINE KENNEDY**
> *Some haute couture definitely is excessive. But if someone is a true "setter of style," it reflects the personality. I always liked simpler lines. And I shopped because I like to shop.*

> **[3]NANCY REAGAN**
> *There is a famous photograph of Mary in a voluminous white gown with black flowers that she wore to that ball. She looked like a chocolate-chip marshmallow.*

> **[4]EDITH WILSON**
> *People criticize you for everything, Mary. You are damned if you do, and damned if you don't.*

> **[5]JANE PIERCE**
> *See? I wasn't the only one overcome by the death of a beloved child.*

We only had one State ball while were in the White House. We were in the midst of a terrible War.[3] How could we entertain and laugh and have a good time while our countrymen were dying by the thousands? We were criticized because we did not entertain; then when we did, we were vilified for having a party "while our countrymen were dying by the thousands."[4] Our only ball was held as our darling Willie lay dying upstairs. I barely remember it because Mr. Lincoln and I took turns sitting with our sick boy. He died shortly thereafter, and I was incapacitated by grief.[5]

Perhaps if I had more chances to *wear* my lovely gowns, I wouldn't have had the need to keep buying new ones. Perhaps under other circumstances, I might have shown *everyone* what an elegant hostess I could be, and could have easily reigned as the social leader in Washington.

> **HARRIET LANE**
> **1857-1861**
> *I suppose this is the logical place for me to put in a word or two. For four years I served as the elegant social leader in Washington while my Uncle James Buchanan was President. Even though the winds of war were swirling around the Capital, the Buchanan administration was well remembered for its excellent social grace. We even entertained the Prince of Wales.*

> **[6]ELEANOR ROOSEVELT**
> *Of course Mary wasn't a traitor. I wasn't a Communist either. But there will always be people who criticize.*

Five: I was *not* a traitor.[6] It is true that some of my brothers fought and died for the Confederacy. My sister Emilie's husband was a Confederate officer who died for his cause shortly after we lost our beloved Willie. Mr. Lincoln sent for Emilie himself. He was always fond of Little Sister, and thought we might comfort each other's heartache. My poor husband had *so many* cares from the War that he could barely spare a tear for his *own* deep heartache. How could he spare time to comfort *me* when I needed him most?

So people said we were harboring traitors in the White House because of my sister. I was as loyal a Union citizen as *anyone*! I never approved of slavery. Never! And I did *not* pass secrets to my brothers, or to General Lee, or Jeff Davis, or anyone else for that matter. All the talk about Mrs. Lincoln being a "spy in the White House" caused us *great* grief. But you know how people like to gossip and spread vicious tales. Mr. Lincoln never *ever* went before Congress to testify about my loyalty. That story was made up of whole cloth after we were both dead for years, done to vilify me and glorify him.[7]

> [7]**MARTHA WASHINGTON**
> *The "cherry tree" story was made up of whole cloth as well. And as for throwing coins across the river, the General was far too frugal to waste money that way!*

But what I really want to talk about came *after* the White House. After my beloved husband was murdered. After my life, as I knew it, was over. I had two surviving sons: Robert, who had recently graduated from Harvard, and Tad, who was eleven at the time.

I've thought a great deal about Robert during my years in eternity. I never figured out whom he favored. He was certainly not a Lincoln—at least not that I know of, since I never knew any of Mr. Lincoln's family. He never talked much about *his* family. Like me, he lost his mother when he was about seven or eight. I don't think he cared for his father. He reminisced occasionally about his stepmother Sarah Johnston, and always with affection, but that was about it. Hmmpf. At least he *liked* his stepmother. I detested mine, which was the main reason for the "extended visit" to my sister in Springfield when I was twenty. Robert looked very much like his namesake, my father, Robert Todd, but I don't think Robert was all that much of a Todd either.

Mr. Lincoln was away "riding the circuit" most of the time when Bob was small, and I think Robert's personality was probably greatly affected by the death of our little Eddy, who died when Bob was six or seven. They were playmates. By the time darling Willie and Tad were old enough to play, Robert (who disliked being called "Bob" by that time) was preparing to enter college. Mr. Lincoln, meanwhile, had become successful, and did not travel quite so much.[8] The younger boys had the great advantage of

> [8]**EDITH ROOSEVELT**
> *No one—absolutely no one—enjoyed romping with his children more than Theodore. He was always a child at heart!*

a father who enjoyed romping with them. Robert and Mr. Lincoln never played. Perhaps that was what was wanting in Robert.

My relationship with Robert had always been very good, until the War and Willie's death. Robert desperately wanted to join the Army. He was twenty-one or -two, and was taking a fearful hazing from his Harvard classmates and the newspapers about his "civilian" status. *I* was violently opposed to his enlistment.

> **EDITH ROOSEVELT**
> *All four of my sons saw action in World War I. I lost my baby. The remaining three also served in World War II. Only one survived.*

> **ELEANOR ROOSEVELT**
> *All four of my sons saw action in World War II. But that didn't stop the gossip about them.*

We were at *War*, and thousands were dying every day. I was *petrified* for his safety. What mother wouldn't be, especially after just losing a son? It wasn't that I didn't *understand* Robert's needs or wishes; it's just that I knew *mine* were more crucial. At least they were at that time. Mr. Lincoln understood and was sympathetic to Robert's view, but he deeply feared for my emotional stability. He charted a middle course. He arranged for Robert to serve on General Grant's personal staff where he would be out of harm's way.[9] Our relationship with Robert began to deteriorate about that time. He said he felt humiliated that his father was personally paying his "Captain's salary," and believed he was being placated. Robert also lost patience with *my* anxieties.

> [9]**JULIA GRANT**
> *Ulys and I both had a fine opinion of Bob Lincoln. He was a competent aide-de-camp, and we always maintained a warm and cordial relationship with him. He never seemed to mind that we called him "Bob."*

Shortly before Mr. Lincoln's death, Robert became engaged to the daughter of Senator Harlan. Her name was Mary, too. Mr. Lincoln and I thought she was lovely, and we welcomed her as the daughter we never had. Then came that *terrible* fateful April night, and whatever control I had on my emotions vanished completely, never to return. The events remain a blur, but a blur etched eternally into my memory. My arm would sting from time to time in exactly the spot where my beloved's lifeblood had splashed on my dress....

> **JACQUELINE KENNEDY**
> *...lifeblood had splashed on my dress...*

Poor Robert had to assume complete responsibility for all the arrangements.[10] The long funeral cortege back to Springfield, the burial, the move from the White House. The whole future of what remained of the Lincoln family. I was *absolutely* no help whatsoever; nay, I was a pitiful burden to everyone during that ordeal. I admit it. I took to my bed for weeks, unable to move, unable to eat, unable to do anything but weep uncontrollably.

> [10]**IDA McKINLEY**
> *Robert Lincoln is an odd footnote in history. He witnessed the assassination of THREE presidents: his father, President Garfield, and oddly enough, my husband. Bob Lincoln was attending the Exposition in Buffalo when the Major was shot.*

> **LUCRETIA GARFIELD**
> *When my husband was assassinated, I steeled myself against any unbecoming display. I did not want to be like Mary.*

> **IDA McKINLEY**
> *When my husband was assassinated, my one wish was to make my husband proud of how well I could behave. I did not want to be like Mary.*

> **JACQUELINE KENNEDY**
> *When my husband was assassinated, I wanted everything to be like the Lincoln funeral except me. I did not want to be like Mary.*

I suppose that's when and why Robert stopped being the "son" and became the "father."

He married in due course, but unfortunately, Robert's Mary, for some reason, disliked me, and made it difficult for me to be near my dear son. He offered more than once to have Tad and me live with them, but I disdained. His wife was cool and remote, and I knew *she* would be uncomfortable.[11] It pained me, since I wished to be closer to my eldest (who, as he aged, looked so much like my dear departed father it was uncanny!) and I wanted so *very* much to be near my little grandchildren. Especially my beloved husband's namesake, Abraham Lincoln the

> [11]**LOUISA ADAMS**
> *Women and daughters-in-law, or women and mothers-in-law...it doesn't matter. It is a difficult relationship. Ask Abigail.*

Second. I wanted them to *know* their Grandmama. I longed to tell them the *true* stories of their immortal Grandpapa. I wanted to pamper them and spoil them, and love them to pieces. But it was quite obvious that one household could not accommodate *two* Mary Lincolns. Our estrangement widened.

My years alone were difficult.[12] Tad, never a strong boy, sickened and died when he was eighteen. I was bereft. I had no one. No husband. Three sons in the grave. One son lost to me by his own distance. There was no one who loved me or who could accept the love I ached to give. I clung to the small kindnesses shown by clerks and servants. I don't think *anyone* could have been as lonely as I.[13]

My emotional health, which had never been robust, became even more frail, but never, *never* was I "incompetent." NEVER! One night, when I was staying in a Chicago hotel, I thought I heard a noise outside my rooms, so I opened the door to look. I was wearing my nightdress and a shawl. Robert was notified and decided that I was "exposing myself in a state of near undress." That was deemed sufficient cause to have me put away. Can you *imagine* such nonsense? I heard a noise. What was I to do? Quickly put on my corset and crinolines and finest ball gown to open the door and investigate?

I sewed my money and bonds into the hems of my petticoats, a common practice. I traveled abroad with Mrs. Keckley, my dressmaker and companion. I could not rely on banks or rates of exchange. An aging woman and a Negress were conspicuous targets for robbery, and I was petrified of sudden foul play. My beloved husband's brutal murder scarred me forever. Since my income was limited and I had no idea how long I might live, I needed to be very prudent.[14] I remembered how Mrs. Madison suffered financially in *her* old age, and how both Thomas Jefferson and James Monroe had to declare bankruptcy in *their* declining years.[15] I was terrified that I would suffer the same dire fate. Is that crazy? It makes

> [12]**NANCY REAGAN**
> *Another candidate for Prozac.*

> [13]**LOUISA ADAMS**
> *Mary was in her late forties when Mr. Lincoln was killed. Her "changing" years were likely contributing to all her miseries.*

> [14]**JULIA GRANT**
> *Prudent? Mary? Spending hundreds of dollars on lace curtains when she lived in furnished rooms? Mary Lincoln was NOT competent to handle financial affairs, and was lucky to have a wonderful son like Robert looking after her.*

> [15]**JULIA GRANT**
> *She tried to sell her clothing—and even some of Mr. Lincoln's shirts. This is not a stable person.*

perfectly good sense to me.

I *was* extremely emotional. I know that. I had insomnia, and when I did sleep, I had frequent nightmares, reliving a twilight version of the terrible events in my life. I had periodic depressions. I was unbearably lonely and friendless. This makes for a sorrowful woman, not a crazy one.

Robert had me sent me away to what was called a private "sanitarium." Oh, he made sure it was the best money could buy, and that I had every "luxury." But I did not have my freedom, and, since there was no such thing as "psychiatry" or "psychology" in those days, there was also no treatment. I will not bore the reader with the things I saw in that place. Suffice it to say, some women there were *truly* "crazy." Some of them screamed all night and tore off their clothing. Some imagined demons chasing them. One even tried to set fire to her room to rid herself of the "devil" that came in through the floor boards. All I ever did was investigate a noise outside my room—and try to be thrifty.[16]

> [16] **BETTY FORD**
> *I never believed that Mary Lincoln was the "crazy woman" that her contemporaries described. I do believe she had problems which today could and would be treated with a high degree of success.*

It was due only to the efforts of a woman journalist who espoused my cause that I was given another "hearing." It took all of ten minutes and I was pronounced "cured." I won't even *try* to dignify that with further comment, save only that my health was further ruined by the "cure," and I spent my remaining days with my sister, wishing only for death to relieve me of all my cares and reunite me with my dear departed ones.

It has also been bandied about, during the last century or so that I was jealous and took immediate and intense dislikes to some people.[17] This is true. I think many people could admit the same. It may not be the finest virtue, but we are not perfect. Perhaps I was more vocal. We don't have to like *everyone*. Even Mr. Lincoln had a few people on his "don't care much fer" list. General McClellan was one, and another was that sanctimonious Edwin Stanton. Neither of us

> [17] **JULIA GRANT**
> *In my own experience, I found Mary Lincoln to be jealous, frenzied, bad-mannered, ill-tempered, and totally unfit to be called First Lady. I have never seen any reason to change my mind.*

"cared much fer" him, the old goat and his pious, "now he belongs to the ages," drivel.

But on the other hand, we were also able to change our minds. Once we knew Secretary Seward better, we *both* regarded him highly, and with affection. He was a fine man.

> **EDITH WILSON**
> *Like Mary Lincoln, I also tended to be less than diplomatic in my dislikes, particularly of those who spoke ill of my husband. That's probably why so many of my contemporaries created such lies and slander about me. I did NOT, repeat NOT, run the country during Woodrow's illness. And even if I did, it is no reason to voice the supposition as if the country were being run by a baboon!*

I had *every* reason to feel a tremendous resentment toward some of my successors. Mrs. Johnson was, I suppose, a nice lady, and, I am sure, better than her disgusting husband. We never met, but she kindly allowed me to stay at the White House until I was well enough to move. But Julia Grant? Why *shouldn't* I feel resentment? Her husband was a mediocre clerk as a civilian, a butcher as a General, and an idiot as a President. But they were lionized!

Every wealthy Republican—and Republicans were *incredibly* wealthy—offered the Grants luxury upon luxury! A mansion in Philadelphia, a mansion in Washington, horses and carriages, silver, jewelry! And Julia Grant lapped it up like a saucer of cream. And she's one to talk about *my* clothes! Hah! When she was First Lady, it was fashionable to expand her already considerable expanse with a bustle, but nothing she could possibly wear would make her less *frumpy, dumpy—or cross-eyed!*

> **JULIA GRANT**
> *I cannot imagine how Mr. Lincoln ever managed to put up with her. She was a total witch!*

> **CAROLINE HARRISON**
> *I thought we all agreed to KINDNESS!*

> **JULIA GRANT**
> *Don't look at me. This is HER chapter.*

And as for the Butcher of the Battlefield, all those rich Republicans subsidized Grant's so-called "business" after the Presidency, and when it failed like everything else he did out of uniform, they were even willing to bail him out.

Then later, when President Garfield was murdered, a "shocked-and-saddened" populace handed over $300,000 to Mrs. Garfield so she could live comfortably for the rest of her life, *which she did*. But me? The widow of the

President who sacrificed his *all* for the country? The widow of the man immortalized as our *greatest president?* I was given one year of his salary. That was it. $25,000, and goodbye, Mary! Later, Congress voted me an additional $3,000. How I was supposed to live comfortably? I had debts. Everyone knew that. I realize that I had my faults, but it still seemed to be a terrible blot on the memory of our greatest, martyred president for his widow to live in cheap boarding houses abroad in order to save money. Nobody was shocked or saddened enough to come to *my* aid.[18] And, when I tried to raise funds by selling some clothing...well, no need to go into that. So if I was resentful, I had every right and more than enough reason.

> [18]**JULIA TYLER**
> *I came to your aid, Mary. It may not have been because of you, but you did benefit a little from my Widow's Pension campaign.*

> **NANCY REAGAN**
> *It's always the money. Always.*

And finally, regarding my opinion about Mr. Lincoln's law partner, William Herndon: I did not like Mr. Herndon any more than he liked me. He dredged up and distorted stories about my husband and a purported "lost love" with an Ann Rutledge, who never even existed, or if she did exist, was merely a passing acquaintance of no significance. I believe he manufactured that entire episode to spite me and cause me pain because I never invited him and his low-class wife for dinner in all the years we lived in Springfield.[19] I always thought Mr. Herndon was lazy, shiftless, uncouth, slovenly, drunken, familiar, and most of all, unworthy of the full partnership Mr. Lincoln gave him. Mr. Lincoln did all of the work; Mr. Herndon sorted the papers and collected fifty percent of the fees. He was also a liar.

> [19]**ELEANOR ROOSEVELT**
> *It is always painful when someone's private life is made public. It's bad enough when it is the truth; perhaps it is even worse when it is a lie that most people want to believe.*

And that's the truth.

ELIZA McCARDLE JOHNSON
1810-1876
First Lady: 1865-1869

Oh my dears, I am deeply touched to be included in this enterprise. Nobody ever paid 'tention to me before. I s'pose it's because when I was the "Lady," I was an invalid. I had consumption. 'Course they don't call it that nowadays. Tuberculosis, they call it now. There were two kinds. Fast and slow. You died either way. Mine was the slow kind. It sapped at me for years.

There ain't much to tell 'bout me. I was born and bred in the eastern part of Tennessee, and 'cept for some time in Washin'ton, and the to-and-from journey, I was never any other place but Tennessee.

I married Andy Johnson when I was sixteen and he barely seventeen. He come to Greeneville with the clothes on his back and a price on his head. Andy was a runaway tailor's 'prentice, tryin' to start a new life for hisself. His folks was pretty much ne'er-do-wells, and his old employer worked him twenty hours a day, fed him po'ly, and whupped him regular.[1] When anybody speaks ill of my Andy, all they need remember is what it must-a took for him to survive that misery. He had-a be tough. And you never saw two harder workin' people in your life than my Andy and me. Times was hard for everyone. The rich ones in our town had a horse 'stead of a mule.

> [1] **MARY LINCOLN**
> *I'm no admirer of Andy Johnson, but I believe that of all the Presidents, he had the worst childhood. Many Presidents grew up poor, but Johnson was brutalized.*

I know Miz Hayes said we should talk 'bout ourselves, but my whole self was bein' a part of Andy's life. Everythin' I ever got he give me, and everythin' I ever done was for him. My life was his life. Even in eternity, my life is his life.

Anyways, Andy set up shop in our little cabin to do tailorin'. I set up housekeepin', and soon enough, raisin' our four babies in one room. His shop was in the other room. Manys a time I'd sit with Andy while he sewed. I'd read to him and rock a cradle. He liked that. I read whatever I could get my hands on. Poems, sermons, some-a Mr. Dickens' stories, but mos'ly the old newspapers. Greeneville was a li'l town; we didn't have a library, and for sure we couldn't afford our own books. Andy didn't care much for the poems and sermons, but he did like hearin' the newspaper talk. He knew some-a his letters and he could write his name, but that was all. So at night, after the young'uns were bedded down, I set about teachin' him to put those letters together, make the words, and read his own newspapers. He liked that the best. I also taught him cipherin'. He was real good at numbers. He had a real knack for it.[2]

> [2]**ABIGAIL FILLMORE**
> *It's hard to imagine how difficult it was to get an education in the early nineteenth century, particularly if you lived in a rural area. In today's world, I would have the equivalent of a 5th or 6th grade education. And I was the teacher!*

My life was bein' a good wife and mother, and takin' care-a the cow and a couple-a chickens and the kitchen garden. Kep' me busy enough. Andy kep' busy too. He was a good tailor. His prices were fair, he did good work, and he was pretty quick about it. As he got to know more 'n more people in Greeneville, we prospered. We bought a place for his tailor store downtown, and we got a bigger house for ourselves. Greeneville was a nice town. We had a good life. A lot better than either one-a us would-a dreamed.

Then the politics bug bit Andy.[3] He started goin' to some-a the town meetin's, and speakin' up for the "mechanics." That's what they called the tradesmen then—the tailors, carpenters and blacksmiths. The "workin'" people rather than the "property" people. And oh, how Andy liked talkin' in front-a folks! He'd get up to make a speech, and he'd be like a fly in honey! He joined

> [3]**PAT NIXON**
> *I doubt I need to say anything more on that subject. Politics can be a real addiction to some people.*

the Democrat party 'cause he thought they cared more 'bout the "mechanics" than the Whigs did. Then he got hisself elected alderman, and state legislator and Congressman, and then United States Senator. I was so proud, I could-a just busted! And Andy, well bein' in the same company as ol' Henry Clay and Daniel Webster and the mighty Thomas Hart Benton...sometimes he was just overcome. "What a great country we live in, 'Lize," he would say, "when a po' uneducated fellow like me can rise up to such a height." Nobody loved his country more'n my Andy. And nobody was prouder of a husband than I was-a mine!

For a long time, when he warn't in Washington, Andy "swung the circle" twicet a year, makin' the rounds-a all the towns in Tennessee. Even the small villages. "If I'm s'posed to represent these people, I have to know what's on their minds," he said. Mos'ly what was on their minds was slavery and State's Rights. And Tennessee was half-for and half-agin' it. Andy said it

> [4]**HILLARY RODHAM CLINTON**
> *Even then "It's the economy, stupid."*

was really about the haves and the have-nots.[4] I never "swung round" with him. It was unfittin' for a woman, and besides, I had-a take care-a the young'uns and the house.[5]

I figure I ought-a say somethin' "important" about slavery, but the truth is, both-a us were kind-a ambiv'lent. Bein' hard workin' plain folks, one step above the po' folks that we used to be, we understood the value-a labor, and the meanness of the rich folks who looked down on people like us and kep' us from gettin' ahead. Andy said that since slave labor was "free" labor, it kep' "free" men, black *and* white, from gettin' work. He figured if everyone was paid wages, the cream would rise to the top, like it always does.

> [5]**LUCY HAYES**
> *I think I was the first "First" who accompanied her husband on political trips. It was great fun! I know Mrs. Polk often joined her husband, but she was the exception, not the rule. And the Polks never traveled during his Presidency. We did.*

He didn't really care one way or the other 'bout slavery as a great moral issue. Matter-a fact, once we was in a position, he bought me a couple-a slaves to help out with the yard work and the washin'—'specially because-a our "surprise." Another baby. That was 'bout the las' thing I needed when I was well past forty and my other children was grown and havin' babies-a their own. Oh I loved our little Frank dearly, but I 'spect my ailments started long 'bout that time, in my weakened condition.

We treated our two slaves a durn site better than Andy's old "employer" ever treated him. But in the actual peckin' order, Andy thought colored folks was pretty much at the bottom-a the heap. Most-a the people (the ones in Greeneville, anyways) thought that way, and ev'body can't be wrong, can they?[6] But we never wanted anyone to be mistreated or denied their basic rights, and that meant any color. Andy never forgot where he come from, so we didn't hold with bein' mean.

> [6]**BETTY FORD**
> *When "everybody" always thinks something, I immediately get suspicious.*

Andy's real feelin's was for the "mechanics" of the world. He hated the "property" people more than anyone, I think. Jus' let a Congressman make a slightin' remark about a blacksmith or a shoemaker, let alone a tailor, and Andy'd light into 'em and give 'em what-for like you never heard. 'Course it didn't make him too popular with the other Congressmen. Andy was also passionate about preservin' the Union. I think he 'bout memorized the Constitution, and said it was mos' important document in the world, 'cept maybe the Ten Commandments

Then the War came, and it came hard to Tennessee. When they said "brother agin' brother" they must-a been talkin' 'bout Greeneville. Folks who was kind and good neighbors for twenty years closed their door to us. They were Secesh, and Andy was not only a Union man, but mighty loud about it. 'Course, whatever Andy thought, I thought. That was how wives did things in those days. 'Sides, he was the smart one. He was the one who got hisself to Congress and on talkin' terms with all the great people we read about in the newspapers. He always made fair sense to me. Don't misunderstand, though. If I thought he was wrong about somethin', I warn't afraid to speak my mind.

> **LADY BIRD JOHNSON**
> *Did you ever think he was wrong?*

Never.

Like I said, the War came hard to Tennessee, and the Johnson family suffered a-plenty. Nobody took care to respect our home like they did Miz Polk's since Andy was the only Southern Senator that refused to resign when the States were secedin'.[7] That didn't help much with his popularity, which always could use a-helpin'. My poor Andy was far too stubborn to meet anybody halfway.[8]

> **[7]MARY LINCOLN**
> *Mr. Lincoln always admired Senator Johnson's courage. Personally, I never cared for him, and always felt he had a finger in the plot to kill my husband.*

I s'pose with all Andy's troubles during the War, what with stayin' in the Senate tryin'-a keep Tennessee from secedin', and then as its Military Gov'nor,

> **[8]ELLEN WILSON**
> *Did I just hear that word "stubborn" again?*

nobody really cared about all my troubles, and I had 'em a-plenty, too. Both my sons and both my sons-in-law went off to fight for the Union, and here I was, past fifty years old with a little one, and startin' to spit blood.[9] My son Charles, the doctor, said I had-a rest and not work so hard. Hah! Easy to say. With the Rebs and the Yanks fightin' over every inch-a

> **[9]HILLARY RODHAM CLINTON**
> *The life expectancy of most women around 1860 was under 50 years of age.*

Tennessee, our supplies dwindled and we had-a make do the best we could with what li'l we had. We went hungry more often than not. Lucky my Martha and Mary were close by to help me with the boy.

Later, when we were s'posed to be safe in the Governor's Mansion in Nashville, there was no guarantee we wouldn't have to 'vacuate or be burned out. There were spies everywhere. Andy took to wearin' a brace of pistols for self defense. I worried 'bout that 'cause on the one hand he was so hot-headed, and on the other hand, he was a poor shot. Sometimes I wonder how we ever managed. And what with all those troubles, there was the personal ones to add to our trials. Son-in-law Stover was a casualty, so my Mary and her young'uns moved back with me to save money and help with little Frank. My strength was failin' badly. Got so's I was confined to a chair most-a the time. Jus' walkin' 'crost a room exhausted me.

Son Charles became a different sort-a casualty. He always wanted to be a doctor so's he could deliver babies and set busted bones and treat the usual ailments. We nigh on busted with pride that the son-a such plain hard-workin' mechanics could go off to a fancy Eastern college and learn such a high profession. Even better, we was mighty proud that we could pay for it! But my Charlie warn't cut out for doin' Army doctorin'. Listenin' to the screams of pain, sawin' off shattered bones; sewin' up bellies with the guts still hangin' out; smellin' the disease and infection that always followed; closin' more eyes in a day than he'd ever close in a lifetime of country doctorin'. No, my Charlie didn't have the stomach for that kind of doctorin'. The whiskey they gave the wounded to ease the pain found its way into Charlie's tent. And more'n more, he used it for his own pain. 'Ventually it killed him sure as a minie ball.

My other son Robert developed the same failin', although it took longer for him to succumb. I think my own greatest tragedy was seein' the two dear sons that we raised; that held such promise; that give us such great pride; to see their lives destroyed that way.[10] I would rather they'd-a been shot.

> [10] **ABIGAIL ADAMS**
> *It seems that in addition to our sisterhood as "Ladies," many of us share the kinship of having dear ones ruined by drink.*

Now like I said, Andy did the politickin', but it don't take a genius t'ask the obvious question: How come a Republican like Lincoln got to have a lifelong Democrat like my Andy for his vice president? Well, the simplest way t'explain a complicated subject is to say thus: President Lincoln needed a "partner" t'appeal to the South, since he had a hunch they'd be losin' the War and comin' back to the fold. And because of this faction and that faction and a few other factions, Mr. Lincoln and Andy run on the "Union" ticket. They warn't Republicans *or* Democrats. Least not on the ballot paper.

> **JULIA TYLER**
> *An invitation for disaster! It was the same situation between "Tippecanoe" and my Mr. Tyler too. It is political insanity!*

> **MARY LINCOLN**
> *You are right of course, Julia. But nobody expected that Mr. Lincoln would be murdered.*

> **JULIA TYLER**
> *Nobody expected that Mr. Harrison would die either. I suppose it made fair sense at the time.*

I s'pose the talk 'bout our sons' problems might-a 'counted for the bad tales they told about my Andy's drinkin'. He'd have a whiskey now 'n again, but like Mr. Lincoln hisself said, "Andy Johnson ain't a drunk." And I say it too, loud'n clear: Andy Johnson ain't a drunk. He'd been sick for more-n a week before the inauguration. Might-a even been typhoid, they said. He was feverish and weak. The doctor prescribed a glass-a strong whiskey to ward off the chill. Andy warn't able to keep food down for days, and the whiskey went to his head. The rest is well known. He was a sore spectacle.[11]

> [11]**MARY LINCOLN**
> *Andrew Johnson's behavior at the inauguration was disgusting and inexcusable. Poor is one thing. Mr. Lincoln was certainly a poor boy. But Andrew Johnson had no.... no....*[12]

I warn't there. My gals and their young'uns and my Frank and I was tryin'-a find whatever trains we could t'come East. The War had done terrible damage in Tennessee, and a-course Virginia was in ruins. I reckon there warn't more than 20 miles-a decent track at a time. The trip took almost two weeks.

> [12]**JACQUELINE KENNEDY**
> *No class.*[13]

Comin' to the White House the way we did, at the time we did, was a tragedy for everyone. Poor Miz Lincoln was overcome with grief, so we was glad to give her time to make her 'rangements. She needed a month. We stayed at Willard's Hotel. Son-in-law Patterson was the new Senator from Tennessee, so we had both gals and their young'uns with us. Good, lovin' daughters are indeed God's blessing.[14]

> [13]**MARY LINCOLN**
> *Right. No class.*

> [14]**PAT NIXON**
> *Amen to that.*

The White House was a shambles. When Mr. Lincoln died, people ransacked the place, actually cuttin' big pieces out-a the drapery and carpets for souvenirs! My Martha and Mary wasn't ones for puttin' on airs. We brought 'em up to do honest hard work. They put on aprons and kerchiefs, got down on their knees, and scrubbed and polished 'long with the hired folks. We warn't proud that way. Soon the place was decent for company. And we done it with the money Congress allowed. Not one cent more. [15]

> [15]**ELEANOR ROOSEVELT**
> *In the twelve years we were in the House, we only put in the swimming pool for Franklin's exercise along with whatever safety and security measures were necessary. There was a Depression and then a War. We were not worried about carpeting.*

'Course I kep' to my chair in my rooms. They was beautiful rooms. Far bigger and fancier than any we ever lived in, 'cept for the Willard. Oncet or twicet I was carried downstairs, but it was too much for me, and I warn't one to draw 'tention to my frailty. People come for a party, they should party. I was near sixty years old by then, and like Miz Jackson or Miz Taylor, I warn't cut out for a fancy life. I could take pride in my daughters' pleasures and in their able handlin' of whatever things needed handlin'.

> [16]**JULIA TYLER**
> *I could have predicted those troubles. I followed events closely, and by that time, I was very familiar with the ins and outs of politics.*

Ev'body was very kind to Andy at first, but the pleasant days were brief. Congress wanted to go one way, and Andy wanted to go another.[16] There was boun'-a be trouble. Tact and political give-and-take warn't my husband's bes' qualities. He was more likely to stand his ground and fight it out come hell or high water. Like I said before, he was nary the most popular man in town.

But the way I figure is this: A president's cabinet is like his family. They should stick together. If some Cabinet member don't agree with the president's policy, he should resign the way the bunch of 'em did with John Tyler. Andy had no problem *listenin'* to other people speak their mind. He respected 'em for it. But when push come to shove, you can't keep a cabinet full of people who are out-and-out agin' you. So when Congress passed this "Tenure of Office Act," which kep' a president from dischargin' a cabinet member if he seen fit, Andy seen it as a bad law, and agin' plain common sense. He insisted it was downright unconstitutional. I don't know 'bout that part. I warn't that smart. But I do know it's a bad law that makes you keep a servant even though he's stealin' from you. And Secretary Stanton was stealin' Andy's confidences and trust and givin' comfort to his enemies. And

LADIES: A CONJECTURE OF PERSONALITIES

this is my *own* thinkin'.

The whole impeachment was a nightmare.[17] Our family tried hard t'keep busy and put on a good face and t'love each other more. But it was a nightmare. I took more'n a dozen newspapers from all over the country, and read 'em every day, cover to cover. I'd cut out important articles, 'specially the ones that were favorable to Andy's cause. I'd wait till after supper, when we had some private time. Then I'd show 'im the stories and try to boost his spirits. I, m'self, had no doubt that Andy would be 'quitted. He done nothin' wrong, other than rub some pow'ful people the wrong way.[18] It was all politics. If Mr. Lincoln still had-a been president, he would-a done the same thing. Well, he would-a had the same policies, anyways. But he might-a handled 'em different.

I remember readin' oncet how relieved President Buchanan was when he lef' the White House. No one could-a been more grateful than me. Andy was angry, but I was glad. We was goin' home where we truly belonged. We had friends there—even the ones we lost touch with durin' the War. We forgave each other and patched up the fabric of our friendship and wove it back together. Sickly as I was, I grew old with my young'uns and their young'uns, 'mongst the people I knew. But the bes' was yet to come. Jus' a few years later, the good people of Tennessee sent my Andy back to the same Senate where he had been impeached. And when he got there, Congress rose as one, to honor 'im.

And one more thing. Eternity is a very special place. Miz Nixon might not-a been able to reach back to me, but I reached forward to her. I walked

> [17]**PAT NIXON**
> *I often thought of Eliza Johnson during our own long nightmare. I wished there were more information about that dear Lady, not just born-married-died stuff. I needed her. And just like when Mrs. Kennedy researched every nuance to Lincoln's funeral, I researched everything I could about Johnson's trial. There was no mention of how his wife or family fared. I think it should be mandatory for a First Lady to keep a private diary of her days. It would be a real gift to her successors. I'm sorry I didn't do it, even though it would have been so terribly painful.*

> [18]**ROSALYNN CARTER**
> *Andrew Johnson was what you could call a Public Relations disaster. Even when he was 100% right, he had a way of turnin' everybody "agin'" him.[19]*

> [19]**PAT NIXON**
> *It sounds familiar, dear. Dick Nixon could have said it was high noon on the Fourth of July, and there would always be people who would swear on a stack of Bibles that it was midnight in November.*

her ordeal with her. And I walked with Miz Clinton, too. And I shed tears with 'em both.

HILLARY RODHAM CLINTON

When so-called "charges" are political or even criminal, it is a terrible ordeal, and strong family love and support are priceless beyond words. But when they are personal and private in nature, it is unbearable. Posterity will all know entirely too much anyway.

JULIA DENT GRANT
1826-1902
First Lady: 1869-1877

I have been longing for my chance to speak out. I have always been overshadowed by Mary Lincoln, and why? Because her husband was shot. No doubt Mr. Lincoln was a fine man, and some people claim he was even a great one. Maybe he was, and maybe he wasn't, but heaven knows, a long line of well-respected men had things to say about Mr. Lincoln, that were not fulsome with compliments.[1] And the things people said about Mary Lincoln…well, I'm too much of a lady to repeat them.

> **[1]LUCRETIA GARFIELD**
> *It's true. My husband was not the greatest admirer of Abraham Lincoln. James said he lacked "strength of purpose."*

For the record, I was the first "First Lady" to recount the events of her life, at least by her own hand. Unfortunately, my memoirs remained unpublished for some seventy-five years after my death, but I did write them.[2] Good manners dictated that one must only say pleasant things about anyone in writing, so I held my tongue, or rather, my pen. But now, with a century twixt me and the reader, I can say whatever I like. Lucy and Carrie made the rules, and I shall be as kind or as unkind as I please. But I shall be honest. *Brutally* honest.

> **[2]MARY LINCOLN**
> *General Grant wrote his memoirs and it was a best seller and made a fortune. Julia probably figured to do the same. Problem was she was a VERY "gushy" writer and had very little to say. And, also for the record, Julia Grant was a jealous person.*

I grew up on a magnificent Missouri plantation called White Haven.[3] My dear parents were devoted to me and my brothers and sisters, and we, in turn, were devoted to each other. It was an idyllic childhood. Of course we had slaves, as did most people of means in Missouri at the time, but our slaves were considered our "family." No one was ever mistreated, nor do I ever remember my darling father selling any of our people or separating families, let alone taking a whip in hand. The bonds of family were sacrosanct to the Dents.

> **[3]MARY LINCOLN**
> *Plantation, my foot. It was farm. A plain ordinary farm. We Todds had the plantation—and the house in town.*

ABIGAIL ADAMS	MARTHA WASHINGTON	LOUISA ADAMS
Has it occurred to anyone how all our Southern Sisters considered their slaves as "family," and that every master was kind and considerate? To hear them tell it, slavery must been a paradise.	*We lived when we lived and where we lived. It was the way it was, and we accepted it as a condition of life. I refuse to be blamed for a society I did not invent. And the Dandridges and the Custises and Washingtons WERE kind masters.*	*Our Southern Sisters, their fathers and their husbands were likely decent masters, and perhaps kinder than most. But there is no excuse, none, for holding another person in bondage.*

In my eighteenth year I met Ulysses Grant, a West Point classmate of my elder brother Fred. He had come to call on us, and, if I'm not mistaken, it was at *our house in town, Mary. We had one too, Mary. In St. Louis, Mary. A far more important city than than Lexington, Kentucky, Mary.* Anyway, it was love at first sight between Ulys and me. Our courtship was perfect and so was our marriage, despite the long distances that so frequently separated us. We wrote to each other nearly every day of our lives.

Above all, Ulysses was a family man. Perhaps it was because his childhood years were wanting in affection that he became so deeply attached to the children and me. His father, Jesse, owned a tannery. He was a boastful, domineering and unpleasant man, and I believe Ulys was always in awe of him. His mother Hannah, while pleasant enough in the few words she ever spoke to me, was a cold and unemotional woman, who I doubt could ever give anyone comfort or encouragement. I always felt that Ulys was far happier in his associations with my family than with his own. My brother Fred liked him from the start; I loved him from the start; and the rest of the Dent family grew to love him dearly as time went on.

The early years of our marriage, although extremely blissful, had its usual trials and tribulations, but I cared not, even though Ulys was a young Lieutenant in the Army, a position where financial remuneration was slight. I traveled with him at every opportunity, and enjoyed it immensely. The life of an Army officer's wife suited me well.[4] And unlike

[4]**MARY LINCOLN**
Julia Grant was built like a safe. Square and thick. And you can see what I mean about her being a "gushy" writer.

Margaret Taylor, I was blessed with a robust constitution and excellent health.

We made friends where'er we sojourned; some of those pleasant associations lasted a half century. When my dear husband was dispatched to fight in the War with Mexico, I returned to my family in St. Louis. I was expecting my first born, and it would have been extremely perilous for me to join my husband near the battlefield on the eve of war. Ulys performed valiantly during those hostilities, and had occasion to meet several people who would factor importantly in our later lives.[5]

> [5]**MARY LINCOLN**
> *Grant actually had very little to do during the Mexican War, and no one of any importance remembered him. Julia Grant tends to get carried away.*

But "speak out!" Carrie and Lucy said. And so I shall, completing all the things that for decency's sake, I omitted from my own personal memoirs. Thus....

In despair and loneliness and with lack of opportunity for his talents, Ulys resigned his Army Commission after the War with Mexico, and we bravely struggled for several years, trying to keep the wolf from the door.[6] My dear father had generously given us several acres as part of my dowry, but unfortunately the land was rocky and not conducive to farming. Ulys tried many other

> [6]**MARY LINCOLN**
> *Ulysses Grant drank himself out of the Army. It was either resign or be dishonorably discharged.*

occupations, all far beneath his great and unrecognized abilities, of which I never had any doubt. But we were not proud. If we could but keep a roof above our heads and provide a decent life for our four dear little ones, we would be happy just being together. My beloved husband would be up long before dawn to labor far into the evening. Laziness was not in his character.

I also rose long before dawn to labor far into the evening, cleaning and cooking and sewing and tending the garden. Oh, I was not a lazybones either! Even though I was bred to supervise the labor of others, I did not disdain doing hard housework myself. I became an excellent cook; much better than Mary Lincoln ever was, anyway.

It is true that Ulysses and I owned two slaves. Actually, they were mine. I had received them as part of my dowry. My darling father insisted that my life was not meant to be mired in toil and drudgery. He had not been completely overjoyed at my marriage. Papa liked and respected my husband, but he was concerned about Ulys's meager prospects, and he so wished his beloved daughter to live in the gracious style of her completely perfect childhood. Ulys did not approve of slavery, and it was often a strain on our

---

[7]DOLLEY MADISON

Julia makes a valid point. When I was forced to sell Montpelier, many of our slaves would have been destitute and without skills to survive. Some of them were old and feeble. I placed most of them with the kindest "masters" I could find, and took as many as was practical with me to Washington City. They could not bear to leave "Miz Dolley," and I could not bear to send them away.

---

limited income to feed and clothe them. He wanted to release them from bondage, but I would never hear of it. They were my family. I had grown up with them since I was a babe. Where would they go? How would they live? It would be inhumane to turn them out into the wilderness with no one to care for them.[7]

Finally we removed to Galena, Illinois, where my father-in-law Jesse fashioned a modest position for Ulys at his tannery. It entailed long hours of frequently monotonous hard work. It also permeated everything with its putrid odors. We dwelt in a small cottage atop a steep hill, and Ulys would walk the steps down every morning, walk them back up for his noonday dinner, and then repeat that procedure in the afternoon. When he made the long climb back up in the evening, he fairly reeked of the hides and the tanning solutions. More often than not, I prepared a hot tub and insisted that he undress and bathe in the yard so as not to afflict our happy home with those foul-smelling chemicals.

I know Ulys was restless at his father's shop. I have a few choice words for my in-laws that I would never allow myself to express during my lifetime (I would never do or say anything then that would cause my beloved husband pain). I put up with both of them for Ulysses' sake and because they, indirectly, were providing the roof over our heads. Hannah Grant had to be the most silent, sullen, humorless, peculiar person I have ever come across in my life. She never had an unkind word for anyone, but then again, she never spoke to anyone.[8] Jesse Grant, however, was an obnoxious and exacting man, and here was my poor, dear husband, nearing forty, and still a clerk. When the position had first been offered, we expected that within a short time Ulysses would be made a partner, like his brothers. But month after month passed, and there were no promotions forthcoming.

---

[8]GRACE COOLIDGE

People accuse Calvin of being silent, but he had a certain charm about him. Those who came to know him always liked him. And, of course, he had that wonderful sense of humor!

Still, we had a strong and loving marriage. The moment my beloved came o'er the threshold of our little cottage on the hill, all was well with the world. It was as if we lived in a castle in Spain! Ulysses flung cares from his shoulders, and basked in the warmth of his loving wife's arms and the merry laughter of his children.[9]

> [9]**MARY LINCOLN**
> *Gushy, gushy, gushy.*[10]
>
> [10]**BARBARA BUSH**
> *She does have a way with words.*

Then came the terrible War destined to rend the country in twain. Ulysses volunteered his services to the Union, which, considering his expert military training and experience, were accepted with alacrity. He was assigned to train the local militia in military drill, a "command" far beneath his ability. But train them he did, and superbly! When those in authority recognized his genius, he was given more commensurate duties.

His rise to the top was long and arduous, plagued with a cadre of jealous superiors anxious to heap calumny upon him. I voluntarily sent our little Fred to serve as his aide. He was a lad of but a dozen years, but I believed it would serve the boy well to be at his dear father's side where he could learn so much. I joined him whene'er it was safe to do so, but mostly I stayed at our home in Galena, caring for the younger children. I often longed to be amongst my own loved ones in Missouri. I worried about them constantly, just as I worried about my beloved husband. I would have much preferred to be with my own family rather than my in-laws, but they were aligned with the Confederacy and it was not considered "safe" or "politically wise."[11]

> [11]**MARY LINCOLN**
> *See? Julia Grant had rebel relatives too, but nobody called HER a traitor.*

But once my brilliant husband's star began its ascent, it gleamed with a brightness that would forever remain aglow. Victory followed victory, albeit hard-fought and hard-won. I began calling my husband "Victor" to commemorate his renown as the greatest general the country had ever known—comparable only to the great George Washington.[12]

> [12]**MARTHA WASHINGTON**
> *There was little to compare. General Washington had nothing to work with. No army, no training, no supplies, no food, no funds and no strong government in back of him. Grant was well trained, with an enormous army, well equipped with food, horses and weapons, and a duly elected sitting government supporting his efforts.*

Now, as to Mrs. Lincoln. She had her say, and now I shall have mine. I met her only once or twice in my lifetime, which was more than sufficient to ascertain her character. Shortly before the end of the hostilities, I had occasion to travel with Mary Lincoln to review the troops in Virginia. Oh! What a terrible scene she made that day! She behaved like the crazy woman she was, or at least was to become. Jealous of anyone who dared remove her from the spotlight! The terrible things she said about me! That I was "waiting in the wings" to take her place! Imagine! Neither Ulysses nor I had any ambitions for the White House whatsoever.[13] If such momentous happenings were ordained by Providence, it was something far beyond my poor mortal powers to prevent. Her behavior was astonishing, to say the least! Her tirade amazed everyone within earshot, and was a devastating embarrassment to her husband. What had started out to be a wonderful, victorious excursion had devolved into a dismal affair. I was fearful of being left alone in her company, lest she prove violent.

> [13]**MARY LINCOLN** *Julia Grant is carefree with the truth. The moment her husband had a victory in the field, she began planning to reign in the White House. She can deny it all she likes. It is the truth.*

After that humiliating debacle, there was no way that Ulys and I would accompany the Lincolns to the theater that fateful April night. It was just as well that we had a previous engagement, or I would have manufactured one. Mrs. Lincoln obviously disliked me intensely, and frankly, I had no intention of trying to court her favor.

The horror of the next few days shocked the nation, indeed the entire world. General Grant and I both admired *Mr.* Lincoln, and believed his tragic death was a great loss to the country. Of course we were immediately sympathetic to Mrs. Lincoln's grief and sent all the appropriate condolences. We were also especially solicitous of their son Bob, upon whose young, untried shoulders would fall the burdens of making all the arrangements for a state funeral.

General Grant and I had come to know Robert Lincoln well. The dashing Captain Lincoln had served as one of my husband's aides during the last months of the War. Bob had wanted desperately to participate in the fray, and struggled against his mother's frenzied desire to keep him from harm's way. (But I sent my Fred, who was only twelve, off to the front with Ulysses from the beginning, didn't I?[14] I believed the exhilarating challenges and demands of the battlefield would prove an excellent education and encourage the character and discipline that a young boy needs. And, of course, his dear father would look after him.)

> [14]**ABIGAIL ADAMS** *I allowed John Quincy to accompany his father to France and serve as his secretary. Johnny was only ten or eleven at the time. I understand how Julia feels, although I had no battlefields to fear.*

I believe Bob resented his mother deeply

for "babying" him. It embarrassed him at college. All the other young men were valiantly going off to War to make their marks. Why was the President's son so "privileged"? Bob did not wish to be perceived as a "mama's boy," or worse, as a coward, neither of which he was.

In all fairness, I cannot fault Mary Lincoln for her concern. It is a natural motherly wish to keep a child from harm. She had lost a son not long before. I enjoyed kinder fortune. I never knew the grief of burying a beloved child. But I know how important it is for a son to "be his own man." Young Bob Lincoln was a fine, remarkably capable and serious lad and did not have his father's reputed sense of humor. I say "reputed" since Ulys had been exposed to some of "Old Abe's" stories and failed to be amused.[15] I have always suspected that Mary Lincoln was just a wee bit jealous of the fine relationship we had with her son, since hers was so poor.

> [15]**LADY BIRD JOHNSON**
> *That may speak more of Grant's lack of humor than the quality of Lincoln's jokes.*

President Andrew Johnson lacked the abilities and character of his predecessor. He called Ulysses to high office and promptly caused him a great deal of distress. My "Victor" was an honorable man, but I fear that he had little political acumen. Those talents did not come naturally to him, and he was caught in the middle of escalating rivalries. I daresay those few years were as intolerable to my beloved as the ones he spent toiling in his father's tannery. At least he could turn away from the tannery each evening. Politics permeates a life, day and night.

Naturally *I* abstained from any activity in politics, although I became an integral part of Washington's social circle. Mrs. Johnson was an invalid, and her daughter, Mrs. Senator Patterson, assumed most of the social responsibilities at the White House. She seemed to be a pleasant young woman, but President Johnson had enormous political problems, and thus little pleasantry emanated from the White House.

Following the Johnson fiasco, my beloved "Victor" was swept into the Presidency by acclamation! I enjoyed every moment. I make no apologies for it. My years as the wife and consort of the President of the United States were perfect bliss! It had been years, *years*, since there was any pleasure in that house! The Lincolns had that devastating War, of course, and Johnson had tumultuous politics and an ailing wife. This was a new day! A new Era! The Gilded Age had commenced!

I immediately launched elaborate plans to redecorate. The Johnson daughters had done their best, but their taste was very plain, to say the least. It suited them, but it certainly did not suit me. Congress was munificently generous with funds for its conquering hero and wanted him to reflect the "coming of age" of our great country. I ordered some of the finest furnishings from the most exclusive shops! It was time that the President's House took its rightful place as the center of a major country of the world, which it truly was!

> [16]**MARY LINCOLN**
> *It was a luxurious mansion. It is amazing how Julia Grant confuses size and quality when it suits her.*

Some people may look askance at us for accepting the gifts bestowed upon us by a thankful nation. We were wined and dined by the most prominent people in the country. We were given a charming house in Philadelphia, although we never lived in that city, and eventually disposed of it.[16] We were given horses and carriages, silver and gold platters and bowls, and exclusive opportunities for investment. And why not? The country was grateful to Ulysses S. Grant, the victorious general who saved the Union. Community groups and organizations clamored to shower him with honors. It would have been unforgivably rude to refuse.[17] My Ulys cared

> [17]**HILLARY RODHAM CLINTON**
> *No comment.*

naught for the trappings of luxury. The only gifts he personally enjoyed were the horses and the cigars. I, on the other hand, could finally indulge my tastes for the exquisite things I had had at my fingertips during my idyllic youth at White Haven.

It was my fondest pleasure to proudly repay my darling father by inviting him to live with us at the White House. Unfortunately, my father-in-law *also* came to live with us at the White House, and I fear they did not get on, as might have been expected. But then again, not too many people fared well with Jesse Grant. Our youngest son, also named Jesse (as a courtesy to my husband, not the elder man), took perverse delight in baiting the two grandfathers into argument over some trivial matter. But true to her nature, my mother-in-law refused to leave her house in Galena, never attended the inauguration and never even visited us. I imagine she must have felt *some* pride in her son, but she never mentioned it.

When our daughter Nellie was barely seventeen, she fell deeply in love with a young, titled English aristocrat whom she met whilst traveling abroad. Her father and I had serious misgivings since she was so young and inexperienced. We tried to dissuade her, but young love, being headstrong, prevailed. And I recalled that I was only seventeen when I fell head-over-heels in love with my dearest "Victor."

It was a grand White House wedding! I don't think there had ever been

116

one like it before! Naturally, a myriad of guests had to be invited: Cabinet members, Congress, the Diplomatic Corps, military hierarchy, and hundreds of new friends that we had made during the years following the conclusion of the late War. Ulys and I, of course, would have preferred something more intimate, but we did have our position to consider. Besides, the country clamored for festivity![18] Nellie received magnificent gifts from every important personage in the whole world! Can you imagine? Kings and Emperors and Sultans sent priceless gifts to my little girl!

I regret that her marriage, four children notwithstanding, was not the blissful union that her parents enjoyed. Nellie's husband had the same predisposition to drink as President Pierce.[19] Divorce was out of the question, no matter what the rationale. A divorced woman would have been totally ruined.

> [18]**FRANCES CLEVELAND**
> *Fiddlesticks. If they really wanted a small wedding, they could have had it. My wedding was attended by family, close friends and only the most important political acquaintances. President Cleveland did not wish to have a circus made of our nuptials. The Grants were thrilled to have the fanfare!*

> [19]**MARY LINCOLN**
> *...and General Grant...*

> **BETTY FORD**
> *Julia Grant enjoyed her limelight, even at the expense of her children. She encouraged her daughter in that disastrous marriage, and when it failed, refused to let poor Nellie come home. Julia liked being the mother-in-law of minor nobility.*

> **EDITH ROOSEVELT**
> *You're not being entirely fair, Betty. It is unfortunate that you were divorced before you married Jerry Ford, but in Julia's day a divorce was a major scandal. It was much easier to avoid the whole situation, and let both parties lead separate lives. Women would travel and visit relatives. Men went to their clubs.*

Whilst on the subject of failings. I suppose it devolves upon me to offer some mitigating remarks about my husband's weakness for whiskey. I do not deny that he fell victim on occasion. Unfortunately, he had little tolerance for alcohol, and it would make its ruinous effect known very quickly. Most of the time, he abstained.[20] But when he was lonely, or under great stress, Ulysses sometimes turned to whiskey for solace and to dull his

> [20]**BETTY FORD**
> *Loneliness and stress are probably the most common reasons people turn to alcohol. President Grant was lucky that he had loving people around him.*

pain. This was not unlike a great many soldiers throughout the centuries. There were even a few occasions during the War when my husband's trusted aide sent for me, since I was the only one who could provide the comfort my beloved needed.

Alas, history has burdened my poor husband with many failures as President. I do not deny that Ulys was an unschooled politician and a trusting man by nature, and whilst his judgment of men was superb on the battlefield, it failed him in civilian life. Of course I would never have spoken even a breath against him during my lifetime, but it is the truth, and I said I would be *brutally* honest. Most of the problems occurred because he misjudged the characters of his friends,[21] but I daresay many of the so-called scandals of the Grant Administration were fabricated out of whole cloth. Small, inconsequential events or oversights were blown far, *far* out of proportion and harmed some of the finest people we knew. To this very day, I *still* believe they committed no wrongdoing save perhaps using poor judgement.[22]

> [21]**FLORENCE HARDING**
> *No one is more sympathetic than I. Warren Harding once told me, "I can take care of my enemies. It's my friends who keep me awake at night."*

> [22]**NANCY REAGAN**
> *And I know a bridge in Brooklyn that Julia may wish to purchase....*

I was proud that my Ulys felt compelled to defend his associates. Loyalty was a quality of all the Grants.

It is also true that some in our family (actually in *his* family) were accused in some allegations of mischief. Even *I, myself,* was suspect. This, of course, is utter nonsense. I handled the money for the family, since Ulys detested keeping the books (perhaps because our finances were so strained it may have depressed him), but I never, *ever* did anything that could even be construed in a questionable or unfavorable light. I don't even have the slightest notion what "cornering the gold market" means.[23]

> [23]**HILLARY RODHAM CLINTON**
> *Uh-huh....*

I am not at all certain that Ulys enjoyed being President. The trappings of office made him uncomfortable. Wearing formal clothing made him uncomfortable. Eating delicacies he could not pronounce made him uncomfortable. I, on the other hand, was enchanted by it! Being First Lady had a great many perquisites that I found most enjoyable. We went to elegant parties with the cream of society, and I, in turn, could reciprocate in grandeur. I rode in a fine carriage.[24] I could finally indulge myself with the latest fashions and the loveliest jewelry and

> [24]**MARY LINCOLN**
> *I declare, if hanging ever became fashionable, Julia Grant would be first in line to the gallows.*

china and silver! I had spent so many years without them.

After eight glorious years in the White House, we decided to travel around the world. Our journey lasted two years and we were treated like royalty. I loved it! We dined "en famille" with Queen Victoria. We met the Tsar and the Kaiser and Monarchs of a dozen countries. It is hard to imagine a circumstance where a simple Midwestern girl could socialize on equal footing with such notables. How could I *not* love such a life!

Upon our return, the opportunity arose for Ulys to seek a third term. Despite all the scandals, my darling husband remained untainted and unscathed, and just as beloved as he was after Appomattox. I waxed enthusiastic about re-entering the White House, but not so my "Victor." He went through the political motions to please me and his numerous faithful supporters, but his heart was not in Washington. He wished to enjoy his remaining years in peace.

Alas, it was not to be. Our son Buck had embarked upon an investment partnership venture and enlisted his father's participation. Seeing as how little would be expected of Ulys other than featuring his illustrious name on the letterhead, my husband, ever the devoted father, acquiesced. For Buck's sake. The rest is unfortunately well known. Buck's partner was an unmitigated scoundrel, and the brokerage failed, leaving our good name once again tarnished and our debts overwhelming. My dearest husband, to his eternal glory, insisted on repaying all the creditors, even though the failure was through no fault of anyone named Grant.[25]

> [25]**MAMIE EISENHOWER**
> *Ike always thought that Grant was a superb General, but that his greatest personal qualities were displayed in his final years.*

As if financial disgrace and misfortune were not enough, my beloved was stricken with an incurable throat cancer. He desperately feared that I would be left impoverished, and we did not wish to burden our children. Mary Lincoln's strife was still afresh in our memory; the "Presidential Widow's Pension" was a paltry sum.

The popular author Mark Twain had become a good friend of ours, and had often urged Ulys to commit his recollections to the printed page. Many erstwhile War commanders were earning fortunes from their memoirs. Ulys had disdained for years; he never fancied himself a writer. But he reconsidered, as a means to repay his numerous debts and achieve future solvency for our family. My dearest love spent his last two years preparing his memoirs in a valiant race against time and the dreaded disease that would eventually conquer. The final notations were made only a week before he breathed his last.

Ulysses S. Grant's funeral was the grandest procession ever to parade on Fifth Avenue. A hundred thousand people lined the streets of New York. Thousands of soldiers marched. A grateful and proud nation subscribed to the erection of a magnificent tomb for him—for *us*—on Riverside Drive. His memoirs earned a fortune, particularly coming on the heels of his tragic death. Those writings are considered by subsequent generations to be the best-written and finest war memorials since Caesar's Commentaries. Ulys would have been stunned—but gratified.

A decade later, unbeknownst to anyone, I also lifted my pen to commit my own memories to paper. Mrs. Polk's *Memorials* had received a brief flurry of interest, and I thought perhaps mine might do likewise. But an old woman's recollections seemed unimportant at the turn of the exciting 20th Century, so they lay packed away in my granddaughter's attic. Nearly fifty years later, they were rediscovered and finally published: the first of the true Memoirs ever to be penned entirely by the hand of a First Lady.

LUCY WEBB HAYES
1831-1889
First Lady: 1877-1881

I am so thrilled! This idea is really working! Oh, thank you, thank you dear Sisters, for your co-operation and enthusiasm! We are finally able to let the world know what we were really like! So now it is my turn.

My father died when I was a baby and I don't remember him at all. My mother was a very remarkable woman, well ahead of her time, raising my two brothers and me with little help from anyone. She did not have the benefit of formal education, other than reading and writing a bit, and of course, the Bible. She was a devout Methodist. But she believed in education, and admired Mary Lyon, whom she had heard about. Mary Lyon was one of the founders of Mount Holyoke College, one of the first schools to provide women with a "higher" education. My mother was determined that I have "opportunities."

The women in Ohio, where I grew up, were barely educated, if at all. There was no need to read or write. We needed the domestic skills. Cooking. Sewing. Tending the crops and putting up fruits and vegetables for winter storage. Most of us still made our own soap and candles, although it was possible to purchase them in town, if you had the money. I learned those skills, too.

In 1846, my mother sent me to the Female Seminary near Cincinnati. There I was exposed to literature, languages, advanced mathematics, geography, history, philosophy and basic science. It was far more than most women my age would ever learn. I enjoyed study and I excelled!

I was still a student when I met Rutherford Hayes. He was ten years older than I, but our families were acquainted. Rud's father had died shortly before he was born, and his mother raised him and his older sister alone, too. We were immediately sympathetic to each other. I was only sixteen then, as fresh and innocent as a sixteen-year-old young lady should be. Two years later, Rud began courting me in earnest. We married when I was twenty.

Like Eliza Johnson, I suppose I could say that Rud's life was my life. We were the most normal-as-blueberry-pie people you could ever hope to find! I always thought we were a lot like Jerry and Betty Ford who came a hundred years later.[1] Good folks, good neighbors—the kind

> [1] **BETTY FORD**
> *I suppose you could call us blueberry-pie people. We liked our neighbors and liked having a good time!*

of people you want to invite for dinner. We were both good natured and always made friends easily and quickly. And we kept them forever. Like the Fords.

Maybe that's one of the problems with history. We expect too much from our leaders. Not everyone is meant to be a hero. Not every leader is a leader because of his (or her) tremendous intellect or sense of command.[2]

Rutherford Hayes was neither a great intellect nor a great commander, but he was definitely a man of substance and exemplary character. I always tried to emulate his fine qualities.

The Fords came "unelected." We Hayeses came "barely elected," and some might say, illegally elected. But the Fords, in their true blueberry-pie American way, were very much needed following the wrenching Viet Nam War, plus the scandals of the later Nixon administration. It was very much the same with us—after the wrenching Civil War, and the scandals of Reconstruction and the Grant Administration.

> [2]**BETTY FORD**
> *There are very few Presidents who had that "sense of command" that Lucy talks about. Washington had it of course, and both the Roosevelts.[3]*
>
> [3]**LADY BIRD JOHNSON**
> *And Lyndon. I don't think people realize his enormous powers of leadership.*

But I am ahead of myself.

No story of our family would be complete without due credit to Rud's Uncle Sardis Birchard. He was a lifelong bachelor, who fared well in real estate, and became a well-to-do Ohio businessman by mid-century. It was Uncle Sardis who financed Rud's college education and sent him East to Law School. It was Uncle Sardis who encouraged Rud's law practice by entrusting him with his many personal and business transactions, which in turn introduced him to some of the most influential people in Ohio. It was also Uncle Sardis who would provide much of the wherewithal for our sons' education. Suffice it to say that Rud and I became "middle class" without serious struggle.

Like Eliza Johnson, "we prospered." Our children came along at regular intervals, and I was a happy wife and mother. We were charter members of the local Literary Society and active in our Church. It was a good, good life.

But during the 1850s, when we were a young family, the war clouds were gathering. Being from a northern state, neither of our families had slaves, but we were far from abolitionists. While we believed that slavery was a sin against God and humanity, we were also very much opposed to the violence that abolitionism was causing. As time passed, everyone was caught up in the furor.

When the War finally came, Rud was forty, but he insisted on raising a regiment and doing his patriotic duty. I was not enthusiastic. We had several young children, and Rud, for all his good intentions, was far more inclined toward a sedentary, intellectual life. Nevertheless, he raised a regiment, and was promptly commissioned as Major.[4] He read all the texts on military training and tactics, and became a fine, if book-trained, soldier. He was eventually promoted to Brigadier General, and enjoyed an excellent reputation, even amongst the "professional" West Point hierarchy.

> **[4]EDITH ROOSEVELT**
> *Even as late as World War I, a private citizen could personally raise and equip a regiment of "volunteers." Theodore "personally" raised the Rough Rider contingent for the Spanish War, and offered to do likewise in the Great War. President Wilson said no.*

I mentioned previously about a "sense of command." Rud had something far better. He earned the respect of his "boys" of course, but he also earned their undying loyalty and affection to his dying day.[5] He loved his men and they loved him in return. We both attended the annual reunions of Rud's regiment until we died, and we were greeted with a genuine warmth and endearment that is rare between soldiers and their commanding officer. We were asked to be godparents of many of their babies; countless little Rutherfords, Hayeses and

> **[5]EDITH ROOSEVELT**
> *And Theodore can claim the same.[6]*

> **[6]MARTHA WASHINGTON**
> *No one enjoyed the love and loyalty of his men more than George Washington.*

Lucys were in the new generation of Ohioans. It is possible to command by love. They preach that in our Church.

Julia Grant joined her husband in the field. I also joined Rud as often as possible. It was not an uncommon practice for wives of senior military officers. Uncle Sardis was delighted to look after his "great-nephews" so I could spend a month or two with my husband. Battles were not fought every day, and often weeks and months would pass and the only action was fought between boredom and tedium. I tried to make myself generally useful in the camp. I did the mending, helped some of the soldiers write letters home, and even tended the wounded. I felt like every soldier's older sister. And I like to think that as the men grew to love Rud, they grew to love me, too.

Billy McKinley was one of the young fellows attached to Rud's Division, and I took to him at once! He was like a little brother to me—only a half-dozen years older than my eldest son. Billy had the sunniest of dispositions,

> **[7]IDA McKINLEY**
> *My future husband was General Hayes' devoted Aide-de-Camp. I believe General Hayes influenced the Major to study law after the War.*

plus a bright mind and strong virtuous character. I don't know anyone who didn't like and admire him. Rud and I both predicted a fine future for that young man.[7]

Rud was wounded four separate times during the War, twice seriously. I knew how important nursing was, since even the slightest wound could quickly become infected—and fatal. As soon as I got word (which sometimes took weeks), I came to camp at once to tend to him personally, thus sparing the overstretched medical staff for more important tasks.

After the war, Rud gravitated into politics. Because of his fine service record, he was easily elected to Congress on the Republican ticket, and later elected Governor of Ohio. None of these honors were actively solicited; they were offered by a community that was proud of one of their own, and honored him with a call to greater service.[8]

> **[8]MARTHA WASHINGTON**
> *As it should be.*

As I said, Rud's Uncle Sardis had made many things possible for us. The War exacted a heavy toll on our own finances, since Rud had relinquished his law practice for four years. And political office, if one is scrupulously honest, which we were, is not a lucrative business.

As Uncle Sardis grew older, he wanted us to make our permanent home with him (when we were not residing in the Governor's Mansion), which brings me to the only bone of contention I ever had with him. Uncle Sardis abhorred slavery, voted regularly for the Civil Rights Amendments granting Negroes freedom, citizenship and the right to vote, and was generous with those charities promoting assistance and education for Negroes. Yet he would not permit a Negro to set foot inside his home. I had developed some type of rheumatism caused by bearing eight children and I required help with the little ones.

Winnie Monroe was essential to my well-being. She had been born a slave, but when she came to us she was a free woman, and I paid her good wages. She was devoted to the Hayes family, and I came to think of her much the same way that Mrs. Lincoln thought of Elizabeth Keckley.[9]

> **[9]MARY LINCOLN**
> *Elizabeth Keckley was the finest woman I ever knew. Negro or white.*

I explained the situation to Uncle Sardis, and suggested that we could provide some suitable quarters for Winnie adjoining his beautiful house. But Uncle Sardis was adamant: No Negroes in his house. I was not about to make a scene or cause trouble between Rud and his usually wonderful (except for this situation) uncle. I thought he was foolish and inconsiderate, not only of Winnie, but of me. Perhaps it was the peculiarities that people sometimes develop with advancing age. But I was adamant too. I needed Winnie. We maintained our own separate house until Uncle Sardis passed on. When his estate became ours, Winnie, to be sure, came to live with us. She also went with us to the White House.

Now about those White House years.

The election that brought us to the Presidency was troubled and suspect. It had been ten years since the Civil War, but feelings still ran high, North and South. Several nasty scandals had plagued President Grant's second term, although the General still remained popular. Rud made it point of honor to refrain from the open electioneering between Republican Senators Blaine and Conkling. They were the front-runners; both involved in scandals of their own. To complicate matters even more, there was also a "reform" candidate for the Republications, but he was perceived as obnoxious and generally unacceptable to a party that did not wish to be "reformed." So the nominating convention sought an unaffiliated, available and honest man.[10] If nothing else, Rud was an honest man. He was also a War Hero, a former Congressman and Governor of an important "Western" State. Even though he was relatively unknown outside of Ohio, those were fine, acceptable credentials.[11]

> [10]**BETTY FORD**
> *We definitely have that in common, Lucy. Jerry deeply wanted to be a credit to his unexpected destiny.*

No one was more surprised than we were when Rud was nominated. It seems that all the obvious choices were objectionable to some faction of the party, and Rud, being the decent and honorable man he was, was probably a good "second" choice for everyone. He did not actively participate in the campaign. He made a few brief appearances, wrote some "open" letters, espoused the party platform, and let the other politicians speak on his behalf.

> [11]**NELLIE TAFT**
> *Actually the most important credential was "Ohio." It was neither a Northern nor Southern State.*

> **IDA McKINLEY**
> *Actively soliciting votes was considered bad taste in those days.*

> **ABIGAIL ADAMS**
> *Since our founding fathers, it had been the consensus that high office was a reward offered by ones countrymen, and should never be unabashedly sought.*

slavery issue had once-and-for-all been laid to rest, but women themselves were becoming an issue of their own. As Abigail Adams said before, they decided to "remember themselves." Some of them wanted to vote, but that was laughable. But they espoused higher education, and even employment opportunities. That was reasonable. Even men began to support those attitudes.

JULIA GRANT
I was absolutely against a woman working unless she was destitute with no one to provide for her. A woman should tend to her husband and children, and, lacking those, to her father, brothers or other male relatives.

MARY LINCOLN
Nonsense! There were many respectable employment opportunities for women. Teacher, dressmaker, milliner. Why the Nightingale Schools for Nursing had become very popular—and respectable—throughout Europe.

JULIA GRANT
Well, I suppose if a woman is truly impoverished. But I personally never knew anyone in such dire straits.

MARY LINCOLN
No, of course not. The Robber Baron families were never impoverished.

But the subject that was quickly becoming "the" moral-political issue of the day was Temperance. Much of the public outcry came from the Women's Christian Temperance Union. It was amazing to me that even without the power of the ballot, women could be an extremely effective political force.

[18]**MARY LINCOLN**
In those days, speech-making, lecturing, and oratory was a form of entertainment. People would come for miles to hear a good preacher!

There had always been preachers and orators and politicians making speeches against John Barleycorn. I remember going to hear dozens of speeches as I was growing up. The whole town would attend.[18] We'd bring picnics. But the decision to refrain from serving spirits in the White House, however, was *not mine*, although I agreed to take the responsibility. Personally, I did not care if people chose to have a glass of wine or brandy. I do not believe that anyone should force his beliefs down another's throat. After all, we live in a free country; we have the right to make our own choices.[19] I, personally, had always declined spirits. Rud had been known to "bend his elbow" on occasion when he was a young man, but he had taken the pledge many years before and was a man of his word. He believed that no one could be faulted for opposing drunkenness and wishing to set a good example. So spirits were banned from the White House, and I became "Lemonade Lucy."

> [19] **HILLARY RODHAM CLINTON**
> *I couldn't agree more. Every time people have tried to legislate morality, it has either caused terrible upheaval, or has failed entirely. We must always remember the lessons of Prohibition.*

To set the record straight, I *never* joined the WCTU, and I *never* liked their members or their policies.[20] I believed in temperance—not abstention. Those women hounded me incessantly, and they used my name and position without permission. I was *very* upset by it, but Rud counseled that I should remain still, unless they said something personally objectionable or liable. I also resented being called "Lemonade Lucy." After all, I wasn't the first "First Lady" to ban spirits. Why didn't they call Mrs. Polk "Sarsaparilla Sarah?"

> [20] **FLORENCE HARDING**
> *Those WCTU women were the most self-righteous group of homely old biddies you ever saw!*

But the WCTU was responsible for one nice thing, however. When they "commandeered" me as their role model, they decided to commission a portrait, which became one of my very favorite possessions. I wore a deep burgundy velvet gown, which made my waistline appear a good deal smaller than it was, and the white lace around the collar accented my chestnut hair, which still had not noticeably grayed. The artist must have taken some pity on me since at least ten years and twenty pounds were removed! Anyway, I loved the portrait!

I was the first "First" to travel officially with my husband during the Presidency.[21] Railroads spanned the continent by then, making travel easier, faster, cheaper and more comfortable. Rud believed that the President should not remain isolated from the people,

> [21] **JULIA GRANT**
> *After we left office, the General and I made a trip around the world and were feted everywhere. I think Lucy wanted to capture some of the pomp and ceremony that came with the Presidency.*

and decided to visit various parts of the country from time to time to see things for himself, and to let the people see him. He invited me to go along, and I agreed at once! I loved traveling. It was not for the pomp and ceremony. That was more to Julia Grant's liking. I just liked to travel and see new places and people.

But like Sarah Polk, I have some serious regrets. I think I was wrong in trying to keep the status quo on what First Lady "behavior" was supposed to be. First Lady "behavior" can be whatever the First Lady chooses. I am sorry I did not use the prestige of my position to do more good. I had no aim save being a wife to my husband and mother to our children. By nature, I was shy and shunned the public eye. But I did have the benefit of higher learning and I should have espoused it wholeheartedly and vocally. It would have been so easy. The timing was perfect. Education for women had become acceptable. It would not have created controversy or scandal. It would certainly have drawn attention away from being "Lemonade Lucy." I would have actually been useful.

Not long after we came to the White House, I received a letter from an old classmate of mine. She had become the dean of a small Womens' College in Pennsylvania. She said, "Help me encourage higher learning for women, Lucy. Be a speaker at our commencement." I declined. I said that my husband would object to my undertaking any tasks that were not purely domestic.

That was not the truth. Rud supported higher education for women. Had our daughter demonstrated an interest, we would have been delighted to send her to college. (Fanny's abilities and proclivities were more social than scholarly, so we did not press.) I know Rud would not have objected at all to my saying a few words at the commencement, especially if I really wanted to. In fact, he would have been pleased. He always encouraged me to participate in community and civic affairs.[22] But I dreaded speaking in public. Just thinking about it made me blush, and I was afraid I would stammer and sound foolish. Mostly, I think I was afraid of what people would say.

> [22]**LUCRETIA GARFIELD**
> *After the Civil War women's organizations and public speaking appearances were becoming popular with our sex. But like Lucy, I was much too shy to even dream about voicing my opinions. I doubted that anyone would listen.*

So instead, everyone said that Lucy Hayes was a lovely, old-fashioned girl who graced the White House with charm and dignity. They said she was a lady who spent Sunday nights with friends singing hymns and serving coffee and cake. Who could possibly object to coffee, cake and hymn-singing? By the time Rud's term was over, he was a popular and well-regarded president. I, the shy, old-fashioned girl, was still the embodiment of the "new woman."

After our White House years, I finally embraced some small "public responsibilities" of my own. I became active in Veteran's Affairs and even assumed a place on the Board of Trustees for the Orphans Home in Ohio. It was Rud's idea that I do so, and of course I always wanted to be useful, as long as I didn't have to make any speeches. But I was always happiest at home, surrounded by my family and friends.

So what is my legacy? Only that succeeding generations call me "Lemonade Lucy," the non-entity in the burgundy dress known only for banning spirits in the White House.

I apologize. I am truly sorry, Ladies. You cannot achieve something if you don't dare. And anytime you dare you will destroy the status quo and be criticized. My husband declined to make hard choices as president, preferring to remain "beloved" and popular among his peers. I also chose to avoid controversy and remain passive, like most of the other women of my time. I could have done otherwise. I should have done otherwise. It is wrong to set a bad example, of course, but just as bad to set *no* example.

Thus I have "organized" our Sisterhood to write their stories. I do not have to speak in public. Thank you all, dear Ladies, for giving me the opportunity to atone for my sins of omission.

NELLIE TAFT

Oh Lucy dear, you are so wrong. When I was 14 or 15, I came to visit you at the White House. You and the President were dear friends of my parents. I will never EVER forget the experience and the tremendous impression you made on me. You were the most gracious, charming, elegant and intelligent woman I had ever met, and I vowed then and there to reign in the White House myself one day—just like Lucy Hayes. Perhaps you did not make history as you might have chosen, but you did inspire another to achieve success. And whatever success I may have had, both as a person and as a First Lady, is due entirely to your fine example.

LUCRETIA (Crete) RUDOLPH GARFIELD
1832-1918
First Lady: 1881

I was the mouse. I was the Lady who melted right into the wallpaper. It didn't matter that my husband, James Garfield, was only president for a few months before he was assassinated. He could have been president for two full terms. I would still be the little mouse.

I suppose most of our personalities can be traced to the manner in which we were raised. Jane Pierce's father was a clergyman and an educator, and she became overly religious and morose. Not that there wasn't cause, poor thing. Who am I to cast stones? My father, Zebulon Rudolph, was an elder in the Disciples of Christ, one of the popular evangelical sects when I was a small child. Father also became one of the teachers at the College of the Western Reserve, later to become Hiram College, in Ohio. Most teachers in those days were clergymen of some sort, since they were usually the only ones with a broad classical education.

In those days, men ruled the world. Women were designed to bear children and keep house. That was what my mother did, and that was what I was brought up to do. Fortunately, for all my father's strict principles of behavior, he also believed in educating his daughter. So in addition to the Bible, I learned some Latin and Greek, and of course, literature, which I dearly loved.

But I also learned at a very early age to keep quiet and keep my feelings to myself. "Obey and behave yourself." Those were my instructions. So I obeyed and behaved myself.[1]

I met James Garfield when we were both in school. My father thought he was not only an excellent student, but a godly man as well. He had also been converted as a Disciple of Christ, and was a true and devout believer. My father encouraged him to become a clergyman and an educator.

[1] **JACQUELINE KENNEDY**
Behaving oneself is not merely a 19th Century attitude. One should always behave. Especially if your life is a fishbowl.[2]

[2] **BETTY FORD**
Mrs. Kennedy is the consummate "behavior Lady." I always admired her, but I wonder if she ever "was." Or did she only "behave?"[3]

[3] **JACQUELINE KENNEDY**
I "was" once, I think. For a little while. Then I learned to behave. And afterwards, "behaving" became my crutch, my solace, my life and my claim to fame. In that order.

I was astonished when James first asked me to go walking with him. "Going walking" in those days was what most young folks did for courtship, particularly if you were poor. James didn't have a dime! (He had logged, worked on a canal boat and did farm chores to pay his way through College and help support his widowed mother.) But he asked me to go walking, little mouse that I was. I don't know what he ever saw in me. I was nice looking enough, I suppose, but I was painfully shy and not very good at conversation. I don't think I knew anything worth talking about, except perhaps books. I always loved to read.[4] So James and I went walking regularly, and talked about books and poetry and religion.

Somehow we found ourselves "engaged." I am still not quite sure how that happened. Perhaps James thought that it would help his future to have a "proper" wife. I suspect my father might have had something to do with it. He probably insisted that James declare his intentions, after the fifth or sixth time we went walking. I suppose I could have turned him down, but I had begun to care for him as well as admire him. And, of course, he was almost sinfully handsome, with those deep, beautiful, penetrating blue eyes. Little mouse that I was, I also believed I might never have another chance with a young man. I had no confidence. Ours was a strange and very long engagement.[5]

I waited for five years, while James went east to Williams College in Massachusetts for additional study and the start of an academic career. At that time, such a distance—about a thousand miles—was like going to the moon! Naturally, he did not return often to Ohio. He was busy making new friends and attachments while I stayed home, teaching basic lessons to the local children, making quilts and preserves, and waited. That was the usual routine for women, and I certainly was not one to challenge tradition. I was obedient. We wrote letters, of course, but our letters were not those of pining lovers eager to be rejoined. Our letters were formal. I could easily read them aloud to my parents, which I did. They

> **[4]LUCY HAYES**
> *I think one tie that binds all of us is our love of reading. We were all particularly well read for our times—better than many of our husbands. And who says that men don't like intelligent women? Hah! Of course they do!*

> **[5]ABIGAIL FILLMORE**
> *Many of us had long engagements while our husbands-to-be finished their education or established themselves in careers. Men had to provide for their wives. I waited nearly ten years[6]*

> **[6]BESS TRUMAN**
> *Harry courted me in earnest for fifteen years before we married![7]*

> **[7]FRANCES CLEVELAND**
> *Grover Cleveland had to wait for me to grow up!*

were filled with details of his studies and his work, and some of the interesting people he had met, and sermons he had heard. My letters were regular and probably very boring. I remarked on the health of everyone we knew and the books I was reading. I mentioned the change of seasons in Ohio. He mentioned the change of seasons in Massachusetts. They were very similar. I said I looked forward to seeing him again. He said the same. This was not a passionate romance. The only "personal" part was his developing a nickname for me: "Crete." Lucretia was too long, he said. And it sounded like a poisoner.

> [8]**ELLEN WILSON**
> *Most people say that Woodrow Wilson was the closest we came to havin' a clergyman in the White House. But Garfield had actually been ordained, although he never was an active preacher.* [9]

> [9]**ROSALYNN CARTER**
> *Then there's Jimmy. He was never ordained, but he surely loves preachin'.*

I would see him on those rare occasions when he returned for a few weeks. We would walk, and talk about books. We talked very little about our future. He still hoped for a career in the clergy but he would speak of his doubt regarding his religious calling.[8] I suggested that he might do well as a professor, since he was educated in both Latin and Greek, mathematics and science, and just about every subject one learned in College. He would tell me how he wished to contribute to the public good, but he did not know how. We never spoke of our "impending" marriage. The relationship was very, *very* proper. He took my arm only when assisting me across the street, or into a buggy. We never kissed. Not once. I had serious doubts our marriage would ever occur. Those doubts became even more nagging once I learned that he had formed a close friendship with

> [10]**JACQUELINE KENNEDY**
> *There isn't anything wrong with good behavior. Perhaps future generations would benefit by "behaving" a little better.*

a young lady in Massachusetts. James had a way with the ladies; they always found him attractive. Perhaps it was those magnificent blue eyes. But James was too devout and religious a man to actually court another woman without first asking me to release him from our understanding. Ours was indeed a courtship of behavior.[10]

Things did not bode well. James was a passionate man. He was enthusiastic and eager about everything, but he had so many doubts. Should he be a minister? Should he be a teacher? Should he read for the law? Should he be a public servant? Should he marry Lucretia Rudolph? I was a timid little mouse. I had no answers for him; not even for the last question. Women weren't supposed to have answers, and I surely did not. Did I love him? In a roundabout way, I suppose he asked me that question, too. There was no way I was going to blurt out the truth, which was that indeed, I *had* grown to love him. Such a confession would be unseemly and I would be considered forward. But I did allow him to read a few selected pages of my diary, wherein I had written of the deep feelings that could only be confided to the private written page. That seemed to quell at least one of his doubts, and so we married. I never, however, dared to ask *him* if he loved *me*. I was afraid of his answer.

Coinciding with our wedding was James' election to the Ohio Legislature. It was a singular honor, since he knew most people in the district. They obviously thought well of him and trusted him. So off he went to Columbus, and started his career in public service. It was a turbulent time, but the slavery issue was one where James had no doubts. Slavery was wrong, plain and simple. Like the Hayeses, we were not abolitionists, but we all were ardently anti-slavery, and fervent supporters of Ohio's Governor Salmon Chase. I believe James was disheartened when Abraham Lincoln was elected President. [11] James never cared for him, although he admitted that Lincoln seemed an honest and decent man. He just didn't think Lincoln had the qualities of leadership. As a matter of fact, right up until his death, James always believed that Lincoln was grossly over-rated, and had it not been for his horrific demise, Lincoln would be remembered as an ineffectual president. We were definitely in Governor Chase's column.

> [11]**LUCY HAYES**
> *Many of Mr. Lincoln's Republican contemporaries held a similar opinion. They considered Lincoln a good and honest man, but they did not think him a particularly effective leader. Rud preferred Chase—or even Seward. I had no preference one way or the other, although I perceived Mr. Lincoln to be the kindest of them all.*

Anyway, James served in the State Legislature only a little while when the War broke out. He enlisted immediately, came home to tell me the news and departed again. He also came home a few times between battles and campaigns, just long enough to leave me with child on more than one occasion. Then off he went again. He had a glorious career in the army, rising steadily and finally brevetted as a Major General. The youngest in the Union Army! People said he was a good and courageous soldier. I wouldn't know. I stayed at home, the way I was raised. I tended to our growing family, buried a baby that James saw only once, and made sure my mother-in-law never wanted for anything either. James and I wrote letters. They were about as passionate as our earlier ones.

Then he was elected to Congress in absentia. His first inclination was to remain with his troops, but President Lincoln personally urged him to come to Washington. So he resigned his army commission and left once again.[12]

> [12]**LUCY HAYES**
> *Rud was also offered a Congressional seat during the War, but he declined to leave his command.*

I was married to a stranger. I saw him infrequently. Our occasional visits were very few with months between. They lasted only a week or so. Sometimes less. Just long enough to expand our family.

As I said before, James was an ardent supporter of our fellow Ohioan, Salmon Chase, who Lincoln had appointed Secretary of the Treasury. Secretary Chase had a daughter, Kate, and the wealthy Chases entertained lavishly. Kate considered herself First Lady in social standing, if not in actuality. I imagine there was no love lost between her and Mrs. Lincoln.[13]

> [13]**MARY LINCOLN**
> *There was no love lost. Kate Chase was a snob of the highest order, and totally disregarded anyone other than her father. Her life revolved around Chase's political ambitions.*[14]

> [14]**JULIA GRANT**
> *It's probably the ONLY thing Mary Lincoln and I agree on. Kate Chase tried to usurp the social prestige that rightfully belongs to the First Lady—whoever she is. When she married Gov. Sprague of Rhode Island, who provided major fortune and major dissipation, I can't say I grieved.*

Miss Chase was elegant, cultured and beautiful. She was also intelligent and politically astute, which made her the most eligible woman in Washington, courted by every Republican man under seventy. Married or not. James was no exception. While I am content there was no untoward romantic involvement between them, he did escort her regularly to the theatre and to parties and lectures and whatever passed for entertainment during the War. As might be expected, word of this reached my ears. This was not the kind of marriage I wanted. The mouse decided to "squeak up."

So I wrote James, "We have been married for nearly five years, and in that entire time, we have only spent a total of twenty weeks together." I offered him a separation, if he chose. I would not stand in his way—politically or otherwise.

I am not sure why he chose to remain with me and strengthen our union. Perhaps it was his religious convictions; we were both devout Disciples of Christ. Perhaps it was political; a separation or divorce would be ruinous to his career. Perhaps it was his growing maturity and feeling of responsibility. Whatever the reason, he immediately took suitable rooms in Washington for our family, and from that point on, we were seldom apart for more than a few days. Our marriage really began then, the children notwithstanding. We began to share more than just poetry and literature. He started telling me about his Congressional activities and his growing interest and expertise in tariff matters. He offered his observations and insights on his fellow politicians. Meanwhile, I began reading newspapers assiduously in order to be conversant with the affairs of the day—and the people involved. I found myself enjoying politics! James and I began to love each other truly. I believe he taught me to love. For certain, he taught me to express my feelings.

During the "season" we lived in Washington, and I loved it! By that time, our income was such that I could afford fashionable clothes, and James encouraged it. He was becoming proud of me. Without wishing to appear vain, I must admit I was pretty, and I had a fine figure, even after bearing seven children.[15] I engaged in activities of my own. I became acquainted with many of the Congressional Wives, and began to come out of my shell. We joined a popular literary society to discuss the latest books. We entertained frequently, and dined out three or four nights a week. Maybe I was still a mouse, but I was definitely a curious one.

> [15]**ROSALYNN CARTER**
> *We hardly ever hear about Mrs. Garfield, but I saw her dresses at the Smithsonian, and would have loved to try them on! She was a little thing. We were probably about the same size.*

There was a surprising side effect to all of this: My husband began to enjoy my company. He enjoyed talking with me and exchanging ideas and opinions and he actually thought I had something important to contribute.[16]

James Garfield's nomination for President was a complete surprise to both of us. He had actively supported another candidate, but the complexities of politics led to a standoff between the "Stalwarts" or third-terms Grant-supporters, and the "Half-Breeds"—those favoring Senator Blaine. James was nominated because, like Rutherford Hayes, he was "available." He antagonized no one. He had everyone's respect, no powerful enemies, and a reputation unscathed by scandal.[17] He was also from Ohio—a "safe" state. Chester Alan Arthur, a New York City "party-boss"

> [16]**LOUISA ADAMS**
> *I would have given a great deal for my husband to "talk" with me as if he thought I might actually have something to contribute. It is ironic the things we envy sometimes!*

> [17]**ROSALYNN CARTER**
> *A politician unscathed by scandal in 1880 was rare.*

(and complete stranger to us), was nominated as Vice President. If James was surprised, Chet Arthur was positively astounded!

There is little more that I can add. My days as First Lady were all too brief. I had been looking forward to it, much to my own amazement. I had acquired sufficient poise and experience during my fifteen years living in the Capital, and felt confident to be the nation's hostess. But within weeks of the Inauguration, I fell seriously ill with malaria and was bedridden for nearly two months. I had just begun to recover when James was shot by an assassin.

> **NANCY REAGAN**
> *The suddenness of an assassination or attempted assassination is probably its most overwhelming aspect. There is no way and no time to prepare. Thank God Ronnie recovered quickly and completely.*

> **BESS TRUMAN**
> *When those anarchists—or whatever they were—tried to kill Harry I was petrified!*

> **BETTY FORD**
> *I went through that experience twice! It has to be some of the worst moments of my life.*

He lingered for several weeks and suffered dreadfully. He lost more than seventy pounds, and was skin and bones when he died. Dozens of doctors examined and poked and prodded and no doubt compounded his great pain.[18] But he never complained. I was with him constantly. For two people who had approached marriage with major trepidations as to its future happiness, we had truly become a devoted and loving couple.

> [18]**BARBARA BUSH**
> *Modern doctors agree that Garfield would have survived with modern medical treatment. He was a young and healthy man. But they didn't believe in basic sanitation in those days. The doctors never even washed their hands before examining his wounds.*

I had no more opportunity to be First Lady than he had to be President. I have no doubt that he would have been a credit to the country!

I was left with five half-grown children, plus my aging father and James' elderly mother to care for. The Country was very generous to its Second Martyred President. My children and I were well provided for. It is to my husband's everlasting credit that all our sons became fine men, well regarded in their professions. His influence upon them was enormous.

I returned home to Ohio where I lived for nearly forty more years. I dedicated the rest of my life to preserving my husband's memory, along with his papers and books and whatever else might be of interest to succeeding generations. I believed it was my duty, and so I did it. The little mouse crept back into her mouse-hole, and was seldom heard from again.

But if it is not too much to add, I think I might have been a good First Lady, if I had had the chance. [19]

> [19]**BETTY FORD**
> *History usually gives the Garfields a "bye," since their term was less than six months. But all indications are that President Garfield could have become an excellent President, had he lived, and maybe we might have even remembered Crete.*

FRANCES FOLSOM CLEVELAND
1864-1947
First Lady: 1886-89; 1893-1897

There are a few of us who knew our husbands since childhood. I knew mine even *before* I was born, or should I say, "he knew me." Grover Cleveland was my father's dearest friend and law partner, and when my father died in an accident when I was very young, it was perfectly natural for "Uncle Cleve" to assume responsibility for my mother and me.

Indeed, one of my earliest memories was walking hand in hand with Uncle Cleve on a summer day in downtown Buffalo a few years after the Civil War. There was a parade for the Fourth of July and he bought me a dish of ice cream. As a matter of fact, Uncle Cleve bought me my first doll, my first party dress, my first high-heeled slippers and my first bouquet.

Mother and I adored Uncle Cleve. He saw to it that we lived comfortably and that I had every advantage during my fatherless childhood, including a college education. I always had a nice crowd of friends—and beaux—and joined in all the parties and dances and activities that girls my age were expected to attend. By the time I went to Wells College, Uncle Cleve was Governor of New York, and a very important man. It was no secret that he was my guardian, so no one thought it particularly strange when bouquets from the Governor's Mansion arrived for Miss Frances Folsom at school.

It was about that time that I began to notice a subtle change in my relationship with Uncle Cleve, or, to be exact, his relationship with me. It was a gradual change, I admit. Perhaps I was just unaware. When I started putting my hair up and lowering my hems, Uncle Cleve began treating his "Frankie," as he called me, as a young lady, and his deportment toward me took on an interesting new tone.[1] He would joke to his friends that he had been "waiting for his wife to grow up."

> [1]**NANCY REAGAN**
> *Get to the good stuff, Frances!*

Mother and I would be invited to dinners or parties at the Governor's Mansion in Albany, which was nothing unusual, since we were considered "family." But *I* was always chosen to be his escort. I was deeply honored, but I saw no "intentions." After all, I was only 18 or 19. What did I know about "intentions?" Nice girls were very *very* sheltered. Uncle Cleve discussed his "intentions" with my mother long before anything was mentioned to *me*. Actually, I believe it may have been Mother herself who intimated that "I

140

might marry the Governor." I was not very enthusiastic since there were two or three young men in my social set whose company I thoroughly enjoyed and I filled my girlish daydreams with fantasies of their romantic gallantries.

Learning to accept my beloved Uncle Cleve as a suitor was not an easy thing. There was no sentimental or passionate romance.[2] There was no romance at all, other than the flowers and gifts and requests to accompany

> [2]**NANCY REAGAN**
> *Come on, Frances! Grover Cleveland was more than twice your age, and your legal guardian since you were a child. He weighted 300 pounds and smoked cigars! I want to know about the wedding night! And so does everyone else!*

him to various gatherings. Most people assumed that Mother might be the object of his suit instead of the chaperone. Sometimes I think she was a little disappointed that she wasn't. When Uncle Cleve (and by this time he preferred me to call him just plain "Cleve") actually proposed to me, he was already President of the United States. He suggested that I take some time to think about it, and oh my, I definitely did think about it. I thought about it a lot. I was barely twenty years old, and my social experience was very limited. I was pretty enough, with a nice shape and pleasant personality, and I had other beaux. I was also having a lot of fun. Cleve was not exactly what you would call a barrel of laughs.[3] There was a lot to think about!

> [3]**JULIA TYLER**
> *Grover Cleveland would never be considered as anyone's beau ideal. My President Tyler, on the other hand, was very romantic. And attractive.*

When he ran for President in 1884, there had been scandalous gossip that he had fathered an illegitimate child several years prior. It was incomprehensible to me that Uncle Cleve could do anything improper, let alone scandalous. So I asked my mother, "What does this mean?" "Well dear," she mumbled, "if a man does not marry young, he has needs to fulfill. Besides, Grover Cleveland did right by the woman and child in question." This, of course, was supposed to explain everything. As you can see, Mother was not comfortable with intimate conversations. (I fear that when my own daughters became of proper age, I failed in the birds and bees department as well.)[4]

> [4]**LUCY HAYES**
> *We all failed in that department. We were all so sheltered!*

Many years later, after having five children with Cleve, I asked him about his illegitimate son. "After all, " I said, "our children have the right to know if they have a half-brother." "It was a long time ago, Frankie," he said, "and quite honestly, I'm not even certain that the boy is mine. Several of my

⁵NANCY REAGAN
I wonder if it ever occurred to Frances that HER father might have been involved—and that perhaps SHE might be the one with the unknown half-brother. Hmm.

married friends were also acquainted with the woman, and when it turned out there was to be a child, I volunteered to assume responsibility. I was the only bachelor and I was financially comfortable. It would spare my friends embarrassment. Besides, even if the lad *were* half-brother to our gang, he'd be old enough to be their father. Let it lie." ⁵

So I let it lie. More than anything, I was an "obedient" child. That's how I was brought up. "Do what your mother tells you. She knows best." Then it was "do what your husband tells you. He knows best." It never would have occurred to me to be rebellious. I was probably more like Grace Coolidge than any other Lady: docile and easy to please.⁶

⁶GRACE COOLIDGE
Thank you for even mentioning my name, Frances. You were First Lady when I was growing up, and you were the idol of every girl in America.

I had many long talks with Mother about the prospect of marrying Cleve. "After all," she advised, "he has loved you dearly since you were born, and would never do anything to hurt you. And being the wife of the President of the United States is an advantage that very *very* few women will ever have." Being First Lady was the least of my concerns. I was young enough and foolish enough to think I could easily manage all the responsibilities as official hostess. After all, I had helped Governor Cleveland on numerous occasions in New York, and was acquainted with many of his political associates. The actual duties of a First Lady were very limited. Planning menus and invitation lists. Choosing flowers and table arrangements. Hosting some tea parties and being on hand to accept bouquets from school children. Writing gracious notes. Nothing demanding. All the girls I knew had been trained since childhood to set a fine table and engage in proper social conversation. My college education gave me insights into literature and music and art. I could hold a fairly intelligent conversation on any number of subjects. "Piece of cake"—as the Modern Ladies would say. I was experienced—at least *that* way.

> **NANCY REAGAN**
> *Frances! Get to the good part!*

> **CAROLINE HARRISON**
> *Nancy! You are embarrassing her!*

> **BESS TRUMAN**
> *Nonsense! Frances is a young girl with modern ideas. Besides, just about every one of us is old enough to be her mother—maybe even her grandmother!*

> **CAROLINE HARRISON**
> *Bess! I'm shocked that you would be so interested in common gossip.*

> **BESS TRUMAN**
> *No hypocrite here, Carrie! All the Trumans loved a good gossip! And Frances was First Lady when I was a little girl.*

But I had a few other things on my mind—like love and romance and courtship. I had read all the latest novels and poems. I could *never* imagine dear old Uncle Cleve fighting a duel for me, or whispering poetic phrases in the moonlight. For sure he would never pine away to a mere 250 pounds.

But being First Lady was dangled in front of me like a magic wand. I would have beautiful clothes and carriages.[7] I would go to the finest places and meet the most interesting people. I would have opportunities no other young girl of my generation could even dream of. Above all, Mother and I would be financially secure for the rest of our lives. Foregoing childish ideas of romance seemed a small price to pay.

Like most young girls at the time, I was very insulated from the "marital" side of marriage. I saw women pushing baby buggies all the time, but I had no idea how these babies were born, although I surmised there

> [7]**JULIA TYLER**
> *Frances Cleveland was the youngest First Lady of us all—even me! And she was very pretty! All the merchants wanted her to endorse their soaps and powders. She was quite the celebrity! By the time Frances was in the White House, I was close to seventy, but I did relive quite a few memories through her. Quite a few.*

was more to it than the stork. Mother explained the "brutal" side of marriage: "There are some unpleasant things that a married woman must put up with," she said. That was as far as her explanation went. As I said, she was not much help with those things.

My girlfriends sought to clarify matters a little further, but their actual knowledge and experience was as scanty as mine. Even one of the girls I knew who was considered "fast" offered little in the way of explanation, except to suggest that I picture President Cleveland in his nightshirt. I admit, we all giggled a lot over that image! And I laughed out loud at the thought of him wearing a nightcap as well!

> **LUCY HAYES**
> *Young ladies and young men were brought up very innocently then. When I was carrying my youngest, my oldest boy was nearly twenty. It's hard for modern people to believe it, but Birch had absolutely NO IDEA that I was going to have a baby up until I actually delivered!*

> **BARBARA BUSH**
> *Come on, Lucy. NOBODY can be that innocent at 20!*

> **LUCY HAYES**
> *On my word of honor, it's the absolute truth! Birch was a little sheepish about his lack of observation, but at least I knew that we raised him to be a decent fellow..... Why are all you modern Ladies laughing?*

But Mother gave me some other very good advice, which I grew to realize as time went on. "Cleve is a great deal older than you are, Frances," she said, "and he is a large man with a huge appetite. Make sure he has a big meal late in the evening, and he will probably fall asleep promptly and not bother you too much."[8] I didn't quite understand what she meant about "bothering" me. After all, he was my own dear guardian. He had done so much for me all my life, how could he possibly "bother" me?

> **[8]NELLIE TAFT**
> *The advice was right on target! Will Taft was even bigger than Grover Cleveland. He was always falling asleep—sometimes even while still at the table! I was always nudging him! Sometimes I wonder how we managed to have three children! But they were all born before Will was 40.*

Nancy Reagan doesn't embarrass me, but I think you will all be very disappointed in the details of my wedding night. It wasn't particularly funny. I wasn't disgusted. It was...well, ordinary. Certainly not brutal, but certainly not passionate or exciting. I think modern Ladies take it for granted that every young girl is looking for a storybook romance. It's probably not until the last fifty years or so that girls thought they could "have it all" with romantic love. And the rate of divorce seems to prove the lie now, doesn't it?[9]

Girls my age were still expected to marry older men. "Love grows with time," Mother told me. It was better advice than she gave about the birds and bees. Just about all my friends married men at least five to ten years their senior.[10] Men had established themselves in a profession or trade by the time they were thirty. They could support a wife. Too many girls who married young men suffered dearly from want of security—especially when the babies started coming.

Grover Cleveland and I were married *in* the White House. We were the *only* Presidential couple to marry *in* the White House.[13] It was a small wedding with little fanfare. Mother and I had practically nothing to do with it. President Cleveland engaged the Minister, wrote out the invitations and planned our honeymoon. His sister Rose, who had assumed the hosting responsibilities for the first year of his Presidency, made the flower and table arrangements and sent for the Marine Band. All I had to do was order a gown and show up.

A brief aside about my sister-in-law Rose Cleveland, since she assumed the "Lady" role for a few months: She was old enough to be my mother, and while we all loved Sister Rose dearly, she was the black sheep of the family. She never married, wrote and published several books, gave speeches in public, and was an ardent

---

[9]JULIA TYLER
You tell them, Frances! An older man who is kind and good to you, who treats you well and considers you the apple of his eye—hah! It's worth far more than a comely lad with a gleam in his eye and empty pockets. I wouldn't trade my Mr. Tyler for all the young men in town!

[10] BETTY FORD
You have to admit, during the past 40 or 50 years, we have had particularly attractive-looking Presidents. Jerry was gorgeous when he was young.[11]

[11]MAMIE EISENHOWER
If you had seen Ike as a young Lieutenant, you would have swooned![12]

[12]NANCY REAGAN
I married the movie star. 'Nuf said.

[13]EDITH WILSON
Julia Tyler and I also married "sitting Presidents," but our actual wedding ceremonies were elsewhere. I was a widow, and those things meant little to me, but I imagine that Julia would have preferred otherwise.[14]

[14]JULIA TYLER
You are so right, Edith. I would have loved the fanfare!

suffragist. Needless to say, Cleve respected those things grudgingly in his sister, but it would have been unthinkable in his wife. My new husband, while fairly progressive politically, was very strait-laced domestically, and it would never have occurred to me to expand my horizons. I was obedient.[15]

> [15]**LUCY HAYES**
> *We were all obedient, dear. That's why we are considered "non-entities." We were never encouraged to have thoughts of our own.*

Immediately after the ceremony, Cleve and I left for a brief honeymoon. He spent the entire time on the train patting my hand and assuring me that he "wouldn't hurt me and I shouldn't be frightened." Hurt me? It was the furthest thing from my mind. I had no idea what he could possibly have meant. But I was definitely frightened, and the more he patted and tried to reassure me, the more frightened I became.

That night, I put on my very prettiest nightgown and climbed into bed. A lamp was lit on the table next to me. There was a light knock at the door. "Come in," I said, in a very thin voice. As the door opened, Cleve's voice boomed out, "Snuff the light, Frank." So I did, and thus was spared my wedding night look at a huge middle-aged man in a nightshirt, robe and cap. I also kept my eyes tightly shut throughout. Cleve tried to be as gentle as a man of his great bulk could be, but the experience was suffocating, to say the least. But I was used to the smell of cigars—every man smoked them then,

> [16]**CAROLINE HARRISON**
> *Ben and I were barely out of our teens when we married and we were BOTH unprepared. But we learned together. We managed.*

and of course, as time went on, I became accustomed to his ways and to what was expected. But I will say this: No young girl should go into her wedding night so completely unprepared as I was.[16] My mother's other advice was right, however. I fed him a hearty meal at eight o'clock, and…well….

We did *not* live in the White House for either of his terms in office. My husband wanted us to have the privacy of a normal man and wife, so he

> [17]**HILLARY RODHAM CLINTON**
> *It was in the 1880s that the gossip magazines started to become popular. And when you are a prominent person, absolutely NOTHING is sacred.*

rented a house in Georgetown and we only stayed at the Mansion during the social season. All the newspaper people and merchants made a big fuss over the new, *very* young First Lady, but I maintained a reserved distance, at my husband's strict insistence.[17] There was even speculation that "President Cleveland was a brutal wife beater," to account for my limited appearances.

I finally had to grant an interview to one of the magazine reporters praising my fine husband, so they would tell the world how happy we were. And we were! Cleve was a very indulgent husband, and permitted me to have whatever I wanted in the way of pretty dresses or hats—and even whatever furnishings I wanted for our Georgetown home. I liked having that separate home, especially during the second term when our children were small.

I was First Lady TWO separate times, since Cleve was our only president elected for two non-consecutive terms. You would be amazed at how popular I was! *I* was amazed, especially since I did absolutely nothing to earn the popularity. Nobody knows about me now, of course, but back then....![18] I suppose being young and pretty gave everybody something to speculate about. However I did entertain nicely and I did all the proper things a First Lady is supposed to do, and since I let Cleve set the rules and the standards for those duties as well as for our married life, I shunned the public eye a great deal.

It was the fashion then to be "at home" one or two afternoons a week. It was similar to the "levees" of earlier times. Ladies would come to call on you—or at least stop by and leave their cards.[20] I never did see the reason for driving a carriage to somebody's house and having your *driver* bring your card inside and leaving it in a little dish. But it was the custom of the day, so I was always "at home" on Saturday afternoon. It was also the custom that any respectable person, male or female, who was appropriately dressed and properly behaved, could stop by the White House to shake hands with the First Lady during the time she was "at home."

> [18]**GRACE COOLIDGE**
> *I was very popular in my day as well. Now I doubt anyone even knows my first name. Or cares.*[19]

> [19]**MAMIE EISENHOWER**
> *And I was extremely popular too. Maybe because everybody "liked Ike." But I was promptly forgotten.*

> [20]**ELEANOR ROOSEVELT**
> *Don't get me started on the business of leaving cards! I always thought it was the most monumental waste of time!*

"You really should change your afternoons, Mrs. Cleveland," a well-meaning House steward advised me. "But that's the only day the shop girls and office clerks are available to stop by," I said. "Exactly," he remarked smugly. I had a great fondness and empathy for the working girl, since many of them were close to my own age and had been orphaned during the late War. It was only recently that suitable and respectable jobs were becoming available to women who needed to support themselves and their families. Had I not been so fortunate in having "Uncle" Cleve as guardian and later husband, I, too, might have been among those shop girls or office clerks. "My Saturday afternoons will stand," I told the steward. "This House belongs to *all* the people, and I like meeting *all* of them."

Not only was I expected to be the social leader of the Capital, but I was supposed to be the leader of fashion as well. I had no special interest in fashion—at least not the way Mary Lincoln or the Julias did. So when a story appeared in a ladies' magazine announcing that "Mrs. Frances Cleveland has decided to abandon the bustle," I was surprised. Nonsense! I never thought about bustles. They had been popular for as long as I could remember. It was what everyone wore, so I wore it, too. But when I received such a quantity of letters inquiring about it, I decided to investigate the story. I sent for the reporter and asked where she had gotten that information. "Oh, Mrs. Cleveland," she said, "my editors demand news about you all the time, and lately there hasn't been any. Rather than be scolded for not doing my job, I manufactured the story. I meant no harm and will certainly offer a retraction, even though I fear I will lose my position." I had no desire to cause anyone to lose her job over my bustle—especially since such interesting employment opportunities had so recently become available for women. So I said we would let it pass, and a few weeks later I ordered a new gown with no bustle. It looked nice, and I received many compliments. Within two years, bustles were a thing of the past. Bustles always seemed to be a great waste of fabric, anyway.

DOLLEY MADISON	**JACQUELINE KENNEDY**	**HILLARY RODHAM CLINTON**
First Ladies are always supposed to be the leaders of fashion. I liked yellow, so all of a sudden every woman in town was wearing yellow.	*And everyone started wearing little pillbox hats and A-line dresses because I wore them.*	*I wish they'd bring back A-line dresses. They look so good on everyone!*

When I was First Lady, the "new woman" of the 1870s had come into her own. The country was growing rapidly with new immigrants, and servants were abundant—and inexpensive. New inventions made housework less a drudge. Ladies had leisure, but unlike Abigail Fillmore's time, they were also educated. Magazines appeared by the dozens, all catering to the fair sex. I became a celebrity against my will, besieged with letters asking for locks of my hair, or one of my "cards." What was my favorite novel or flower? What

148

hand cream did I like? Hundreds of women wanted one of my special recipes. (I didn't know how to cook, but the White House steward was kind enough to provide an easy and inexpensive recipe to pass along.) Would I allow a song to be dedicated to me? Would I be godmother to someone's baby? I was constantly answering letters. By Cleve's second term, I had become a mother. Now the letters were filled with requests for advice. What soap is best for washing children's "didies"? What is the proper bedtime for a six-year-old? For heaven sake! I was barely twenty-five! I was no expert!

But the one serious contribution I made, or helped to make, came during Cleve's second term. He had been complaining of a severe toothache, and I finally insisted he must have it treated. The dentist was alarmed at what he discovered, and called in several doctors who confirmed the diagnosis: cancer of the jaw. Immediate surgery was essential. But the timing was poor. The country was in the midst of what they called a "panic." The economy was in a serious downturn, and Cleve was convinced that if word got out that he had a cancer, it would have dire effects. "We cannot wait," I insisted. "The doctors believe they can remove the cancer and that you will recover. We must take that chance. You remember how General Grant suffered during his last years from cancer."[21]

We told no one. Not the Cabinet. Not the Congressional leaders. Not his secretaries and the staff. Not even our families.[22] The half-dozen doctors and dentists involved swore a solemn oath of secrecy, and we slipped away on a yacht, which had been turned into a hospital. An expert technician fashioned a rubber jaw, made to Cleve's exact measurements. When that device was inserted, it would be hard to know that half his jaw had been cut away.

"You are crucial to the success of this deception, Frank," Cleve told me. "You will have to filter my calls and appointments for a while until I am recovered."[23] We needed to make an announcement once we returned from our "cruise," so we said that the President was suffering from an abscessed tooth which was causing him pain and had to be removed. An abscessed tooth, while serious, was not something

> [21]**JULIA GRANT**
> *Ulys suffered unbearably during his last year. He seldom complained, but I could see how he was wasting away, and how much pain he was in.*

> [22]**BARBARA BUSH**
> *Can you imagine trying to get away with something like that today? A President can't even get a haircut without making headlines!*

> [23]**EDITH WILSON**
> *Hmmpf. I did the same thing for my husband, and people accused me of running the country.*

that would plunge the country into economic turmoil.

I received callers in his place and begged their indulgence for my husband's "poor toothache." I handled his important correspondence similarly, asking that matters wait a few days until "the President had recovered from his ailing tooth." It worked. No one suspected. The doctors were true to their pledge, and I don't believe word leaked out about this until long after his death fifteen years later.

And finally, for all nosey posterity, we had a very happy marriage. As I said, we were married for more than twenty years and had five children. After Cleve died, I was only a little past forty. A few years later, I married a professor of archaeology at Princeton University.[24] Then I disappeared from the public completely, living the quiet life of a professor's wife.

> [24]**JACQUELINE KENNEDY**
> *Frances Cleveland and I were the only Presidential widows to remarry. Nobody gave it a second thought when she did, and everybody had too much to say when I did.*

In the late 1940s, when I was in my eighties and widowed for a second time, I was invited to a dinner at the White House, and was escorted to the table by none other than the victorious General Eisenhower. Ike was probably puzzled why he was escorting old "Mrs. Preston" to dinner, and assumed that I was a Truman relative. When I said that I was delighted to be back in the dear old House again, Ike asked, "Oh, have you been here before, ma'am?" "Why, General, I lived here for eight years," I said. "I was married to President Cleveland." I was First Lady before Ike was born.

CAROLINE SCOTT HARRISON
1832-1892
First Lady: 1887-1892

When Lucy Hayes first approached me about writing in our own voices, I leapt for joy! I always resented the fact that I was relegated to the bottom of the pile in the "First Lady" category. And why? I never understood why, unless, perhaps it was because of Ben. He tried his best, Lord love him, but he was not popular as President. I, however, was a *wonderful* First Lady!

Name a quality a woman was supposed to have in the 1880s, and I had it.[1] I was intelligent, but not *too* intelligent. I was educated, but only in the socially acceptable subjects. I was plump and buxom, but not fat. I had a cheerful disposition (as opposed to Ben's sanguinity), and I was talented. I was a superb cook, an immaculate housekeeper, had a fine contralto voice, and frequently sang the solo part at Church. Above all, I was a painter.

It was all the rage to paint on china in those days. Flowers, wildlife, birds, children's faces…you name it, I painted it.[2] At home in Indianapolis, I set up a small studio in our house. I gave lessons in china painting. Once or twice a week, several of the young women in town would come to paint their saucers and plates. I can't tell you how many people would compliment me on my original designs.[3] I liked painting flowers the best.

Speaking of flowers, I had a gift for gardening as well. The White House conservatory was never as beautiful or as bountiful as when I was Lady of the House. I was in that conservatory every day, supervising the gardeners, advising on cuttings and making suggestions for new

> [1]**HILLARY RODHAM CLINTON**
> *If a poll were taken among us as to who was the best housekeeper, Carrie would win in a walk! Not a speck of dust escaped her eagle eye. And in those days, being a good housekeeper was the highest compliment you could possibly pay a woman.*

> [2]**ELLEN WILSON**
> *Ah was a painter. Ah wanted to be a professional artist like Mary Cassatt. When Ah 'tended the Art Students League in New York, Ah was considered quite talented. But then, a-course, after Ah married, mah ambitions became merely mah hobbies.*

> [3]**JACQUELINE KENNEDY**
> *When we restored the White House in 1962, we came across some of her china-paintings. They were lovely.*

arrangements. We had fresh flowers every day! If any government colleague was ill or bereaved—or had a new baby—flowers promptly arrived from the White House…"compliments of President and Mrs. Benjamin Harrison." I frequently sent bouquets to the Veterans' Homes in the area to cheer the men who fought so nobly during the late unrest. The Harrisons would never forget our valiant soldiers!

Government service, particularly military service, was a tradition in Ben's family. His grandfather, General William Henry Harrison was the "hero of Tippecanoe" during the War of 1812. He was also President for a month. I never knew the old gentleman, of course, but Ben had some boyhood memories of him. And his great-grandfather and namesake, Benjamin Harrison, signed the Declaration of Independence. He was also one of George Washington's adjutants and the first Governor of Virginia. My great-grandfather also served in the Revolution, so I suppose it was natural when the Daughters of the American Revolution was founded, and I was First Lady, that I was asked to be its first president. I accepted. It was a great honor.

Interestingly enough, the "Daughters" did not plan to establish their own society. All they wanted to do was to apply for membership in the recently-formed "Sons of the American Revolution." The "sons," however, refused the "daughters." I was personally offended. I had a son, Russell; I also had a daughter, Mamie. Both of them were great-great-grandchildren of the illustrious "first" Benjamin Harrison. Why should my daughter be denied her birthright?[4]

> [4]**BETTY FORD**
> *Hear, hear.*

Needless to say, I was enthusiastically involved in the establishment of the D.A.R. and contributed generously. And, before some of the modern Ladies take issue with the D.A.R., let me assure you that our charter and intentions were patriotic and benevolent. We all claimed a noble heritage and wished to repay our ancestors by perpetuating their glorious memories and espousing civic activities.

> **ELEANOR ROOSEVELT**
> *We Roosevelts had a fine family tree. Our ancestors came to this country in the seventeenth century.*

> **EDITH WILSON**
> *I am a direct descendant of the Indian Princess Pocahontas. That's royalty, no?*

> **JULIA GRANT**
> *My family always said their lineage went back to Denticus, one of Caesar's legions. All the men in our family had Roman noses.*

> **ABIGAIL ADAMS**
> *Judging from our family name, I suppose we go back to the Creation. Now can we stop this nonsense?*

While we are on the subject of "fine family trees," please do not assume that Ben came from a wealthy aristocratic family. Far from it. The Benjamin Harrison of Revolutionary fame had several children, and his lands and estates were divided amongst them. William Henry Harrison was a military man of comfortable, but certainly not abundant means, and he had *ten* children to provide for. Ben's father was the youngest son, and inherited little. My own family tree was similarly "genteel." That meant "socially acceptable, but poor." My father was a minister-professor, like several of the other Ladies, and Ben was one of his students. So when Ben and I were married at the tender age of twenty (despite our parents' exhortations to postpone our plans till we were older), we set up housekeeping with little more than our devotion, good intentions and determination to work hard and succeed.

Although Ben had read law with a prominent attorney in Indianapolis, success did not come easily or quickly. We managed; we did not prosper. While Ben was a fairly good orator, he could be diffident and uncomfortable in personal interaction. A successful law practice depended heavily on referrals; few colleagues referred clients to Ben. We made a modest home in a small two-room cottage, and the meager income Ben received from his practice was supplemented by his service as clerk to the court. Those were hard times for us. There was at least one occasion when Ben seriously considered abandoning the law entirely and becoming a storekeeper. "At least we could feed the family," he said.

I learned from the start to make a dollar do the work of three. I made everything I could: the drapes, our clothing, the furniture covers. I knitted and sewed; I crocheted and baked. I set up a kitchen garden and canned the produce. I wasted nothing. And my house, small as it was, became a charming showcase. Our friends and family always admired my taste and talents for home-making. "Carrie, I don't see how you do it," they would say. "Such a lovely place on such a small budget!"

Ben was a great help at home. First thing in the morning, before he went downtown, he chopped enough wood for the day. When he came home for his noonday meal, he would fill several buckets of water, so I could do the washing and cleaning and bathing the babies.[5] We had no servants, and certainly no slaves. I was nearly forty before we could afford a girl to help in the house. We did everything ourselves—for a very long time. Like I said, we

> [5]**BETTY FORD**
> *Let's hear it for Ben! She washes and cleans and cooks, and he brings the water and everybody claps! Amazing!*

managed; we did not prosper.

Despite the military tradition of his family, Ben was very reluctant to serve in the Civil War. It was certainly not from cowardice or lack of conviction. He was no slacker. He was concerned about providing for our family. Our income, even after ten years of marriage, was still modest. He even considered using our limited savings to purchase a replacement! But the Governor of Indiana told Ben that if he could raise a regiment, he could lead it! An officer's pay would provide for the children and me, so Ben hung a flag and a sign outside his office window, announcing that volunteers were wanted. Within the week, Ben was the commander of a regiment. And, for the record, he was an excellent and brave officer. He received several battlefield promotions, and by the time he mustered out, was a Brigadier General!

Naturally, Ben's distinguished service record was instrumental in helping his law practice once the War ended. We finally began to prosper. We bought a house in town, and I filled my days making it into one of the loveliest. Once Ben's professional success was assured, it was merely a matter of time before he was asked to stand for public office. With the politics of Reconstruction being so factional and complicated, it seemed the better part of valor to elect an honest man of good repute.[6] His previously limited political activity was to his benefit. A Senatorship soon followed.

> [6]**EDITH ROOSEVELT**
> *Great emphasis was put on Civil Service reform. People should be qualified for the jobs they hold, and neither hired nor fired because of their political affiliations. When Ben Harrison was president, he appointed Theodore as a Civil Service Commissioner. We were a newly married couple, and it was our first experience living in Washington—which we loved! Of course Theodore took his position very seriously, and made quite a name for himself.*

Then, because a Senator was appointed by the State Legislature in those days, and they generally rotated the office amongst their own, Ben was duly retired after his term. But in 1888, he was resurrected as a safe candidate from an increasingly important State. He was nominated for President. I mentioned that Ben was not a popular President. This is true. He was not a popular man. Decent, absolutely. Capable, of course. Well-

> [7]**LUCY HAYES**
> *Rud had all those qualities, but he was also personally delightful. Everyone who knew him liked him.*

intended, without question.[7] But even though he espoused the "right politics at the right time," he had few real supporters. What Ben lacked (and I, *ahem,* had in ample quantity) was charm. People said he was a cold fish. I can't argue that.[8]

But back to me! I suppose one of the reasons history has consigned me to the dustbin was because I wanted to tear down the White House and build a new one. Don't look at me like that! There were dozens of prominent people who felt as I did back in 1889. First off, it was falling apart.[9] It leaked. It creaked. The termite damage alone was a threat to the foundation. Something was always breaking or coming apart. I personally lived in fear of fire. The place would go up like a tinderbox.[10]

Secondly, there were not enough "family" bedrooms, let alone quarters for guests. And our extended family was substantial. Besides the two of us, there was our son Russell, serving as Ben's secretary, plus his wife and children, and our daughter Mamie, and her husband and children. We also invited my elderly father, my widowed sister, and my widowed niece, who served as *my* secretary, to live with us.

Thirdly, there were all sorts of

> **[8]IDA McKINLEY**
> *After the Cleveland administrations (the man with only enemies), with Mr. Harrison as the "sandwich" (the man with no friends) people were thrilled when my Major became President. He had charm in abundance! Everyone liked him.*

> **[9]BESS TRUMAN**
> *Sixty years later we had to do the same thing. The wood was so rotted upstairs, that the leg of our piano broke right through the floor. It took nearly two years before we could move back in. This time, it was reinforced with steel beams.*

> **[10]MARY LINCOLN**
> *Carrie is right. Even 25 years earlier when we were there, the House was in sore need of repair. I always worried when my boys would play in the attic. There were rats!*

modern conveniences that we wanted to install. The years after the War produced an enormous revolution in industry. The latest inventions abounded and were affordable, but the White House kitchen hadn't been changed since well before Lincoln. I insisted on a good stove and oven and ice boxes. We wanted a telephone system, modern plumbing and electricity. Mr. Edison personally came to the White House to determine the feasibility of putting in the necessary wiring for electric lights. It was not feasible—at least not in its present condition. "The chance of fire is much too great," he said. That settled it. Congress named a committee to evaluate the situation. I was on the Committee.

I personally thought it would be most cost-efficient to tear down the

> [11]**JACQUELINE KENNEDY**
> *Some of those old designs are still in the archives. None of them were "right." We are fortunate that wiser heads prevailed and the old, dear White House was remodeled and not demolished.*

> [12]**EDITH ROOSEVELT**
> *Carrie was probably more right than wrong in her assessment of the House. By the time we arrived only a dozen years later, we had to do another extensive overhaul. The repairs authorized during the Harrison years were woefully inadequate.*

> [13]**JACQUELINE KENNEDY**
> *I would have given my eye teeth to have some of the things that Chester Alan Arthur threw away! He had superb taste!*[14]

> [14]**PAT NIXON**
> *When Mrs. Kennedy redecorated the White House, she had reproductions made of some of the antique furniture. When I was Lady of the House, I set about to find some of the original furnishings and have them "donated" back where they belong.*

hundred-year-old House, reclaim whatever was of value, and start again. I said we should build a new Presidential Mansion worthy of the great nation we had become. After all, our position was equal to that of Kings and Emperors and Czars, all of whom had magnificent palaces. And here we were, the American President and his family, living in a House with rats, spiders, decayed floors and one bathroom.

We asked several well-known architectural firms to submit designs.[11] There were a couple of models I liked very much. But there was a big clamor in Congress not only about the expense, but about the sentiment of being the House of Jefferson and Lincoln, etc., etc.... Anyway, funds were authorized to do some structural remodeling, which included electrifying the place as well.

I've never been too proud to admit when I am wrong, and I don't mind admitting that I was wrong about wanting to tear down the White House and put up a modern mansion.[12] The House is a national treasure and should always be maintained in the original. Styles change; tradition is timeless.

When the remodeling was complete, I set about to make sure there was a place for everything and everything had a place. I inspected every corner. President Arthur, who had preceded us by a few years, had fine and sophisticated taste, but it wasn't mine. Anyway, he had sold off countless old chairs and tables—some dating back to Dolley Madison. Dozens of wagons had carried away his so-called junk.[13]

So imagine my surprise when I went rummaging through the attic and

156

discovered the remnants of dozens of beautiful chinaware services from past administrations. It was only natural (since I was very knowledgeable about china) that I begin a serious collection and documentation of the various settings. The White House Steward was happy to assist, and we pored over records and invitations and menus and whatever photographs and sketches were available. Today it's one of the most popular of all White House treasures: The Presidential Dinner Services. Just think! A hundred years later, chinaware companies copy and sell cups and saucers all modeled after the ones I fished out of the White House attic in 1890.

We had a big gala affair to "christen" the new-and-improved White House. Mr. Sousa's Marine Band played some of his lively marches, and there was dancing far into the wee hours. And we had electric lights! One of Mr. Edison's electricians was prevailed upon to stay on permanently at the White House to maintain the new lighting system.[15] We were petrified of turning the switches on and off. One time we kept the lights on all night when our electrician was away since none of us would dare touch that switch.

By the time we dwelt in the House, the President's wife had become a "personage." Like Frances Cleveland before me, I received more than a hundred letters and invitations each week. I suppose word got out that I was an excellent cook, so I was flooded for my favorite recipes, which I was happy to send along. Courtesy dictated that all letters be acknowledged and answered. It would be terribly rude to ignore the people who were lending us their House. There was no way I could respond to all those letters and invitations, supervise the new construction, take charge of the D.A.R. *and* host and attend the various functions that filled the First Lady's schedule. I was constantly being asked to make appearances, to make donations, to sponsor various events, and to receive visitors. I did so as long as my health permitted. My niece Mary was a godsend! She handled much of the correspondence and filled in for me numerous times.[17]

[15]**SARAH POLK**
We had converted the White House to gas lighting during my husband's administration. Luckily we kept candles on hand, since the gaslight failed at our "gala" and we would have been totally in the dark.[16]

[16]**JULIA TYLER**
No, food, no wine, no dancing and no lights. What fun!

[17]**EDITH ROOSEVELT**
I believe Carrie was the first "First" who had an actual social secretary. After that, it became an essential part of the First Ladyship. I would have been lost without one!

I was also one of the oldest First Ladies. I was nearly sixty and my health began to fail. I was diagnosed with tuberculosis, although they still called it consumption. Eliza Johnson had the "slow" kind. I had the "fast" kind. I died in the White House within months. It was devastating for Ben, since it came on the eve of his nomination for a second term. He lost that election but I suppose he didn't have his heart in it anyway. Our marriage had been a happy one. We were a good balance of temperament.

Ben returned to our home in Indianapolis and resumed his law practice. He had always been fond of my niece Mary, and a few years after my death he married her. It was a natural decision, since she had nowhere to go, and he had our big lonely house in Indianapolis.[18] (Of course, not being blood relatives, they could not live together without the blessings of matrimony.) They even had a child together—when he was seventy! The reason I mention it is because it created dreadful strife within the family. I wish there were some way I could have blessed that union and kept everyone together. Both Russell and Mamie were shocked and angered that their father would remarry in his advanced years. And his new wife being a family member and having a half-sister younger than their *own* children scandalized them! They refused to have anything to do with their father![19] I am sure Ben was devastated. When he died, our children didn't even attend his funeral. But they didn't understand him. In his own way, he was like Woodrow Wilson twenty years hence: a man who needed a woman's presence in his life. The loneliness can be unbearable to a man accustomed to the comforts of marriage.

> [18]**ABIGAIL FILLMORE**
> *Several years after my death, Mill married a widow in Buffalo. Our children had both died, and I can understand his loneliness and need for family life. I would not have wanted it any other way.*

> [19]**NANCY REAGAN**
> *I keep telling you. It's the money. It's always the money!*

Anyway, I said my piece, and I am thrilled that Lucy came up with this idea. And, as I think about it, history is wrong to leave me so far behind. Some of the other Ladies have expressed regret that they contributed little. I am proud of myself. I believe I made a real contribution as First Lady. No, I *KNOW* I made a contribution.

IDA SAXTON McKINLEY
1847-1907
First Lady: 1897-1901

Of all the Ladies, I had the best and most wonderful husband. The best, the most patient and the most devoted. You see, I, too, was an invalid.[1] Ladies like Jane Pierce or Margaret Taylor could plead infirmity to avoid the rigors of being a White House hostess, or their own feelings of social discomfort. Like Eliza Johnson, I truly was unwell. But it didn't start out that way.

I was a lively girl back in Canton, Ohio, when I came of age after the Civil War. My father was the town banker, who espoused some very novel ideas about a woman's role in life. He believed a woman should be self-sufficient. After my formal schooling, I actually worked in his bank as one of the cashiers. I loved working in the bank, since it released me from housework, which I disliked, and I got to meet people, which I did like. I was pretty and outgoing. Several of the likely young men in town seemed to think so anyway, and I went to all the usual dances and parties and socials! Oh yes, young Miss Ida Saxton was definitely one of the most eligible ladies in town and she thoroughly enjoyed herself!

One of those likely young men was Major William McKinley,[3] a young attorney, just back from the War, trying to establish a clientele and reputation. We courted for a proper amount of time, but I was smitten from the beginning. The Major had every quality I could possibly want in a husband, not the least of which was his constant, unflagging devotion to me. There are some people who say he spoiled me terribly. There are still more who say I was cloying and demanding. Perhaps there is truth in all of it.

[1] **JANE PIERCE**
I don't know why Ida persisted in trying to maintain the role of First Lady. She was not up to it and should have retired. It would have been the sensible thing to do.[2]

[2] **ELEANOR ROOSEVELT**
Sensible perhaps. But some people believe that disabilities are there to be overcome, not merely forborne.

[3] **LUCY HAYES**
Billy McKinley was attached to Rud's division during the War and rose quickly in the ranks. I knew him quite well, and was drawn by his obvious talents and energy. I thought of him as I would a younger brother.

[4]**BETTY FORD**

Ida was a pathetic case. History ranks Ida in the same category as Mary Lincoln, Jane Pierce and Florence Harding. Very, very difficult for their husbands to deal with.[5]

[5]**LUCRETIA GARFIELD**

I suppose coming after the more active roles First Ladies took following Julia Grant, if Ida retired to her room, it would be like a throwback to a bygone era. Times were progressive. Besides, there isn't much to do in one's room, day after lonely day.

Anyway, we married, and we had four wonderful, happy years together. We were both popular among the young "smart set" in Canton and had a large circle of friends. We entertained often and dined out two or three times a week. It was a very active social life. Then, as nature would have it, our family began to grow. I was thrilled, and so was the Major. We both adored children and wanted the traditional large Victorian family. Our darling Katie was the apple of our eye. The Major and I doted on her. The country was prospering, the Major's law practice was prospering and our marriage was prospering. Then Fate pointed its deadly finger, and everything turned dark, at least for me.[4]

First my beloved mother died, which was a severe blow, since I loved her dearly. And then came the cholera epidemic that took our darling Katie. I was with child again, and…well, our adorable baby Ida lived only a few months. Child-bearing was not easy for me, and perhaps the cholera had invaded my system in some way. The doctors said it affected my brain. I don't know. Whatever it was, my health was destroyed, and I fear it cast a deep shadow on the Major's life as well. I had nervous "spells." I also developed severe rheumatism, which made it difficult for me to walk.[6]

[6]**BETTY FORD**

Ida had epilepsy. People didn't mention that disease by name in those days. It was considered in the same category as insanity—or worse. She also had a type of rheumatic arthritis, which became crippling over the years. The pity of it is, that with today's medical advances, she could probably have led a reasonably normal and active life.

Needless to say, I was devastated in more ways than one. The loss of my babies was unbearable, made worse when the doctors told me I must never again have children. That, of course, was prevented in only one way, thus my ability to be a complete companion to the Major was forever curtailed. But my dearest and most beloved husband never permitted my infirmities to lessen his love for me. He never even looked at another woman, and for the rest of his life, always referred to me as his "dear wife Ida, the prettiest girl in Canton, Ohio." In his eyes, I would always remain the lively young woman of our early years, and, I chose to see myself only through his eyes. The Major threw himself into his law practice and his political activities. I had to make a choice: I could completely withdraw to my room and live the life of a fading flower, or I could do as much as I possibly could to be a part of my husband's expanding world. I chose the latter, feeble effort thought it might have been.

Invalidism had ceased to be fashionable by that time. Women like Lucy Hayes, my husband's good friend, set a different standard for late Victorian wives. We were expected to be active and productive.[7] Our education was not merely limited to music and art and domestic duties. We were trained to take an interest in civic affairs and to participate in the growing number of public and charitable activities suitable to our talents and interests.

> **[7]LUCY HAYES**
> *I was always involved in community affairs in some way or another. The last quarter of the Nineteenth Century was the start of a big movement toward Women's Clubs and other civic associations.*

We were raised to be well-rounded wives for men of distinction. I was raised that way and I wanted to participate. My body was woefully frail, but my spirit was always strong![8]

> **[8]ELIZA JOHNSON**
> *I s'pose I was fortunate that I could withdraw from public life durin' Andy's presidency. If I was to be active, 'specially durin' that troubled time, it would-a killed me. 'Sides, I would-a been such a burden to everyone.*

When the Major was elected to Congress, I went to Washington with him and tried to make whatever social rounds my poor health permitted. I needed a cane and couldn't walk for very long without becoming exhausted, and I dreaded being in public without the Major, in case I had one of my nervous spells. But I made a few good friends and was grateful for their kindness and their company. I became active in some charitable organizations and participated according to my limited abilities. I could crochet, so I made slippers by the dozens for the poor, or for the Veterans' Homes, or for whoever could use them. I read a little, but I found that excessive reading increased my nervousness. Besides, I was never the intellectual type like Sarah Polk or Abigail Fillmore. If my health had been good, I would be dancing and socializing and making the rounds of all the parties. I was more like Julia Tyler. I liked parties. I think my beloved husband was the only one who understood the longing of the butterfly forever trapped in the cocoon.

> [9]**NELLIE TAFT**
> *In 1908 there was another election of two Williams: William Howard Taft and, making his third losing attempt, William Jennings Bryan.*

The 1896 election was the first of the contests between the two "Williams": William McKinley and William Jennings Bryan.[9] This election started a revolutionary style in electioneering. Mr. Bryan was considerably younger than the Major and very energetic. He was the first presidential nominee to meet and greet people face-to-face and "stump" the country. Before that, "stumping" was only local; the theory being that a Presidential candidate was above common politicking. Asking for votes was unstatesmanlike. Quite naturally, in deference to convention and my poor health, the Major stayed home in Canton, and let people come to our front porch. How they flocked to our house! I loved it! I was able to join him and smile and say "how-de-do," or sit quietly in my rocking chair, crocheting. No one needed to know of my infirmities. I was so close to the Major then. I could share this important time in his life without it being a strain on either of us.

Managing the campaign was the Major's close friend, the wealthy Mark Hanna, who brought his considerable business acumen and pocketbook to politics. If Bryan was defying convention by his personal appearances, Mark

> [10]**LADY BIRD JOHNSON**
> *Historians usually refer to the election of 1896 as the first "modern" political campaign. The candidates advertised heavily and spent what was considered a tremendous fortune on electioneering.*

Hanna was defying convention by advertising. He had millions—yes, millions—of handbills printed and distributed, and for the very first time, he introduced a celluloid button that said "McKinley." People could pin it to their clothing. Sometimes it even had the Major's photograph. It was very exciting.[10]

I don't want to imply that I'm sorry that the Major became president, but I suppose, to be very honest, I would have preferred to have him all to myself in our happy little home in Canton. The nature of my illness was embarrassing. Walking with a stick was common enough, and when I didn't have severe pain, I could manage nicely. But I lived in terrible fear of my nervous spells. I never knew when they would occur or how long they would last. Sometimes weeks or even months passed without having one. Other times I would have them so often it frightened us.

The Major was the only person who knew how to help me during those spells, so when he became President, he insisted on some changes in the formal protocol. I always sat *next* to the President, rather than opposite him. And he *always* escorted *me* into the room, rather than the next "ranking" lady, or guest of honor.[11] It was well known to our guests that Mrs. McKinley was an invalid and needed special consideration. No one ever objected.

I was dreadfully lonely in the White House. My attempts to participate in social affairs were limited, and I was unable to venture out. My little group of friends came to visit me from time to time, bless them, but I made very few appointments, since I didn't wish to disappoint people by canceling at the last moment. Most of my time was spent crocheting. I must have crocheted more than a thousand pairs of slippers for charity. They were quick and easy to make. It didn't cost much and I could turn out a pair in a few hours. Every organization that requested a "presidential" contribution got a pair of slippers hand-made by Mrs. McKinley. I refused no worthwhile cause. They were frequently auctioned off, and I am told that a great deal of money was raised because of my woolen slippers. At least I did something useful.

[11]**PAT NIXON**

When Ida had a seizure, her face would become grossly contorted. Guests would be uncomfortable, since they didn't know exactly how to react. McKinley would throw a napkin or a handkerchief over her face to spare everyone embarrassment. In my later years, I had a stroke and was disabled. I can understand how Ida felt.[12]

[12]**NELLIE TAFT**

No one understands better than I. I had a stroke when I was in the House, and it affected my face and my speech. I had to withdraw from active life for quite some time. By the time I was well enough to resume all my activities, Will was no longer President. But I would NEVER have appeared in public if I had had Ida's problems. I personally think it was very selfish on her part to inflict such a burden on the President.

But it was my wonderful and devoted husband who was the light of my life and my true comfort. He took the time to stop by my room during his busy day to see if I was all right. We would lunch or supper together—only the two of us—as often as possible. I received three or four scribbled little notes from him every day just to let me know that he was thinking of me. Some evenings, we would sit quietly in our rooms, drinking coffee and reminiscing about those long-ago years when we danced and laughed and rocked our baby to sleep and were so happy.

The Major's White House office window faced my sitting room. Every day at two o'clock, he would go to the window and wave his handkerchief to me. I would be sitting by my window waiting for his gesture of love. I waved mine back. There were times when he was elsewhere in the building, but he would always return to his office at two o'clock to wave his handkerchief. Every day. He knew how much it meant to me, and how nervous I could get if he were late.

Many people said he was a saint. Some said he was a fool. I have no doubt he could have been a far greater president if he didn't have to worry so much about me.[13] But to my beloved Major, I was still and always "the prettiest girl in Canton, Ohio." That came first.

When he was shot, his first thought was for me. "Be very careful how you tell my wife," he told his secretary. I summoned every inch of courage that I possessed so I could remain with him during those few days before he died. "I would *not* have one of my spells," I commanded myself. I would be the comfort to him that he had always been to me.

After he died, I went back to Canton and lived my remaining years with my sister. Funds were raised by popular subscription for the magnificent McKinley Memorial, in a majestic setting, high on a hill. I attended the ceremony. It was my last public appearance. I wrote some letters, organized the Major's personal papers, continued my crocheting and tried not to be a burden to my sister. Amazingly, during those few years of my widowhood, my nervous spells disappeared.[14] Perhaps the Major saw to that from Heaven. Perhaps I just wanted him to be proud of me.

> [13]**ELIZA JOHNSON**
> *The other Ladies asked me to speak history's opinion-a Ida. She had all the advantages: wealth, education and social standin'. 'Course her ailments were a pow'ful handicap. But Ida was a whinin' and demandin' and inept First Lady. At least Jane Pierce and I "retired" and I for one, took an interest in the events of the day and tried to be useful. Ida was burdensome. She thought only about herself. She is prob'ly right about her husband bein' a greater president if he didn't need to cater to her whims so much.*

> [14]**BETTY FORD**
> *It is always amazing how much we are able to do for ourselves when we are obliged to stand on our own.*

EDITH CAROW ROOSEVELT
1861-1948
First Lady: 1901-1909

There wasn't a time I didn't know Theodore Roosevelt, and think I loved him since I was five. His younger sister Corinne was my best friend, and the Roosevelts were particularly kind to me, since (I learned as I grew older) my family, the Carows, were "to be pitied." My father was an improvident alcoholic, leaving my mother to raise my sister and me in "genteel poverty." The Roosevelt family of New York City, on the other hand, led active and exciting lives, and I was thrilled to be invited to tag along, which I did all the time. By the way, that's Roosevelt with a "Roo" not a "Roe." Eleanor was a "Roo" married to a "Roe."

When I had grown out of my awkward adolescence and Theodore stopped looking at me like another sister, I was sure I would marry him. By the time he left for Harvard, everyone assumed that we had an "understanding."[1] So did I, more or less. After all, nobody knew him better than I did. No one! We shared so many interests.

What I didn't know, however, was the secret place in his heart that made room for Alice Lee. I never quite understood the attraction. Granted, Alice Lee was pretty and had a pleasant charm, but she was no match for him, either in intellect or interests. The fact that the Lees were a wealthy, well-connected Boston family and I was poor couldn't possibly have been an issue, since none of the Roosevelts were snobbish.

My heart was truly broken when Theodore married Alice Lee. I was not one to shed tears, but there must have been a very soggy private corner deep inside me with all the tears I didn't shed.[2]

> [1]**MARY LINCOLN**
> *Mr. Lincoln and I had an "understanding," and then we had a "misunderstanding" which left me with no groom. My heart was truly broken, and I had to face the entire town as a jilted bride. We were both prideful people, and several months passed before we were able to talk again, and clear the air. I never doubted his love for me, but I did have some doubts about his desire to become a part of Springfield "society." His background was so different from mine.*

> [2]**LUCRETIA GARFIELD**
> *I was another one who wasn't given to emotional outbursts. It doesn't mean we don't feel things deeply.*

And since I was such an old and close friend of the family, and since there had never been any *declared* understanding between Theodore and me, I couldn't avoid being in Alice's company on occasion. I steeled myself against any show of emotion and even danced at their wedding. It would have been rude, and Theodore would have been deeply hurt had I stayed away. And, of course, the resulting gossip would have been intolerable.

During the three years of their marriage, which people said were happy, I didn't see Theodore at all. I maintained my close friendship with Corinne, although I never confided to her the depth of my hurt. My own nature was reserved, and my family's fortunes were strained, thus my social life was much more quiet than the rambunctious (and wealthier) Roosevelts. I read and sewed and saw a few select companions, and I tried not to wallow in my disappointed hopes. The eligible young men I met on occasion never came close to having the vitality and scope that I had always loved in Theodore. They were unbelievably dull by comparison, and I could not abide dull. I expected to remain unmarried, although the thought of spending the rest of my life with my waspish mother and tiresome sister made me shudder.

Alice Lee died from complications of childbirth on the very same day and in the very same house where Theodore's mother succumbed to typhoid fever. It was Valentine's Day. I ached for his double loss, and for baby Alice, who would never know her mother. Theodore was inconsolable.[3] He left the baby with his older sister Bamie, went out west, bought a ranch and became a cowboy.

Two years later, I ran into him by accident. He had come home on one of his infrequent visits and whether Corinne had planned it that way or not (and Theodore, I came to learn, specifically gave instructions that he did *not* want to see me), we did run into each other. By that time, he was a handsome, athletic young man who was deeply involved in politics. I had become a decent enough looking young woman with intellectual tastes.

[3]**NANCY REAGAN**
I knew that Ronnie had been married before, but during all the years of our marriage, I never even gave his first wife a thought. It is to her credit and my benefit that she always took the civil and courteous high-road, and never aired the grievances that led to their divorce. On the infrequent occasions that I was in her company, she was invariably polite. So was I.

Of *course* Theodore wanted to see me. He was just confused, and probably embarrassed. I'm sure he knew that I had been hurt, but men don't know how to address those feelings so they avoid them. We never spoke of Alice Lee. *Never.* Theodore behaved as if those five years never happened, and that I was the same old Edie he had known and loved as a child. His diary, however, had an entry a few days after Alice's death, noting that "the light had gone out of his life forever." I don't believe that for a minute. He was grieved, for certain. Perhaps a small light went out, but oh, the other lights that went on!

Our courtship was brief and circumspect. Victorian proprieties dictated that a widowed spouse pledge eternal fidelity to the departed one. Theodore was very Victorian. He was actually ashamed of himself for falling in love again, so we had a very small wedding in Europe. I was twenty-five by then, and grateful beyond all comprehension to be marrying the man I had always loved.

It was *I* who insisted that baby Alice live with us at Sagamore Hill, Long Island. Bamie adored her and wanted to adopt her. "Absolutely not," I told him. "She is *your* daughter, and now she is *our* daughter, and will be sister to any children we may have together."[4] He agreed reluctantly, probably because he felt she would be a constant reminder of her dead mother. Perhaps she was, but he never acknowledged it.

Alice was indeed a constant reminder to me, since she grew up to have her father's exuberant personality, but looked *exactly* like her mother. I tried *very* hard to be a good mother to her and to love her as deeply as I did our other five. It was not easy. Alice was a difficult child, indulged to a fault by her adoring Lee grandparents. But we managed to achieve a good relationship, and she was always a devoted sister to the other children.[6]

> [4]**JULIA TYLER**
> *It was fortunate that Alice Roosevelt, difficult woman that she became, was fond of her half-siblings. Unfortunately Letitia Tyler's children loathed the seven I had with their father. I suppose it was the age difference. Also the inheritance money.*[5]

> [5]**NANCY REAGAN**
> *It's always, ALWAYS the money.*

I had also known Eleanor since she was born. Her father Elliott was Theodore's brother, so we grew up as if he were *my* own brother as well. It was unbearably sad about Elliott; a boy so full of promise, with the sweetest disposition of them all, turning to drink and opiates. And it was sad

> [6]**ELEANOR ROOSEVELT**
> *It is not commonly known, but I also had a half-brother. Before my father's death, he was involved with a woman, and there was a child. It was kept very hush-hush. When I was middle-aged and living in the White House, we exchanged a few letters. I was deeply devoted to my father, and could not, in all conscience, turn away from his son—legitimate or not. After all, I had been given so much throughout my life, and that poor man had absolutely nothing.*

> **[7]ELEANOR ROOSEVELT**
> *I spent a good deal of time with Uncle Theodore and his family. It was not comfortable for me, since they were everything I was not: Good looking, athletic, daring, and every one of them a born leader. I was tall and gawky, plain as a post, physically and socially awkward, and scared to death of just about everything.*

about Eleanor, too. I mean, poor dear, an orphan at ten, shadowed by Elliott's misfortunes, raised by a fuddy-duddy grandmother and strangely eccentric aunts and uncles. We tried to befriend her and invited her to Sagamore Hill every summer.[7] Our Alice was the same age, tall and slender. There the similarity ended. Alice was a boisterous Roosevelt, and Eleanor disappeared into the wallpaper. Where Alice's slenderness was willowy and graceful, Eleanor's was gangly and awkward, and unfortunately, poor thing, her mouth and teeth were hopeless.

But, it's MY section, not Eleanor's.

The Roosevelts were not the wealthy family most people think. We were comfortable by most standards of the day, but definitely not wealthy. Theodore had a substantial inheritance that was constantly overdrawn, what with his unproductive ranch in the Dakotas and all the expenses of our large house at Sagamore Hill. His government salary, in all his lower-level positions, was pitifully small. He received royalties from the many books and articles he wrote, but they were hardly best-sellers. Theodore would not receive substantial income from his literary efforts until after his Presidency. My own "inheritance," on the other hand, paid for a new hat once in a while.

I had been brought up to watch every penny; therefore, I became the family bookkeeper. It was a never-ending and usually losing battle to keep our ends met. Theodore, like most men, needed whatever he wanted

> **[8]NELLIE TAFT**
> *I am sympathetic on that issue. Will's salary as a public servant was never sufficient for the type of entertaining we needed to do, let alone the causes we were expected to support. Fortunately, Will's wealthy brother Charley was devoted to us, and helped supplement our income.*

whenever he wanted it, and our home was filled with books and paraphernalia that he "absolutely had to have." Our few quarrels centered on his spending.

I couldn't begin to count the times I would put a $20 bill in his pocket, the equivalent of $100 or more today, and at the end of the day it would be gone. He could never offer an explanation or accounting. "Edie, I just don't know where the money goes," he would say sheepishly. It was always a few books, membership dues to one of the dozens of clubs and societies he supported, an old out-of-luck friend, a political contribution…. I could go on and on.[8]

When Theodore was Civil Service Commissioner under President Harrison, we lived on a meager salary in Washington and supported Sagamore Hill as well. But Theodore made his presence well known very quickly, and we hosted the most important people of the day generously and frequently. I doubt that any other minor official figured so prominently in Washington society. But Theodore was never one to be pushed into the background.

Not that I minded hosting our dinners! I loved it! The conversation was always brilliant, since only interesting guests were invited. On any given evening we might discuss a Supreme Court decision, Act II of Hamlet, the history of Lithuania and the proper way to skin an elk—all before dessert. Theodore was conversant on all those subjects. And I didn't just sit idly by, limiting my conversation to "Would you like more coffee?" No indeed! I participated eagerly and with substance.[9] I was as voracious a reader as Theodore, although my tastes inclined more toward arts than sciences. Theodore had a passion for hunting and natural science. It was a childhood hobby he never outgrew.

> [9]**LUCY HAYES**
> *By the beginning of the 20th Century, an educated woman was no longer an anomaly. Ladies were coming into their own. A prominent man was expected to have an educated wife.*

Every year, he went hunting for a month or two. I know modern readers must be appalled at the thought of a man leaving his wife and six children to go hunting for such a long period of time, especially when communication systems were practically non-existent. But I seldom complained, even though my "vacation" consisted of moving our large household, including servants and hundreds of books, back and forth between Washington and Sagamore Hill.[10] But the children were boon companions to each other and always discovered ways to entertain themselves.

It would be a lie to say I did not miss Theodore or desire his company. I missed him dreadfully, and his company was always a delight. It would also be a lie if I said I didn't harbor some resentment at being stuck at home while he off on one of his

> [10]**NELLIE TAFT**
> *Edith Roosevelt was an iceberg. Nobody got a rise out of her. Nobody ever knew what she was thinking, if indeed she ever thought about anything other than herself—and Theodore.*

"bully" adventures in some Godforsaken place out west. But I would keep my irritation in check by remembering that he might still be married to Alice

Lee, and I might be wandering through third-class European hotels with my mother and sister. Those thoughts would always be enough to make me count my blessings.

My youngest son, Quentin, was born shortly before the start of the Spanish-American War. I had always had relatively uncomplicated childbirths, but this time I developed an internal abscess and was seriously ill. The doctors could not locate the source of the infection and offered little hope. They prepared Theodore for the fact that I might not live. He was totally distraught. I am sure he was dredging up memories of losing his first wife in childbirth. But amazingly, it did not, nor would not, prevent him from "going off to War."[11] He told his closest friend, Henry Cabot Lodge, that it would be a tormenting decision, "but I would leave Edie on her deathbed rather than fail to participate on the battlefield." Other women might be angry or devastated, but I knew him better than anyone. He knew he was powerless to do anything for me, but he could possibly accomplish a great deal for his Country.[12] That having been said, I recovered. And Theodore and his Rough Riders made history. It carried us into the White House.

> [11]**MAMIE EISENHOWER**
> *"Duty, honor, country." It doesn't say anything about "family." Thousands and thousands of men have left their homes and loved ones when duty called. It is always wrenching, and unbearably lonely.*

> [12]**NELLIE TAFT**
> *Not to mention his ego.*

It was an exciting time for the whole country! We were full of the hope and promise of a new century. Theodore was the perfect leader for the time! It may surprise modern readers, but I was a particularly admired First Lady for many years. There were some people who said I was the only First Lady who never made a mistake.[13]

> [13]**NELLIE TAFT**
> *Bah, humbug.*

I know the Grants enjoyed their White House years, but I doubt any other family, moderns included, had as much fun as we did! Of course we were shocked at President McKinley's death, but Theodore jumped in with both feet. And the rest of us jumped in right behind him. We were the liveliest, most innovative, fun-filled family that ever lived there. Every day was a new adventure! Every problem was a yet-to-be resolved challenge!

We made the most extensive renovations to the White House since the Madisons rebuilt it in 1812. Naturally, I was involved in all the plans. The House was eighty years old and in a dreadful state of disrepair. The renovations the Harrisons had made were found to be woefully inadequate.

No offense to Carrie, of course, but Congress had taken the easy way out by merely repairing what was absolutely necessary.[14] They failed to consider the long term. Major structural changes had to be implemented just for safety, to say nothing about convenience! And the wiring that the Harrisons had installed for electric lights and telephones? Why in ten years they had become completely obsolete! [15]

We hired the finest architectural firm in the country, and I supervised every step along the way. Constructing the West Wing was our major contribution. We needed the office space so the downstairs ceremonial rooms could be truly ceremonial, and the upstairs rooms strictly private. I totally redecorated from top to bottom! We had to! We inherited thirty-year-old furnishings from the Grants, and not only were they old, frayed and out of style, but they looked more suitable to the lobby of a Saratoga Hotel than the Executive Mansion.[16]

I know there are some people who shrink at the thought of adorning the White House dining room walls and fireplaces with hunting "trophies." I understand. Taste changes with time, and I might not necessarily decorate the same way had I the opportunity for another chance. But the White House was to be our home for seven years. This is what Sagamore Hill was like, and we wanted to be surrounded by the things we loved. Moose and buffalo and bear abounded.[17]

I suppose I could discuss politics. I could discuss Theodore's unwise remark not to seek a second term of his own. I could discuss the Panama Canal. I could even discuss his ill-fated "Bull Moose" campaign that did serious damage to the Republican party. But while I was always interested in current events and the people involved, this is *my* story, and the real "me" was Theodore's wife. That alone was an exhausting job! It was not always easy to keep up with Theodore. His boyhood lasted a lifetime. I did not have the

> [14]**CAROLINE HARRISON**
> *I agree with you. We did only what was considered necessary at the time.*

> [15]**LADY BIRD JOHNSON**
> *Technology is technology. The modern age had begun.*

> [16]**JULIA GRANT**
> *My decorations were exquisite! Everyone said so. I spent a fortune, and had the best decorators in the country provide the furnishings! Besides, what's wrong with a Saratoga Hotel? We were frequent visitors to Saratoga hotels and thought the furnishings were magnificent!*

> [17]**NELLIE TAFT**
> *I remember having dinner at the Mansion and wondering if the carcasses on the walls and the food on my plate were one and the same creature. It was perfectly dreadful.*

171

legendary Roosevelt vitality; I required a little sleep now and then.

Some of my contemporaries considered me to be the "cold fish" among the raucous Roosevelts. Not so. I ran and hiked and rowed and swam with the pack. I examined the rock collections, the spider collections, the butterfly collections, the frog collections and even the (ugh) snake collections.[18] Why I remember Archie telling one of his little friends, "When Mother was a little girl, she must have been a little boy!"

Don't let my quiet demeanor fool you. I had my cares and worries like anyone else. Theodore was a glutton for high-risk activities. When he hunted, he didn't hunt partridge or duck. Not Theodore. He went after moose and grizzly bear! The more dangerous it was, the happier he was. When he went

to Cuba during the Spanish-American War, it was unthinkable that he would sit still and let the professional soldiers carry on.[19] Oh, no! Theodore had a permanent seat in harm's way, and each time he set out on one of his "bully adventures," I had to prepare myself to become "the Widow Roosevelt." But I couldn't let him see my fears or concerns. That wouldn't have been sporting. If he had to worry about me, he wouldn't be able to have a good time. And, after all, that was probably what he loved most about me: I was sporting.

He lost an eye, a good part of his hearing, and carried a bullet in his chest from an attempted assassination. He had been bitten, clawed and scratched by countless animals. And each time he got up, it was with a smile on his face and a desire for more. Sometimes when I think about it, I amaze myself at how "sporting" I was.

After his Presidency, what else was there for him to do but go hunting? "Don't worry about the trip to Africa, Edie," he assured me. "The Smithsonian Institution is sponsoring and financing this project, and we'll have a large and well-equipped party. You can meet me in Egypt this time next year." So I bided my time for a year and met him in Egypt. I loved to travel, and no one should miss seeing the Pyramids if they have the opportunity. By that time I was quite used to long separations while

Theodore was having his fun.

His trip to South America was another story. By that time he was well past fifty. The exploration party, which included my son Kermit, was small. They would be thousands of miles from civilization, in jungles infested with who-knows-what kinds of poisonous insects and plants. And crocodiles. And (ugh) snakes. I pleaded with him not to make that trip. We had just become grandparents! He could sit back as an elder statesman and reap all the rewards of "the good life." "But I have to go, Edie," he said. "It's my last chance to be a boy!" He was probably right, but he had the longest childhood of anyone I ever knew!

So he went and he nearly died. At one point, he was so ill that he urged the group to continue on without him so as not to be a burden. Of course that was unthinkable. I barely recognized him when he came home months later. He had lost 60 pounds.

"Now you can stay home with the family," I insisted. "We can still go to interesting places, but we'll stay in hotels and travel by rail or motor car." He agreed. I looked forward to having him to myself—and enjoying "the good life."

But no sooner had War broken out in Europe, than Theodore started making plans to equip and command a volunteer regiment just like the Rough Riders. Dozens of his ex-soldiers wrote him to say they were ready to enlist! But President Wilson, whether it was for political reasons, or because he just had more sense, denied Theodore's request.[20] Theodore persisted and lobbied intensely. Wilson denied the request four times. It was almost enough to make *me* a Democrat! Instead, the lion sent his cubs. Ted, Kermit and Archie would do their patriotic duty and volunteer even before the United States had entered the Great War. They were all wounded

[20]**EDITH WILSON**
Woodrow also found Theodore Roosevelt engaging, and actually liked him personally. But, like McKinley, he thought him rash and headstrong.

and they were all decorated for conspicuous bravery. My baby Quentin became an airplane pilot for the French Army when he was just twenty.

When the news came that Quentin's plane had been shot down—no survivors—it broke Theodore's heart. And mine. He was never the same. His health had been failing, especially with relapses of those dreadful tropical diseases. He was only sixty when he died, but he packed three lifetimes into those three score years.

When Theodore died, the light went out of *my* life forever, even though I lived on nearly thirty years more. I traveled extensively, enjoyed my grandchildren, and winced at the thought of Eleanor as "permanent" First

Lady. I buried two more sons during an even Greater War, and, due in no small part to Eleanor, dissolved into the ranks of the non-entity First Ladies. But that is fine. Theodore is the one to be memorialized, not I. Nothing else would be sporting.

HELEN (Nellie) HERRON TAFT
1861-1943
First Lady: 1909-1913

So now it's my turn. Yes me, Nellie Taft. I'm the one to ache for. Oh, we all know about "poor" Jane and "poor" Ida, and "poor" Mary with all their problems. But how about "poor" Nellie: the one who wanted to be First Lady more than anything? The one who practiced and rehearsed, and spent every waking moment preparing for her ascension. And then....

I was born in 1861. That says it all. I was born 100 years too early. I should be forty years old today! Then I wouldn't have to worry about being First Lady. I would make my own run for the presidency![1]

> [1]**HILLARY RODHAM CLINTON**
> *Go get 'em, tiger!*

Our family was prominent in Cincinnati, my father being the close friend and law partner of Governor, and later President, Rutherford Hayes. Lucy Hayes and my mother were also dear friends and the Hayeses stood godparents to my younger sister. When I was fourteen or fifteen years old, our whole family was invited to the White House as their guests.

I don't believe anything made such an impression on me as that magnificent place. It wasn't just the beautiful furnishings, or the fact that it was the biggest house I had ever been in. It wasn't even the fact that there were dozens of servants and wonderful food and fine entertainment. It was the seat of power from which great things were accomplished, and it would never be boring! Even as a child, I instinctively understood that. And I wanted to live there more than anywhere else in the world.

I immediately went into training. Mrs. Hayes was a college graduate, and I suspected her successors would also be well schooled. Since I was an excellent student, my parents were delighted to encourage my higher education. I announced to my father that I wished to study law. He replied, "I have no doubt you would excel in your studies, Nellie, but I don't think you could earn a living, which you would truly need to do, since you would consign yourself to spinsterhood. No man wants to marry a woman lawyer."[2] Thus ended my law career. I studied music instead and taught piano. I chose it

> [2]**EDITH ROOSEVELT**
> *Nellie was always the candidate. Theodore always thought she was a much better one than her husband. I don't know. I always liked Will Taft. Nellie, on the other hand, lacked the most essential quality for politics: Tact. She had none.*

because it was socially acceptable. I had some small talent and a sincere love for music; I did not like teaching.

What I did like, however, was the salon I helped start amongst the "younger set." Cincinnati was one of the major cities of the Midwest, filled with culture. The sons and daughters of prominent families flocked to our Sunday afternoon teas. That's where I met Will Taft. He was a big, *BIG*, genial fellow of exceptional character. He had a keen mind and the sweetest disposition of any man I ever encountered. I was more serious, and I admit, no raving beauty, although my looks were pleasant enough, and I always had a decent figure. Certainly better than his. He had graduated at the top of his class at Yale and had just been accepted at the Bar. His family was even more prominent than mine. Suffice it to say, we were both well-connected socially and politically, and it was a match of destiny. It boded well.

Right from the start, we embarked upon a life of public service.

There was, and probably still is, one major drawback to a life of public service: Money, or lack thereof. Public service does not pay well, considering what is expected both politically and socially.[3] For instance, public servants are expected to contribute generously to the party that elected them. Nowadays, I don't think they are allowed to mandate it to lower level public servants, but when we were young, even the lowliest clerk gave generously and frequently to party coffers.

And, if you were a higher-ranking public servant, as Will was as a Circuit Court Judge, you were also expected to patronize charities, public causes and artistic endeavors. You could never say no to anybody because contributions would be printed in the newspapers and you would be conspicuous by your absence. We certainly couldn't have it bandied about that "Judge Taft was opposed to the Orphans' Home or some-such because he neglected to contribute $20 for the subscription." And, if you were ambitious for advancement, you also needed to "see and be seen." Entertain. Attend the proper events. And naturally, your wife was expected to present the proper image, with stylish gowns and gloves and hats, and all the accessories.

Needless to say, I bought whatever clothing I could best afford, joined everything, subscribed to everything, donated to everything, went to everything, and served on countless committees for countless organizations.

[3]**LOUISA ADAMS**
Nellie is right on that account. If people wondered why the "noblesse" handled the "oblige" it was because they were the only ones who could afford it.[4]

[4]**HILLARY RODHAM CLINTON**
Hasn't changed a bit, Louisa.

Do you have *any* idea how much it cost to provide oysters and pheasant and champagne to fifty or sixty guests every month or two? Don't ask![5]

Fortunately, Will's older brother Charles owned the largest and most important newspaper in Cincinnati—if not the entire Midwest. He had also married the only child of a bona fide millionaire. They both adored Will, and were unstintingly generous in supporting his career. I don't know how we could have ever managed all our social

> [5]**SARAH POLK**
> *Most people don't realize that the President was expected to pay for his hosting responsibilities from his own pocket. Do you wonder why we rarely served food or beverages at our soirees? We couldn't afford it! In those days there was no allowance for entertaining.*

obligations on Will's meager government salary if not for Charley and Annie.

Of all the Presidents who were lawyers by training, Will was probably one of the best. Certainly he was the one who loved it the most. It was not a political stepping stone or a "well-I-don't-know-what-else-to-do" career choice, like so many of our other presidents.[6] Will had a real calling. He served as a Circuit Judge on the Appellate Court early in his career, and never ever wanted to be anything

> [6]**EDITH ROOSEVELT**
> *You see what I mean by tact.*

but a Judge. Bor-*ing*. Full of old men and dull women. He didn't hear cases on exciting murders or frontier justice, or the stuff that makes for storybooks and legends. He did plain old-fashioned business law. Bor-*ing*. I hated it.

I, on the other hand, never *EVER* gave up my White House memory, which, as I grew older, became less memory than burning ambition. When President Harrison appointed Will to be Solicitor General, I think I would have thrown all 300 pounds of him out the nearest window had he declined! I was half-packed by the time he finished telling me about it! I didn't care that I had a small child and another on the way! I was going to Washington! I was going to hobnob with all the people who counted! I could sniff opportunity at a hundred paces, and here it was! My ladder to success!

Once we were established in Washington, I set out to join, attend, donate, participate and know everyone, especially in the younger up-and-coming group. Will could go sit with the old men in frock coats if he wanted, but I intended to make up for it. But he insisted I call upon every wife of every Supreme Court Justice, so I did. All nine of them. They were all old enough to be my grandmother, and behaved accordingly. And they all wore black. Bor-*ing*.

It was during our sojourn in Washington that Will met up with the tornado-in-spectacles, Theodore Roosevelt. They struck up a fast and firm friendship. Will liked Theodore at once, but then again, Will had no taste. He liked everyone. Theodore probably found Will useful. Theodore used people. Will was attracted to Theodore's enthusiasm, exuberance and broad interests; Theodore admired Will's steadfastness, loyalty and solid judgment. But of course, a judge is *expected* to have judgment.

Theodore Roosevelt also paid considerable attention to the "older" gentlemen of Washington, but he courted men like Henry Adams and John Hay, two of the most intellectual and interesting men in town. I longed to be invited to one of *their* "afternoons," and certainly could have arranged for an invitation. But Will preferred the Judicial set. He said he was more comfortable with them. *Excruciatingly* bor-*ing*.[7]

> [7]**EDITH ROOSEVELT**
> *I wonder if Nellie ever realized that her husband was 'bor-ing.' And she wasn't exactly the soul of wit, either.*

Fortunately more exciting times were in store for us.

It did not hurt anyone with political ambition to come from Ohio during the decades following the Civil War. It became the cradle of several Presidents. William McKinley was an Ohioan. We had been casually acquainted with the McKinleys for some time, and I always made it a point to be particularly solicitous of Mrs. McK. She had a "nervous" condition and rarely made public appearances, but I asked after her, and sent her notes and flowers.[8] All the right things.

> [8]**IDA McKINLEY**
> *Nellie was always kind and considerate. I thought she was a fine asset to her husband.*[9]

> [9]**EDITH ROOSEVELT**
> *How could Nellie possibly fault Theodore for "using people?" She did the same thing!*

Some years later, when he was President, McKinley appointed Will Governor-General of the Philippines. The United States had acquired the islands as part of the spoils of the Spanish-American War. We really didn't want to be there and nobody else really wanted us there either. But like or not (and there were many people *very* much opposed to it), we became caretakers of a country besieged by at least a dozen different revolutionary factions. Will was a fortuitous choice. He had judgment, honesty, diplomatic skill, and above all, the personal geniality to become a very popular Governor-General. The Filipinos loved him, and he loved them.

I adored the Philippines. I admit I was hesitant at first; a new country, new surroundings, a new language, and me with three small children. Robert was nearly ten, Helen five or six, and Charlie still a toddler. But adventure was something I always embraced, and I look to that period as my finest and happiest hours. In the Philippines, I *was* the First Lady. And I thrived! I worked with architects and gardeners developing the parks and promenades. I subscribed to the Symphony and Libraries and Museums and every cultural endeavor. I supported all the charitable and civic organizations formed to educate and care for the downtrodden. I sincerely believed in every one of those activities! No hypocrite I! And I hosted some of the grandest ceremonies and state dinners they ever had on those islands. I oversaw everything. No detail was too small to escape my attention. It exhausted me, but I loved it!

I rode in War Canoes! I rode for several hundred miles on muleback through the jungles—wearing a long skirt with petticoats and a corset![10] In the rain! It was an exciting time! Even Theodore Roosevelt was impressed by my

> [10]**HILLARY RODHAM CLINTON**
> *Thank goodness I never had to wear a corset!*

stamina and sense of adventure. Edith was probably green with envy, since all she did was go rowing on Long Island Sound.

But when President McKinley was assassinated, Theodore became President. He offered Will a Supreme Court Justiceship or Cabinet Position. Much as he had always longed for a seat on the highest bench, Will declined. He said there were important projects pending in the Philippines, and he wanted to see them through. As I said, Will was a man of exceptional character. It was one of the things I dearly loved about him.

A year later Theodore offered Will the post of Secretary of War. More accurately, Theodore *demanded* that Will accept. *I* demanded that Will accept! Secretary of War was a very important position in those years. Very visible. It was *the* stepping stone to the Presidency, especially with a President like Theodore Roosevelt. Will was not enthusiastic. He preferred the Supreme Court. It had always been his greatest ambition. But it wasn't mine. Nobody, but *nobody,* ever hears of the wife of a Supreme Court Justice. I would be buried alive amongst eight old men and eight dull women always dressed in black. Death by boredom! No sir! I had my eye on only one spot, and I didn't care who knew it.[11]

> [11]**EDITH ROOSEVELT**
> *There was no one in Washington who didn't know about Nellie's ambition. She was not a subtle person.*

Perhaps it was a reward for our devotion to

our "Little Brown Brothers" as people were calling the Filipinos (a nickname I detested, by the way), but Secretary of War Taft and I were asked to make a State Visit to the Orient. Japan, China, Korea! I was thrilled! I loved to travel, especially to exotic places. The only drawback to the trip was that we had to play chaperone to "Princess Alice," Theodore's incredibly spoiled and arrogant daughter. She was just like her father; always drawing attention to herself, and taking attention away from *us*, the *official* representatives of the United States of America. Alice Roosevelt and I became mortal enemies, although she was always fond of "Uncle Will" and my son Robert.[12]

> [12]**EDITH ROOSEVELT**
> *The Tafts were a classic example of 'loved him, hated her.'*

When Theodore stupidly announced that he would not seek a second term after his election in 1904, he knew it was a mistake as soon as the words slipped from his mouth. Everyone else knew it too, including his wife. She was remote, but she wasn't a fool. But it paved the way for my big, strong, genial Will, who made a lukewarm, halfhearted, "if-you-really-want-me-to" effort to achieve this great goal. But I had it all planned. What a wonderful First Lady I would be! I would support the arts and culture! I would host elegant balls and entertainments! I knew just what to do and how to do it. I would socialize with the most important people in the world, and they would all know Nellie Taft. I had spent years planning it. I would leave a legacy for the future! Our tenure in the Philippines was merely a dress rehearsal.

> [13]**CAROLINE HARRISON**
> *It had been customary for the incoming President to ride with the outgoing President. Wives rode in a separate carriage.*

I insisted on riding in the carriage beside Will to the inauguration and I entered the House in triumph![13] Of course the first thing I did upon entering the House was to remove the antlers and grizzly heads that adorned every wall. After all, this *was* the official residence of the President of the United States, not a frontier souvenir stand.

> [14]**EDITH ROOSEVELT**
> *It was scandalous! Nellie Taft finagled Cadillac to give them two automobiles free of charge—in exchange for the right to use the "donation" in their advertising campaign. We would never have stooped so low.*

Then I arranged for the President and his family to have suitable transportation. It was 1909—the age of the automobile, and here we were, still riding in horse buggies. The Cadillac Company was delighted to accommodate us.[14] There was precedent for this arrangement. Dozens of mercantile establishments in

England were thrilled to provide the Royal Family with goods and services in exchange for being "Shirtmaker to the King" or "The King's Potter." Why not? The President should ride in a manner becoming his station. And we certainly couldn't be expected to pay for it from our own pockets. Then I proceeded to have all the "visible" White House servants dressed in livery. I wanted us to look elegant.

I also engaged a professional housekeeper to tend to the everyday maintenance of the House. I couldn't be bothered worrying that the brass doorknobs required polishing. I had other priorities. Mrs. Jaffray was a superb housekeeper who supervised everything from turning the mattresses to planning the family dinners. As a matter of fact, she stayed on at the House long after we had departed.[15]

But Fate can be very capricious. Only a few short months after Will's inauguration, we took a pleasure-cruise up the Potomac. I was overcome and fainted. At first we thought it was the heat, although, Lord knows how hot it had been in the Philippines, and I never fainted or complained. But it wasn't the heat. I had had a stroke.

> [15]**BESS TRUMAN**
> *Mrs. Jaffray overstayed her usefulness. She was probably the worst housekeeper I ever saw, and was an insubordinate and bossy old battle-axe to boot. Harry fired MacArthur and I fired Mrs. Jaffray. The Trumans would not abide insubordination.*

Will was beside himself. He spent every moment he could spare at my side. And I spent the next four years learning how to talk again and how to read again. Oh, I understood everything. I knew everything that was going on, but I couldn't communicate. I couldn't be part of it. I confined myself to my rooms so people wouldn't see my distorted face, or how I embarrassed myself when I tried to eat. I found myself being ashamed for my condescending treatment of "poor" Ida McKinley.

When Will and I celebrated our Silver Wedding Anniversary, I decided to have a party.[16] Even though I was unable to perform a good many of my formal duties, I had recovered sufficiently to host a "private" party. At first we decided to draw the line at just our "nearest and dearest," but the line kept expanding. The Cabinet needed to be invited. And the Court, of course. And the Diplomatic Corps. And the Leadership of Congress. And the other

> [16]**LUCY HAYES**
> *Nellie probably remembered the Silver Anniversary party that Rud and I had in the White House. We requested no gifts, and it was mostly a family affair.*

[17]**FLORENCE HARDING**
We were thrilled to be invited to the Taft's anniversary party—even though we had never met them and Warren Harding wasn't even holding office at the time.

[18]**EDITH ROOSEVELT**
The Tafts received a virtual mountain of silver as "unsolicited" gifts from everyone who wasn't nailed down! Hah! At least a hundred thousand dollars worth of silver trays and bowls and compotes! It was dreadfully tasteless. But then again, Nellie was always bourgeois.

[19]**ABIGAIL ADAMS**
Nellie is correct. When John fell out with Thomas Jefferson it affected him beyond words. It didn't bother me nearly as much.

members of Congress. And the Ohio political hierarchy.[17] And on and on and on, until it became a colossal event. I know a lot of criticism was leveled at me for having such an ostentatious party and for accepting the gifts which our guests offered.[18] But I also remembered when Nellie *GRANT* got married, and when "Princess" Alice *ROOSEVELT* got married they received wedding presents worth fortunes! Probably in the millions of dollars by modern standards. And truly, it was not our original plan. It started out to be for close friends and family. And it just grew…like Topsy.

Will was never more than an average president. I know it. Certainly this country has had far worse. But Will wanted very much to be his own man, not an oversized shadow of his predecessor. Will was a cautious man. A conservative man. Maybe even a little bor-*ing*. He was totally unaccustomed and emotionally unsuited for political infighting. And here I was, unable to help him. I longed to advise him who his real friends were, who was paying lip service and who he needed to beware at all costs. My intuitions and insights were *always* accurate. But my words were garbled and my writing made no sense whatsoever, even though my mind was absolutely clear as a bell!

So some of the disenchanted politicians went tittle-tattling back to Theodore, who was making a triumphal assault on Africa, killing everything in sight for the Smithsonian or the National Geographic Society, he claimed. He stopped off just long enough to take a bow in all the capitals of Europe, and came running home to shake his head sadly at Will, poor Will, and express his grave disappointment and concern. And Will, poor Will, had no idea what he had done or had neglected to do to make Theodore turn on him so viciously.

Do not think for a moment that men don't suffer the pains of broken friendship.[19] They do. Will was devastated. What little heart he had for the Presidency was totally gone, especially after

LADIES: A CONJECTURE OF PERSONALITIES

my illness. He ran for re-election in 1912 because he felt obliged to the Republican Party, and possibly to vindicate his good name, which as far as I was concerned, needed no vindication. The results were a foregone conclusion, since the Republicans were so deeply split. Theodore and his Bull Moose Party were back in the fray. Will was defeated and Woodrow Wilson, the Democrat, became President. I never *ever* trusted Roosevelt. Ever.[20]

> [20]**EDITH ROOSEVELT**
> *Nellie Taft was a prime example of the expression, "I'd rather be right than President." Even her husband said that Nellie would rather give up being First Lady than forego the opportunity to say "I told you so."*

I left the House with almost as much relief as I had joy in entering it. All my dreams and ambitions had been dashed in ways I could never have predicted or prevented. Perhaps it was hubris for my vainglorious desires.

Will went on to even greater service. He served as Law Professor at his beloved Yale for a few years, and then on Wilson's Labor Relations Board. He and Wilson had grown to like and admire each other. Then, when Warren Harding became president, my husband was offered his lifelong dream on a silver platter: The Chief Justiceship.[21] What a wonderful way to end a long, noble and fine career!

> [21]**FLORENCE HARDING**
> *Perhaps it was a "thank you" for the honor of being invited to their anniversary party when we were nobodies. But in all fairness, Taft was suberbly qualified. It was one of Warren Harding's finest appointments.*

By that time, my recovery was nearly complete, so I did something no other First Lady had done before, or so I thought. I wrote my memoirs. They were published immediately. I even received royalties.[22] It would be several years after my death before Julia Grant's autobiography was discovered.

> [22]**JULIA GRANT**
> *Perhaps my "memories" were not the work of a professional author, but Nellie's were not very good either.[23]*

I outlived Will by more than a dozen years and I even managed to finally outdo Theodore and Edith Roosevelt. Their offspring never added luster to their family name. Unlike my avowed enemy, Alice Roosevelt, who did absolutely nothing *worthwhile* in her extremely long life except demolish everything and everyone with her acerbic tongue, my daughter obtained her Master of Arts Degree and went on to become the Dean of Bryn Mawr College.

> [23]**MARY LINCOLN**
> *We were all gushy writers. That was the way we were taught.*

My son Charles had a long and distinguished public career in Ohio, and

[24]**LOU HOOVER**

Bob Taft was a fine man. He first met Bert and me during the Great War and was our devoted friend for the rest of his life.

the Taft family great-grandsons *and great-granddaughters,* more than a century later, lead the State in public service. And my son Robert came very close to being President himself, after serving for nearly twenty years in the Senate.[24]

No mother could ever have been more proud of her children. Not Abigail Adams. Not Barbara Bush. Perhaps I learned a new meaning of the word legacy.

ELLEN AXSON WILSON
1860-1914
First Lady: 1913-1914

If y'asked me what Ah would like more than anythin' else in the whole world, Ah would say "time for mahself." Ah don't know how many other Ladies would put it at the top of their list, but it is surely mah first choice, since Ah never had very much of it. Ah was one-a those people who attracted responsibility for others like a magnet. Not that Ah'm complainin'. Not at all. Ah dearly loved every one-a our family, and was happy to do for 'em whatever Ah could. But Ellen Axson the artist, Ellen Axson the person, the just-plain-me, Ellen Axson wanted time to reflect, to create, to dream, to wonder, and to be relieved-a everyone else's cares and needs and burdens. In mah own little cubbyhole hideaway. Time. And space.

Ah was born in Georgia in 1860. Need Ah say more? It was a dreadful time for mah parents. Mah father was a minister, and even in the best-a times, ministers are not well off. We depended on the kindness and generosity of a parish that had been decimated. The kindness and generosity was real; the means were exhausted. A-course Ah don't remember those early years, but it left painful scars on mah poor father, since he suffered from cripplin' melancholy throughout his life.

We had a spread-out family. Ah was the eldest, mah brother Stockton, six years younger. Then came Eddie, when Ah was sixteen. And finally, mah baby sister when Ah was twenty. The last was prob'ly responsible for mah mother's early death. Ah don't believe children should come so far apart.[1] They never become playmates.

> [1]**ELIZA JOHNSON**
> *When my youngest was born, I already had grandkids. Li'l Frank had four other "parents" rather than sisters and brothers. It warn't easy for 'im, 'specially with me bein' sickly.*

The few early years Ah remember were happy, since Ah was surrounded by lovin' and devoted kin and dozens of friends. We all did the best we could for each other. By the time Ah was seventeen or eighteen, Ah had become a fairly proficient artist, at least that's what mah teachers said. They predicted a future for me teachin' school or givin' art classes. Or doing china paintin' like Carrie Harrison. And maybe even bein' paid for it.

When Mama died, mah father fell into one of his deep melancholies so we were all split up and sent to kin. Ah felt dreadful about it, a-course, but what could Ah do? Ah was only twenty, with no income, no home, no means-a supportin' myself, let alone mah brothers and infant sister, and a father, who, bless his soul, was no help whatsoever.

Then came the two great miracles-a mah life, and Ah truly b'lieve they were miracles, because never in mah wildest dreams would Ah have ever hoped for 'em to happen. First was the miracle of meetin' Woodrow Wilson. Ah always had plenty-a friends and beaux, but Ah was not inclined toward marriage. Ah was much too concerned with tryin' to earn a livin' so's Ah could provide for mah family. But Woodrow, a minister's son himself, came to town, attended our Church, saw me and decided to come callin'. He was very attractive. Tall and slim, with a very serious demeanor, which belied his warmth and delightful sense-a humor. Most people who knew 'im well would comment on the sense-a humor. The warmth? That was reserved for only very close friends and family.[2]

> **[2]PAT NIXON**
> *Dick Nixon was like that too. He did have a good sense of humor—in his own way. But there was also a very real warmth saved only for his nearest and dearest.*

Our courtship lasted quite a while, punctuated by volumes-a letters. We discovered so many interests in common, and our characters were similar. We both enjoyed serious and philosophical conversation. His letters endeared me from the start. Woodrow was indeed mah lover, mah husband, mah dearest friend and trusted confidante, and above all, companion. And Ah was his.

The second miracle-a mah life was the opportunity to attend the new Art Students' League. How a young girl-a only twenty-one could be sent, unchaperoned, to New York City was beyond anyone's imagination! But Ah suppose mah uncle, with whom Ah was livin' at the time, found it easier and more practical to let me study in New York City than to support me in Rome, Georgia. Ah was only another mouth to feed. The Art Students League was free. Ah had inherited a little money, which would pay for mah room and board, and Ah suppose mah uncle trusted the Lord to keep an eye on the minister's daughter in New York City and keep tongues from waggin' in Rome.

In the 1880s there were very few women who were "professional" artists.[3]

> **[3]CAROLINE HARRISON**
> *I would have given anything to have had an opportunity for serious art study. I dearly loved working at my easel.*

Ah had heard-a Rosa Bonheur, the French woman who had won a prize at the Academe des Beaux Arts. And Ah had heard about Mary Cassatt, an American painter. A Southern belle like me. She earned a livin' by commissioned portraits.

Maybe Ah could do the same. While the Art Students League accepted female students, it did not take us seriously. We were s'posed to be "Sunday" painters. Hobbyists. Doin' the china. But Ah wanted pastels and oils and water colors. On canvas. Not china. *And* Ah wanted the respect-a mah peers.

Mah classes were what you'd expect: "You have a lovely talent for paintin', Miz Axson, and we know you will take much personal pleasure from it." That was a polite way-a sayin', "Go home, get married, raise a family and paint china like Caroline Harrison." Not to demean Carrie's talents, but Ah had no interest in china paintin'. Then one evenin', Ah left an unfinished water color on mah easel, signed "EA." Next mornin', there was a long note attached from one-a the teachers, offerin' praise and constructive comment. It was what Ah'd been longin' for! "EA" made an appointment with the teacher, who was stunned to find that the "E" was for Ellen, and not Edward or Elmer. Since he couldn't renege on his praise or comments, from that time on, mah work was taken more seriously. Ah steadily improved.

Meanwhile, Woodrow, who was finishin' his studies at Princeton College in New Jersey, would visit me in New York, and take me to dinner or to the theatre. He encouraged me with mah artwork, although he, too, assumed that mah "career" would become mah "hobby" once we married.[4] He was right. When we married, mah very first goal was to provide a home for mah siblin's. Woodrow was generous to a fault with 'em, and within a few short months, Ah had a ready-made family with a six-year-old brother, two-year-old sister and our first daughter on the way. And we were always havin' long visits from Woodrows, Wilsons and Axsons. We never had an empty house.

> [4]**NANCY REAGAN**
> *Most of us who had budding careers were expected to become full-time homemakers once we were married. I did.*

Our three girls were born within five years. Like Ah said, Ah don't b'lieve in spread-out families. Ah wanted our children to be playmates, which they were. We became a 'specially close family. Woodrow adored his girls, and Ah b'lieve he was truly happier with daughters instead-a sons. He was a ladies' man; not in the sense-a romance, but in the sense-a enjoyin' a woman's company.[5]

We were married jus' about thirty years, and I spent jus' about all of it doin' for others. Ellen The Constant One. Ellen The Tower-a Strength. Ask me if

> [5]**NELLIE TAFT**
> *Woodrow Wilson was not immune to the charms of women. There was a Mrs. Peck with whom he carried on a lengthy and rather ardent correspondence. It became quite a scandal when he ran for the presidency.*

Ah objected. A-course not. Ah was the Minister's Daughter, the First Born, the Giver-a Care. The li'l ones needed me. Mah brother Stockton was very demandin'. He suffered from the melancholy that plagued our father. Woodrow had chronic bouts-a depression and intestinal troubles which modern doctors would say were stress-related. Woodrow worked terribly hard in those early years. He was a strugglin' young professor, writin' books and articles and always givin' extra seminars. We needed the money. Teachers—even at a university—had a pitiful income.

Woodrow was an excellent speaker, and thus in great demand in academic circles. His seminars were always filled. Few men ever worked harder to prepare. He would spend hours writin' and re-writin'. And a-course, after the children were asleep, he'd invite me in to listen to his speech and comment. Ah enjoyed those times together, just the two-a us. We had so few of 'em. He was either goin' off to his lectures, or we had family obligations. Then there were times he was so overworked and exhausted that Ah *insisted* he go off alone for a few weeks just to rest. Our alone-together time was definitely limited.

BETTY FORD
I think it must have been common for a man to take a separate vacation back then.

NANCY REAGAN
Sure! Women didn't work, so what did they need a vacation "from"? And if they ever did go away, it was usually to visit relatives.

BARBARA BUSH
I don't suppose they even thought about a "family" vacation...

LADY BIRD JOHNSON
I don't think "family" vacations got really popular till after World War II. Who could afford them durin' the Depression?

Money was always tight. If there was anythin' left in the purse after the rent and necessities, it went for Woodrow's books. He, like Thomas Jefferson, "could not live without books." Woodrow was an intellectual man, and keepin' that intellect fulfilled and challenged was essential to the well bein'-a our entire family.

When we first came to Princeton, Ah was duly invited to the social affairs that professors' wives used to give for each other. "You'll recognize Miz Wilson easily," they'd say. "She'll be in a brown dress. She always wears the same brown dress. Ah think it's the only one she has." They were right. That dear brown dress was mah best dress. Dresses were expensive! Our budget couldn't buy books *and* dresses. Books won. Ah never even *considered* buyin' art supplies.

LUCY HAYES

For some reason people are always curious about women's dresses. I had conservative taste. My high necked, simple gowns were criticized. The ladies' fashion industry had hoped I would stir up business, since I was more comely than my predecessor, Julia Grant.

JULIA GRANT

When I was able to afford the latest styles, I intended to have them. Besides, Ulysses always thought I was comely. Always.

CAROLINE HARRISON

Of course you were, Julia, dear. And that's the only thing that really matters: if your husband considers you comely.

JULIA GRANT

I WAS comely.

But when Woodrow became President-a Princeton University, and later Governor-a New Jersey, our finances took a turn for the better. The girls were mostly grown, and less needful-a mah time. Mah brothers and sister were off on their own. We could engage sufficient household servants to manage the large number-a guests we were expected to entertain. There were seldom less than a dozen for dinner every night.[6]

So Ah finally found mahself with some uncrowded hours, plus an empty upstairs room

---

[6]**EDITH ROOSEVELT**

As our husbands rose in political circles, the amount of entertaining required of us was staggering!

---

with good northern light. Ah was in heaven. Canvases and paints were taken from the trunk. New brushes were purchased. A "do not disturb" sign was placed on the door. Ah could paint to mah heart's content, and even if it was only for mah own pleasure, what a pleasure it was! Ah even submitted mah work to New York galleries, and was delighted when a few were accepted. The family was surprised at "Mama's talent," but Ah had always known that Ah was better than just a "Sunday painter."

When Ah submitted a canvas for a show in New York, Ah reverted to "EAW." No one knew mah identity. Since Ah was the Governor's wife, Ah did not wish to call attention to mah position. The canvas stood on its own and "EAW" won a prize.

Those were the wonderful years—when Woodrow was a University President and then Governor. We had our sorrows and losses, but by and large, Ah was never happier. As the girls grew into adults, Woodrow and Ah spent more time together, and Ah even had some time to mahself. We'd take a cottage for the summer near Cape Cod. Ah'd go with mah daughters, and Woodrow would join us on weekends. The girls disappeared in their own activities with their friends and beaux, so Ah had time to paint, and establish friendships with many-a the other artists who frequented the Cape. We'd discuss our work and our philosophies, and argue their merits and flaws, and the hours would pass much too quickly.

Ah was stunned when the Democratic Party chose Woodrow as their nominee. Ah was sure they would choose William Jennings Bryan again. Neither Woodrow nor Ah were enthusiastic about Mr. Bryan, but then again, we weren't enthusiastic about Woodrow runnin' for President either. He could be very stubborn and difficult. Ah was concerned that his lack-a political "give-and-take" might make trouble with the party bosses. Woodrow was a scholar, not a politician. In New Jersey, party bosses ran the show, but nobody ran Woodrow.

The Republican split between Theodore Roosevelt and William Howard Taft gave Woodrow the Presidency. Ah determined to make the best of it. Ah figured Ah'd set up a studio in the White House in some out-a-the-way room with good light. Just a couple-a hours a week for mahself and Ah'd be happy. But not long before the election, Ah began feelin' unwell. Nothin' specific, just a general malaise and tiredness. So Ah watched my diet, drank a "tonic," took brisk walks when Ah could, and tried to rest as much as possible.

But Ah wanted to do some good and leave mah mark. One-a the Senate wives pointed out a dreadful slum—within walkin' distance-a the White House. It was a disgrace![7] Those dilapidated eyesores were at least fifty years old, with no sanitary facilities or runnin' water. Ah was determined to have 'em torn down, and solicited all the political support Ah could find. The slums were eventually demolished. Thinkin' back on it, Ah realize how naïve Ah was. Tearin' down an eyesore is one thing; but we never thought to plan for its replacement. Or the *dis*placement-a dozens-a impoverished Negro families who had nowhere to go. Ah

> [7]**JULIA GRANT**
> *I remember when those buildings were built! They were originally temporary barracks for Union soldiers during the War. Afterwards, they were sold to freed Negroes at a very reasonable cost. I urged some of the White House staff to purchase a house as insurance for their old age.*

hope history isn't too unkind to me for bein' so short-sighted. Had Ah lived, Ah'm sure we would-a followed up with a campaign for new housin'.[8]

By the end-a mah first year in the White House, it was impossible to hide mah weakenin' health. The social duties had grown enormously since Miz Lincoln or Miz Grant. Ah received hundreds-a letters every week, and a score-a invitations nearly every day. Woodrow depended on me to listen and comment on all his speeches. Two-a our daughters were gettin' married and White House weddin's are much more elaborate than the kind you'd have back home. Our doctor said Ah had Bright's Disease, a kidney ailment which, at the time, was usually terminal. Ah knew from the start Ah wouldn't survive, but we waited till it was inevitable before we told Woodrow. He had so many other problems, not the least-a which was the tinderbox in Europe that would explode into The Great War on the very day of mah funeral.

Ah told Dr. Grayson, and Ah told my girls, and Ah told Woodrow, that if fate provided another companion for 'im, it would be the dearest wish of mah heart that he remarry, and that mah daughters accept his new wife in friendship and affection.[9] Woodrow needed women around 'im. He thrived on their pamperin' and attention, and was desolate by 'imself. The cares-a the world were on his shoulders, How could a despondent and lonely president even begin to cope?

So let me anticipate history's question to EAW: Had Ah lived, would anythin' have been different? Would Woodrow have been different? It's foolish and presumptuous to think Ah would-a been able to persuade Woodrow to compromise on the Treaty of Versailles, and that we would-a joined the

> [8]**ELEANOR ROOSEVELT**
> *I remember Mrs. Wilson's campaign to rid Washington of a squalid slum. I applauded her efforts. I was just a young housewife at the time, and my support was meaningless. But I remembered her warmly when I became First Lady and undertook similar projects of my own. Had she lived, I am sure I could have counted on her support.*

> [9]**EDITH WILSON**
> *I always treasured the memory of Ellen Wilson even though we never met. Her daughters accepted me with open arms and we always maintained a cordial and enduring friendship. How many step-mothers can say that!* [10]

> [10]**JULIA TYLER**
> *I would have liked to have had a cordial friendship with Mr. Tylers "first" family. We might have been companions—and they could have been a support for their half-brothers and sisters.*

League of Nations and the world would-a been safe for democracy and we'd-a lived hap'ly ever after. Woodrow was as stubborn as the worst Georgia mule. After all, he was a Capricorn. And then a devastatin' stroke played havoc with his disposition. But Ah do think Ah might-a been able to keep 'im from some the stresses and strains that ruined his health to begin with.

Edith Galt was a wonderful wife to Woodrow, and Ah bless her forever, but Ah wasn't cowed by 'im like she was. After all, Ah married a strugglin' young teacher near mah own age. *She* married the President of the United States, fifteen years her senior. She would do what Woodrow said—right or wrong. Had Ah lived and remained in good health, Ah would-a been able to speak mah mind without his doubtin' mah loyalty or steadfastness. He always relied on mah judgment. And perhaps, just perhaps, Ah might-a been able to help smooth all his adversarial relationships. Diplomacy was not his best quality. It was not Edith's best quality either, and Ah had been smoothin' things over for Woodrow for years.

But (and possibly because-a his frailties, physical and otherwise), Woodrow has gone down in history as one-a our greater presidents; Edith, in her weakness, is judged as a strong First Lady, and Ah, the tower-a strength for the whole Wilson family, am completely forgotten. Thus the vagaries and ironies-a life.

EDITH BOLLING GALT WILSON
1872-1961
First Lady: 1916-1921

Oh the vagaries and ironies of life! Eternity has a sense of humor. There was a time when men and women sneered, "*SHE* is running the country," meaning me. Of course that wasn't true. Today modern women say with pride, "*SHE* ran the country."[1] It still isn't true, but it does make me smile, and for a very long while, I did not smile.

I was born a few years after the War of Secession, into an old Virginia family that traced its lineage back to Pocahontas. We were reduced to genteel poverty just like everyone else in Virginia after the War—unless you were in abject poverty. "Learn charm and grace and womanly things, Edith," my father said. "Marry well and provide for yourself, and if possible, provide a little for your family." So I did. In my early twenties, I married Norman Galt, a well-to-do jeweler in Washington, DC. He was several years my senior, but he was good to me and to my family, and ours was a happy marriage. He died when I was 35. Since we had no children, I was his sole heir. I started "working" in the jewelry store, mainly to occupy some empty hours, and also to keep an eye on my rather substantial inheritance. People said I had a good head for business, and a flair for dealing with the customers. I enjoyed working.

A few years later, I became acquainted with Woodrow Wilson's cousin, Helen Bones, who lived at the White House and assisted with the social duties. She invited me to tea one rainy afternoon. In all my years living in the nation's capital, I had never been inside the Mansion. There I was, dripping wet, with mud on my shoes, and who do we meet by chance, but the President, who promptly invited himself to our tea party.

President Wilson had recently lost his wife, and from what I subsequently learned since he was delightful at our very first meeting, had been suffering from near-crippling depression. Not only was he mourning his dearest companion of thirty years, but the Great War had been raging in Europe, and had placed him under enormous strain.

Our next few encounters were always as Cousin Helen's friend. "Bring your friend Mrs. Galt for dinner," he would say. Or "perhaps your friend

Mrs. Galt will join us for a ride this afternoon." Naturally it didn't take me long to realize I was being courted in a very circumspect manner, since the first Mrs. Wilson had been dead less than a year. Interestingly enough, the entire Wilson family, including his three grown daughters, encouraged our courtship even though it became a major political liability. It was much too soon to even *think* of the President courting, let alone proposing marriage, which he did within six months. "People will gossip," I said. "They will make your life miserable, and I don't want you to be unhappy on my account. We must wait until after your Presidency." I adored Woodrow and would have been happy to wait and marry him as ex-President.

²BARBARA BUSH
I surmise from pictures that Edith Wilson was around my size. Maybe even a little taller. "Little Girl" indeed!

"Nonsense, Little Girl," he said. "I will be miserable every day without you in my life!" Woodrow always called me "Little Girl."² Why, I'll never know, since I was nearly 5'9" and weighed…well, let's just say I was statuesque. Not fat, but definitely not willowy. But "Little Girl" I was.

We married quietly, in my house. "Gossip be hanged," Woodrow said, and who was I to contradict a man fifteen years my senior, a noted University President, several eternities ahead of me in education and intellect, and the President of the United States of America besides?

Even before our marriage, Cary Grayson, Woodrow's doctor and our mutual friend, took me aside and told me that the President frequently suffered from headaches and gastric problems, mostly due to stress. "What he needs, Edith, is regular exercise, relaxation and a happy home life. It will be *your* job to make sure he gets it." It became my first priority.

NELLIE TAFT
Will loved golf and played often. But he wasn't very good at it.

FLORENCE HARDING
Warren Harding enjoyed golf, too. He liked most sports, but his abilities were only average.

MAMIE EISENHOWER
Ike was a good golfer. He was a natural athlete. He was probably the first president—aside from Teddy Roosevelt—whose athletic prowess was noted during his term in office. I was never much of an athlete.

BETTY FORD
I think all modern Presidents are fairly good athletes—maybe Nixon not quite so much. But good physical and mental health goes hand in hand with plenty of exercise.

We took up golf. Every morning, weather permitting, we rose early and played nine holes. We were very poor golfers, but the walk was invigorating, and we laughed a lot!

I would be telling a downright lie if I said I didn't enjoy being First Lady. I loved it! Photographs taken in the early years of our marriage showed me smiling and laughing and thoroughly enjoying myself. And while most people saw Woodrow as serious and scholarly, I saw him as a man who whistled all the popular songs of the day, was a good dancer, and loved to tell jokes! And as far as the "job" of being First Lady? I was 43 years old. My years as Mrs. Galt taught me well. So did my "Southern" upbringing. I was perfectly comfortable assuming the social duties and public appearances that were expected.

Oh, we were very, *very* happy. We entertained appropriately, considering that it was Wartime, and went to concerts and vaudeville shows and baseball games.[3] We believed in being visible. The people liked it. Woodrow never had a problem with the *people*. Only the *Congress*. Even when

> [3]**ELLEN WILSON**
> *Woodrow enjoyed the theatre and seein' the latest vaudeville acts. Most people didn't know he was a natural mimic, and loved imitatin' the performers.*

there was a Democratic majority, they were apt to negate Woodrow's initiatives. Congressmen were far more conservative than my husband. And Woodrow, who had been a student of government since his youth, had some wonderfully progressive ideas.[4]

Woodrow tried desperately to prevent our involvement in the Great War. He deplored the thought of American boys losing their lives over the boundaries of failing European empires. He patiently explained to me that the War was really about the rotting decadence of old autocracies, and

> [4]**EDITH ROOSEVELT**
> *Mostly stolen from Theodore's initiatives.*

Kaiser Wilhelm's aggression was merely a symptom and a trigger. Woodrow was a very smart man. I don't think people really knew *how* smart.

But the Great War made its way to our shores, despite every effort to avoid it. I volunteered with the Red Cross and made sure I was frequently photographed for the newsreel cameras. I knew the importance of public relations even then, and realized that one picture of me in a Red Cross uniform would inspire hundreds of other women to volunteer. They did. And I instituted the "wheatless" and "meatless" days, to conserve food for our soldiers and our Allies. I even bought a flock of sheep to graze on White House grounds. It freed the gardeners for more useful work. When the sheep

⁵ROSALYNN CARTER
I can just imagine what people would say if I "decoded" delicate secret messages for Jimmy! The thought would never have entered either of our minds!

were sheared, I sent a pound of their wool to each State to be auctioned off for War Bonds. I am told the wool raised thousands of dollars. Yes indeed, I enjoyed being First Lady! I was good at it! And Woodrow was happy to have me near. He set up a desk for me in his office, so we could work side by side. He even taught me some of the secret codes so I could decipher messages and save him time.⁵

Then, of course, there was Theodore Roosevelt breathing down his neck with his endless requests for a battlefield commission. I didn't care for Theodore Roosevelt. I didn't doubt his patriotism or personal courage, but I believed that he was "grandstanding" for attention. He was anxious to have the Republican nomination in 1920.⁶

⁶NELLIE TAFT
Edith Wilson is right about the grandstanding Theodore. He couldn't bear being out of the limelight. Will, on the other hand, admired Wilson, and I believe the feeling was mutual. President Wilson appointed my husband as head of a wartime commission.

When American boys were dispatched, the Great War came to a swifter end for our being "Over There." During those awful months, Woodrow determined that the carnage and devastation must never happen again. It must be a "war to end all wars" he declared, and set about compressing his three decades worth of governmental scholarship into a course of action for the future. I daresay no other President was more qualified to do so—not even Madison or Jefferson! I was absolutely in awe of him! We were inseparable, and I learned from him daily! I didn't support his views merely because he was my husband and I loved him; I agreed because it was good common sense!

Woodrow took a very bold step! He appointed himself to the Peace delegation, and became the first President to leave the American continent during his term. What a thrill it was to sail to Paris! When I suggested that

⁷EDITH ROOSEVELT
Talk about grandstanding....

he consider including more "members of the loyal opposition" in his entourage, Woodrow disdained, believing they would be their usual nay-saying selves, and get in the way. He didn't want anyone in the way.⁷

A conquering Caesar could not have been more enthusiastically welcomed! Every day brought another ten invitations and a dozen huge bouquets! We were entertained by all European officialdom. The British, the French, the Italians—and even the minor countries! Everyone wanted to meet the great President "Weel-son!" And since protocol required us to return the courtesies, I was kept extremely busy preparing "our turn" as host.

I loved every minute of it! There I was, covered with orchids, laughing and having a wonderful time! But underneath all the charm and outward enthusiasm, Woodrow was suffering.[8] His delicate digestion rebelled against the finest cuisine in the world; his nerves were frayed by his inability to convince the Europeans to prepare for a lasting peace. Woodrow would come back every night with a raging headache. "Those fellows only want one thing," he would explode in frustration. "They want revenge! Territory and reparations! They don't give a damn about a lasting peace. They can't understand that bankrupting a former enemy is not in anyone's best interest! Or maybe they just don't care."

> **[8]ELLEN WILSON**
> *Ah would-a recognized those signs right away. Woodrow had suffered a few "breakdowns" durin' the thirty years-a our marriage. Ah knew the headaches, the temper flare-ups, the restlessness, the insomnia. Rest, exercise and a change-a scenery usually helped.*

I must digress. Woodrow was a wonderful and brilliant man, but through my long life (and I lived to be nearly ninety) and through eternity, I have grown to realize that he had similar failings as John Quincy Adams and Andrew Johnson. They could not be budged from their natural intransigence if they thought they were right. They never realized they could have achieved 90% of what they wanted by just giving back 10%.

Woodrow was no match for the wily European poker players who were accustomed to bluff, bombast and power. And, after all, it was *their* borders and economies that were in dispute, not ours. Woodrow was right. They only wanted territory and reparations. The entire European continent was bankrupt financially, economically and morally. They weren't interested in any lasting peace, especially if they had to give back anything. It would have required a much shrewder politician to achieve that goal—if it could have been achieved at all.[9]

> **[9]ELEANOR ROOSEVELT**
> *Franklin and I went along as a minor part of the Wilson entourage. I was very impressed by President Wilson, and believed wholeheartedly in all he was trying to achieve. I think much of my own political philosophies took root in Wilson's idealism.[10]*

> **[10]LADY BIRD JOHNSON**
> *Idealism is a wonderful thing. We all need to have stars to reach for. But idealists seldom make good Presidents. At least, not during their own lifetimes!*

The League of Nations was the dearest wish of Woodrow's heart. He had spent hours and hours preparing its outline and defining its goals. "Think of it, Little Girl!" he said. "If countries had a mechanism to discuss their grievances and find reasonable solutions, we could avoid war and the dreadful bloodbath that takes millions of lives!" Woodrow's political enemies said he gave away entirely too much in return for Europe's acceptance of his "League," but with a Treaty in his pocket, we came home. Then all his troubles began.

Congress wanted no part of any "League of Nations." "We are a peace loving country, bounded by two great oceans. We have no business trying to settle all the quarrels in Europe," they said. "Those countries haven't been able to live in peace with each other for thousands of years. A League of Nations isn't going to change anything, and it will cost our country millions of dollars!" [11]

Woodrow's ideas were sound. After all, he was brilliant governmental scholar and a decent, patriotic man who was deeply committed to the best interests of the country. It was just hard for him to understand that some of his adversaries were also brilliant governmental scholars and decent, patriotic men, who were deeply committed to our best interests as well. [13] The political battle lines were drawn, and they raged.

> [11]**FLORENCE HARDING**
> *This point is very well taken. I was always interested in politics and I was totally against a League. Oh, it sounded very good in principle but it would be impossible in practice.* [12]

> [12]**BESS TRUMAN**
> *The same was said about the United Nations a generation and millions of lives later.*

> [13]**EDITH ROOSEVELT**
> *Henry Cabot Lodge was Wilson's implacable enemy—and our dearest friend for 30 years. Prior to his becoming Senator, Cabot had been a professor of governmental studies, and considered a "wunderkind" at Harvard. Perhaps the rivalry wasn't merely political. There were some obvious personal jealousies as well between "Harvard and Princeton."*

I suppose if we had been married longer, I would have recognized the signs of Woodrow's imminent collapse. With Congress proving hostile, he insisted on taking his case to the "people." Dr. Grayson objected strongly. I objected strongly. But Woodrow had become extremely set in his ways, and after all, he *was* the President of the United States. We went on a cross-country speaking tour to promote the League, and he collapsed from exhaustion. We rushed back to Washington where he had a massive stroke a few days later.

It was a dreadful time. That is when my "stewardship" began.

After the initial shock, and my subsequent relief to learn that Woodrow would survive, many decisions had to be made. My *own* inclination (and that of his chief advisors) was that Vice President Marshall should be called on at once to assume responsibilities until such time as Woodrow sufficiently recovered.[14] My husband, whose mind remained clear despite his frail body, was adamant. "Tom Marshall is a nice enough fellow, but he's a namby-pamby. He'll give away every objective I fought so hard for!" Frankly, I didn't care one whit about the Treaty or the League or Europe or anything else. My only concern was for my husband's health and welfare.

The *doctors* made the final decision. They said if he were forced to relinquish his responsibilities, it would kill him. He would lose the will to live.

"The President must deal only with urgent matters. And no politicking!" they said. "He must be kept quiet and comfortable, and work only an hour or two a day. And you," they told me, "must funnel all his decisions to others."[16] I demurred and suggested that his Cabinet be charged with those duties. "I'm not qualified to handle those responsibilities," I said. "The 'qualified ones' will be too political," the doctors reminded.

So I funneled the decisions and tried to limit his work. That is *all* I did. I do not deny that it was an awesome responsibility since the decision about what was and what was not urgent was left to my discretion.[17] So the gossip started, and I was accused of running a "petticoat" government and other rude and untrue statements. I held my tongue. But I changed. I changed from the outgoing, happy, laughing woman under the big cartwheel hat with the

> [14]**PAT NIXON**
> *When Ike had a heart attack, Dick assumed a great many presidential duties. I think it was the first time in history that a Vice President was entrusted with those responsibilities while a president was still alive. We don't realize how recent the importance and qualifications of vice president has become.*[15]

> [15]**LUCY HAYES**
> *That is true. When Rud was nominated, we had never heard of Vice Presidential nominee William Wheeler. He was selected to "balance" the ticket geographically. Vice Presidents were always non-entities. Like First Ladies.*

> [16]**FRANCES CLEVELAND**
> *I only funneled Cleve's appointments and correspondence for a couple of weeks. Edith funneled for a year and a half!*

> [17]**HILLARY RODHAM CLINTON**
> *Who runs the agenda runs the meeting.*

flowers. My face grew sterner and my lips tighter. I did exactly what the doctors advised, the very best way I knew how. I kept endless hours, nursing a sick man, responding to thousands of letters of support and affection, maintaining a proper correspondence with all the dignitaries who proffered their sincere friendship, running a huge mansion, and trying to determine where the everyday workload should be funneled—and what was and was not urgent.

I had no education or background for this. I didn't even know my husband that long or well to be able to "read his mind." But as Woodrow recovered, he helped me winnow the non-essentials. "That can go to State," or "that can go to the Attorney General," he would say. "Those fellows can handle it just fine."

Of course people complained and said nasty things, as people are wont to do. Even Woodrow's most loyal aides became quarrelsome. I had no time for quarrels. I began to understand Woodrow's temperament better: "If you aren't with me, you are against me." He had a point. I was deeply hurt and offended by the gossip coming from "devoted friends" of the president. He had surrounded himself with the brightest and most progressive advisors, who he believed were completely loyal to his purpose. Well, I might not have been the smartest person in the world, but I was smart enough to know who my friends were, and these "smartest and brightest and most loyal" proved to be anything but! I couldn't discuss those matters with Woodrow in his condition. It would have hurt and upset him. So I tried my best to disassociate ourselves from the wolves in sheep's clothing, and do the best job I could to protect my sick husband from attack.[18] I learned to be what some people call a "good hater." I *never* forgot or forgave the treachery of some of his "friends." And when they wrote their memoirs some years later, and said untrue and unkind things about the Second Mrs. Wilson, what could I expect? I gave as good as I got.

> [18]**ELEANOR ROOSEVELT**
> *Edith Wilson considered herself the wife of a sick man who happened to be President of the United States. In truth, she was married to the President of the United States who happened to be a sick man. I found myself in that position as well. The office takes precedence over the personal relationship.*

Naturally delegations from Congress called on Woodrow—ostensibly to wish him well, but in reality to determine his incapacity. I sat in and took detailed notes, at my husband's expressed order. "I don't want those fellows to mix my words up, Little Girl," he said. "You write it all down, so they won't try to pull a fast one."

200

I hated those last years. I knew how ill Woodrow was. I also realized that while his mind was clear, certain physiological and mental changes had occurred to make him more irritable and fixed in his ways.[19] Little things troubled him far out of proportion. And he was positively consumed by the need for the League of Nations, although it became apparent that Congress would vote it down.

The 1920 election was between two Ohio newspapermen whom nobody had ever heard of before: Cox and Harding. It was really about the League. Harding won; the League lost.

I purchased a charming townhouse in Washington when Woodrow retired. We led a quiet life during those few remaining years. Woodrow read a great deal, we bought a projector and screen and watched the latest moving pictures, and of course had many visitors and voluminous correspondence.

> [19]**FRANCES CLEVELAND**
> *After Cleve's cancer surgery, he became a changed man. He was always stubborn, but he became positively unmovable. It damaged his second term and his overall reputation. Presidents need to be flexible.[20]*

> [20]**BARBARA BUSH**
> *I don't think flexibility is a common quality of Presidents. Besides, in the political world, "flexibility" can be construed as wishy-washy. It is a very hard call!*

When he died, it was a blessing, since his poor body had suffered for so long. The outpouring of grief from a "grateful nation" appeared to me to be completely hypocritical to the grief they caused him while he lived. When Senator Lodge requested permission to attend the funeral service, I adamantly refused. He had nothing good to say about Woodrow during his lifetime; any temporizing after the fact would be inappropriate, to say the least. Lodge stayed away.

I lived on for nearly forty years, blessed by great energy and good health. I became a "professional widow" in every sense of the word.

I spent those forty years doing everything I could to further enhance my husband's reputation, which, by the Second War-to-End-All-Wars, had become revered. I was invited to every opening session of the League of Nations, which limped along without American support. I went gladly, accepting every accolade that was always proffered. I helped restore Woodrow's birthplace in Virginia into a national historic site. I traveled extensively. Whenever there was a parade or memorial to the Great War or to my late husband, I was there—smiling and waving! My hats changed with the times. I did not. I served as an advisor on a motion picture about him. Woodrow would have been thrilled, since he loved the movies! It won the Academy Award for best picture! And, of course, when successive Presidents

invited me to the White House, why of course, I went. I only lived down the street.

And I wrote my memoirs. I was unaware that Julia Grant had written hers many years before, since they weren't unearthed till I was an elderly woman. But Nellie Taft's reminiscences had received some modest success, and I believed that my "stewardship" would be of interest. Besides, some things needed to be set right. My book also met with modest success. And I was a better writer than Nellie Taft—or Julia Grant.[21]

[21]**MARY LINCOLN** *If you like gush. Most of us were not particularly good writers. We wrote the way we were taught. Gushy-gushy-gushy! Eleanor wrote well, but Abigail Adams was the best writer of us all—by far!*

What I didn't do, however, was become a person in my own right. I could have been one. I had every opportunity. I knew all the right people. I had the prestige. I was even financially secure. I know Eleanor Roosevelt would have been thrilled to have had my support for her many activities. She asked often enough. But if it did not pertain to Woodrow Wilson, I abstained. I was still old fashioned enough to know that my place in history was as a wife. Besides, I didn't wish to expose myself to any more criticism than has already been leveled at me. I've had quite enough, thank you.

ELLEN WILSON

Ah cannot say that Ah could-a prevented Woodrow's failin' health. Or his failin' disposition. Ah cannot even say that Ah might-a prevented the "so-called treachery" of some-a his advisors. But Ah was not a good hater, and took some pride in mah ability to smooth and soothe. Ah had many friends in Congress and in the Cabinet. Ah would not-a refused Senator Lodge a place at Woodrow's Memorial Service. It would-a been tacky. He had always been nice to me. Ah definitely would not-a been a professional widow, however. A-course Ah would-a supported everythin' that brought honor to Woodrow's memory, but Ah would-a retired to Princeton or Cape Cod, and taken comfort in mah art. And Ah would-a continued to sign "EAW" so that "Mrs. Woodrow Wilson" would not get the credit for Miss Ellen Axson's talent.

222

FLORENCE KLING DeWOLFE HARDING
1860-1924
First Lady: 1921-23

Let me just say at the outset, I did *not* kill my husband. I don't deny I would have loved to wring his neck sometimes, but I loved my husband. He was my life.

I was five years older than Warren Harding.[1] I was divorced with a young son, and lived with my harsh, overbearing father, who never let me forget that my first marriage had failed, just as he predicted. Since I was struggling to support myself

> [1]**NANCY REAGAN**
> *I heard she was EIGHT years older than her husband.*

and my baby by giving piano lessons, my father offered me a devil's bargain, and he was definitely a devil. He offered to raise my boy as his own—provided I stay out of his life. What a terrible choice! But my survival instincts were stronger than my maternal instincts so I reluctantly agreed. I maintained some general contact with the lad of course, and once he became an adult, our relationship became closer. I suppose some women are just not meant to be mothers.[2]

> [2]**JANE PIERCE**
> *I cannot imagine a woman making such a choice! Motherhood is the most sacred duty a woman has.*

When I met Warren Harding, I was nearing thirty, and he was the handsomest man in Marion, Ohio. He was also the most eligible. He had just bought a small newspaper, and was trying to drum up local business. I wanted him and I got him. But Warren Harding had an eye for the ladies. I always knew it. Women liked him, and why not? He was handsome, with a wonderful shock of wavy hair that became white and distinguished-looking as he aged. He had a ready smile and kind word for everyone. Maybe too ready and too kind, since he never could say no. His father used to say it was a good thing Wur'n wasn't a woman, or he'd be in the "family way" all the time.

It is not easy for me to bare my soul. I spent my entire life keeping it well hidden. I kept no journals, wrote few letters, had few close friends. But I owe it to Mrs. Clinton and Mrs. Kennedy, and no doubt others to come, to open my heart so they can close theirs.

Not long after we married, I developed a chronic kidney disease. Modern antibiotics would make my problem no more than a treatable nuisance, but in the 1890s, it was life-threatening, incapacitating me for months at a time.

Of course those "wifely duties" became impossible.

> **[3]IDA McKINLEY**
> *Why not? My Major was completely faithful to me, and I was unable to fulfill those "wifely duties." But then, the Major was an exceptional person. A saint.*

I am neither naïve nor a fool. I never expected Warren Harding to remain completely faithful to an ailing wife.[3] I expected him to patronize the usual places that men go to from time to time to fill those needs. Discreetly. But Warren Harding was a romantic man. He preferred the chase and the conquest and the trappings of the affair. And, being a newspaperman, he loved to memorialize each amour with letters and photographs and souvenirs. That was bad enough. But he had appalling taste in women.[4] All of 'em. Once he became prominent, they all wanted something—mostly favors for keeping quiet.

> **[4]LOU HOOVER**
> *Florence is right about Harding's taste in women, herself included. She was a shrewish woman with a sharp tongue. I'm sure it wasn't easy for Harding to be married to her.*

Early in our marriage we became very friendly with a couple named Phillips. We exchanged visits and dinners. We even vacationed together. Carrie Phillips and I were boon companions. We shopped, traded recipes, curled each other's hair—"girl things." This went on for several years, until I learned that she was Wur'n's mistress and had been for most of those years. A knife in my heart and a knife in my back. I was doubly betrayed.[5]

> **[5]ELEANOR ROOSEVELT**
> *Lucy Mercer was my secretary and "friend." I know what it is like to be doubly betrayed.*

After the "Great Row," I had to make some choices. I was surely not the first, nor would I be the last, to experience such treachery. But in 1902 or 3 or 4, I had few options. We could divorce, of course. I was the injured party. But I had already been divorced once; a second would ruin me, and I had tried so hard to rebuild my reputation. There would be no divorce. Never!

I could languish and devote myself to imaginary ills—like Jane Pierce, and my own mother, for that matter. But I had languished enough during very real illness, and I appreciated the blessings of good health. No, much as I disliked the old goat, I was my father's daughter. No languishing for me.

I suppose we could have remained together-but-apart. Whether "apart" means leading separate lives or just being emotionally remote making each other miserable is something else again.

Or, I could turn a blind eye and make a life within a life.[6] I took the easy way. I smeared on a coat of grit and vowed I would never be hurt again. Embarrassed? Yes. Angered? Often. Humiliated? Regularly. But hurt? No more.[7]

I devoted myself to myself. I had a nice enough figure so I treated myself to the best clothes I could buy. I tried every cream, every powder, ever mixture to keep my complexion smooth. Unfortunately, I tended to wrinkle no matter what I did. I had my hair "marcelled" to look young and fashionable. I doubt it worked. I finally relied on hats with thick veils, and avoided the harsh glare of daylight. If I was going to make the best of it, it would be at my best. I held my head high.

I also devoted myself to the *Marion Star*. Our newspaper. I know modern historians want to say "Florence Harding ran the newspaper." It would be easy to take the credit. My ego could certainly use it. But it wasn't true. Florence Harding ran the marriage, but Warren Harding ran the paper. He decided the tone and wrote the editorials. He decided what and whom to support or oppose. It was generally according to the popular opinion of the day. The Republican opinion.

Once, when Wur'n was ill, I helped out for a few days. The office was a shambles! The janitor had no concept of clean, so I put it to right. I also put it in order and I stayed for fourteen years. I found my niche in the circulation department, making sure the advertisers paid up. My husband was lax about money. Never wanted to hurt anybody's feelings.

I supervised a dozen or so ragamuffin newsboys and made sure their accounts tallied. What small maternal instinct I had was lavished on those boys. Perhaps it was guilt about failing my son. Both Wur'n and I truly liked children. I taught those boys manners, and insisted they use "sir" and "ma'am" to the customers. I found out when there was trouble at home (which was often) and arranged a square meal for 'em more times than I can count. I'd give 'em handkerchiefs and combs at Christmas, and nearly every week, I'd bring in fresh-baked brownies or cookies as a treat. I was a good baker. The boys loved me. Warren Harding ran the paper, but I was there to

---

[6] **JULIA GRANT**
When my daughter became unhappy in her marriage, she chose to remain apart. A divorce would have been ruinous—even though her husband was an abusive and drunken fool. She spent months at a time with us—and with other friends and family.

[7] **JACQUELINE KENNEDY**
I don't care how much grit you use, there is always hurt. Every time.[8]

[8] **HILLARY RODHAM CLINTON**
Hear, hear.

mind the store.

It was a good arrangement. It left Wur'n free to do his beloved "bloviating," as he called it.[9] As a prominent citizen, he was a popular speaker for the Rotary or the Elks or the Chamber of Commerce. He'd talk the usual blather about the Country and the Flag and Free Enterprise.[10]

> [9]**HILLARY RODHAM CLINTON**
> *It also allowed time for his many extracurricular activities.*

> [10]**BARBARA BUSH**
> *There's nothing wrong with Country, Flag or Free Enterprise. It's a good thing to hear periodically.*

I didn't mean it to be disrespectful. I just meant that it was non-controversial.

My marriage was like walking through the paces. I had covered myself with so much grit that I barely realized how lonely I was. Mary Lincoln admitted her loneliness, but it was nothing compared to mine. Mary had a husband who cared for her and respected his marriage vows. She had children. She had sisters to provide familial comfort. She had memories. I had nothing and no one. Warren Harding and I went along amiably enough, between hellish rows over his succession of chippies. I know I was no great prize: an older wife with chronic health problems. He, on the other hand, grew handsomer as he aged. I just wore thicker veils and higher collars.

Naturally the attractive and eloquent editor of a thriving Ohio paper caught the attention of the Republican bigwigs. He was "brought along." I was in heaven. I foolishly assumed he would behave himself. He didn't. But I loved politics, and, having no obligations at home, was free to travel with my husband, which I did all the time. He needed watching. I met all the political leaders and developed my own rapport with them, and not just as "Mrs. Harding." I was "The Duchess."

Wur'n started calling me "Duchess" half in affection and half in derision, since I suppose I was a bit dominant. But the name suited me, and the people who called me "Duchess" did so with respect. They'd come regularly to Wur'n's famous poker games. Those men loved their cards, cigars and whiskey. I didn't play poker or smoke cigars of course, and my health forbade any liquor, but I was the bartender. I mixed the drinks.

Time would prove that some of our political chums were less than completely devoted to the public welfare, but at the time, they were bright with promise. They were also good company. Fun to be with! Don't look to me to turn on a friend unless I've been personally wronged. Same with Wur'n. We were nothing if not loyal to our friends. More's the pity, I suppose.

I was always more politically astute than Warren Harding. I not only enjoyed "politicking," I understood it. I also understood Wur'n. I knew his strengths and weaknesses. His strength was his likeability. He was delightful. Hail-fellow-well-met. Do-you-a-favor-any-time. He was very, *very* good at meeting and greeting and making friends. His weakness? Everything else. And he could be such a ninny sometimes!

In 1912, Warren Harding became U.S. Senator from Ohio. We were thrilled!

I expected a new life in Washington. I bought a brand new wardrobe and filled my head—and heart—with thoughts of new people and good times. Little did I realize how unhappy I would be. The Congressional wives were less than cordial. I was considered elderly and provincial, my new wardrobe hopelessly "outré." Oh, I went to the large gatherings, but I received few calls, even though I diligently left my card everywhere. And, soon after our arrival, I had another long bout with my kidneys. This time I was near death. Doc Sawyer, our dear friend and family physician, came and stayed for weeks, nursing me back to health.

My husband was genuinely concerned and solicitous of my condition. We never "hated" each other, despite his finding entertainment elsewhere. It is sad. Nearly every other First Lady was blessed with a happy marriage and a devoted, loving husband. I was not.[11] I suppose Heaven must have pitied my empty life so I was given a great blessing: Evalyn.

> [11]**LOUISA ADAMS**
> *There are many ways to have an empty and unhappy marriage. Infidelity is only one.*

My story would not be complete without my dearest friend, Evalyn Walsh McLean. No two people could be more unlikely. She was nearly young enough to be my daughter, and was the pampered child of one of the wealthiest and most prominent men in the country, married to a man even more spoiled and more wealthy. She was a dear friend of Alice Roosevelt Longworth and together they generally dominated Washington society.[12] I was hopelessly middle class. But wonder of wonders, Evalyn and I took to each other at once and

> [12]**NELLIE TAFT**
> *Hmmpf. Gives you an idea of what Washington society was like!*

became inseparable. Her husband Ned was equally at home with Wur'n and his friends. They all liked cigars, poker, whiskey and, I suppose, the "dollies." The McLean's Georgetown mansion became our second home.

Evalyn helped me choose fashionable clothing, took me to concerts and made sure I was invited everywhere. She also had one of the kindest hearts I've ever known. We would go once or twice every week to visit wounded veterans, bringing flowers or books or other special treats. I helped 'em write letters home, I read to 'em, played card games with 'em—it was a wonderful feeling to be useful and needed.[13]

Evalyn also introduced me to Madam Marcia, an astrologer with extraordinary psychic gifts. Just about everyone I knew consulted Madam Marcia. Now before everyone jumps all over me about my fascination with a lot of "hooey," let's just say that I've never met anyone who wouldn't like to glimpse the future. Is it a crutch? Of course. But everyone needs some kind of crutch. Jane Pierce needed her Bible and prayers. Ida McKinley needed her husband waving his handkerchief. And I, who had so little pleasure in my life, needed some hope that I might find a little happiness.[14]

Madam Marcia predicted that Warren Harding would be elected President in 1920, but would not survive his term. My common sense told me it was foolishness. Warren Harding was an unexceptional Senator with no national reputation. I don't think he had even introduced a piece of legislation! There were certainly more qualified candidates. We'd be the first to admit that.

> [13]**ELEANOR ROOSEVELT**
> *Nothing eases a sad heart like being useful to others.*

> [14]**NANCY REAGAN**
> *The Duchess is right about that. Whenever there is worry or care or unhappiness, people need to have hope. And if they can glimpse the future, why not?*[15]

> [15]**MARY LINCOLN**
> *I have always believed in the spirit world. There are many things in the world that we can never know. Some people have true gifts.*

On the other hand, the Republicans were hopelessly split between the Old Guard and the Progressives. There was no front runner. Our political friends in Ohio assured us that a deadlock at the convention would eventually prove key to Warren Harding's nomination. But even with their support and Madam Marcia's assurance, I had grave doubts. I doubted my husband's competence to be President. I doubted my competence to lead Washington society. But then again, how competent was Franklin Pierce? Or Millard Fillmore? Decent enough men, but certainly not brilliant. And I? Well, Evalyn McLean would help me.

The rest is history. After a hopeless deadlock, the Republicans united behind Warren Harding. I was worried that his shenanigans would come to light. Politics were separate from a man's private life—at least they were then, but the little tarts were willing, nay, anxious, to profit from their liaison with the Presidential nominee. The Republicans actually paid a lot of money to retrieve some of his indiscreet letters. I thought I knew about most of his girlies, but it turns out I didn't know the half. It was the first election where women voted, and they voted for Wur'n overwhelmingly. They were probably attracted by his good looks and easy smile. He won in a walk. I suppose I was the first "First" to vote for her husband.[16]

> [16]**ELEANOR ROOSEVELT**
> *Not quite, dear. FDR ran for Vice President on the Democratic ticket that year. I, too, voted for my husband. It was the first and only time he lost.*

It is not disloyal for me to say that Warren Harding was ill-suited to be President. He was; it's a fact. But marital peccadilloes aside, he was a decent and kind man who only wanted to be well liked and have everything run smoothly. He figured if he named the best men available to positions of authority, he would accomplish both goals. Some of his appointments were excellent: Charles Evans Hughes to "State" and Herbert Hoover to "Commerce." And, of course, appointing former President Taft as Chief Justice of the Supreme Court was one of his finest acts.[17]

> [17]**NELLIE TAFT**
> *Harding made an old man very very happy. Of course Will was also eminently qualified.*

My goal was to be an "accessible" First Lady. We had enough haughtiness with Edith Wilson and Nellie Taft. I answered every letter, and was delighted to send my favorite recipes to anyone who asked. I posed for the newsreel cameras and even greeted the tourists who came to the White House. I gave a huge garden party for ex-soldiers from every Veterans' Hospital in the area. They came with canes, crutches, in wheelchairs and on stretchers to enjoy the Harding hospitality. I personally shook hands with more than five hundred of 'em! It was the happiest day of my life.

Wur'n and I didn't talk about politics as much as we used to once he became President. He was too busy during the day—and at night, he liked to relax with his Ohio pals. When we first had an inkling of "hanky-panky," we couldn't—and didn't—believe it! We had known some of these people for years! Long before *anyone* could have conceived of Harding as President! It probably never occurred to 'em that Wur'n would bear the brunt of their crimes against the country, but invariably, the President is responsible.[18]

> [18]**BESS TRUMAN**
> *We all know where the buck stops.*

There were suicides, resignations, accusations and a swirl of evidence of wrongdoing. Meanwhile, my kidneys failed again. I was past sixty and doubted my body could suffer any more punishment. Wur'n was also suffering. Chronic indigestion—at least that's what Doc Sawyer said. He said it was from stress and worry and too much rich food. He was right about the stress and worry and rich food, but he was wrong about the indigestion. Warren Harding had a bad heart, but we didn't know it, and we never dreamed of questioning Doc's diagnosis.

> [19]**HILLARY RODHAM CLINTON**
> *I was always there for Bill, despite our private woes.*

Once again, after several weeks, I began to recover. Wur'n was genuinely glad. I had always been there for 'im, despite our private woes.[19] His world was crumbling, and he didn't know why. He had done nothing wrong. He never took a dime from anyone, and the ways our "friends" were accruing vast sums were beyond our comprehension!

His death was a blessing—and a complete shock. He seemed the picture of health. No wonder suspicions arose as one scandal after another began to surface. I didn't kill him. The doctor didn't kill him. He didn't commit suicide. He had a heart attack—brought on by stress, worry and rich food.

Even as his body lay in state, Evalyn and I burned hundreds of letters and photographs and whatever evidence I could find—not of any *public* wrongdoing—only of our *private* life. He was dead; let him rest in peace. Let me rest, too.

Six months later, another of his little tarts popped up out of the woodwork. Nan Britten had been a neighborhood child who used to come by the house for gingerbread or cookies. She was always a precocious one. Even at twelve years old, she behaved, well…I suppose it wasn't surprising she

> [20]**LADY BIRD JOHNSON**
> *It was the truth, Florence, and you know it. The child was his.*

turned out the way she did. She claimed to be the mother of Warren Harding's child. Nonsense! Some young boy was probably responsible, and she just wanted money like the rest of 'em.[20] That little trash left no stone unturned trying to make me pay for her bastard, but I wasn't about to give her a cent. I was sure she had a string of young men enjoying her favors.

I died a year after Wur'n. I had nothing to live for. My memories were unhappy; I left no legacy. My husband left a tarnished reputation. I had all our personal papers locked away for fifty years, hoping that by then, history might treat us both with a little kindness. Neither of us should have been in the White House. We knew it.

GRACE GOODHUE COOLIDGE
1879-1957
First Lady: 1923-29

When Calvin Coolidge was courting me, my friends said, "Grace, I don't know what you see in that Coolidge fellow. He has the personality of a fish!" My father was no better. "Don't encourage that Coolidge chap, Grace. He'll never amount to anything. You can't get six words out of 'im." My mother told me, "Grace dear, there are a dozen young men in town eager for your company. Why waste your time with that Mr. Coolidge? He's the most anti-social person I ever met!"

Mother had a point. I had no lack of suitors. It was always one of my happiest blessings to make friends easily and keep them forever. But Mother didn't realize how persistent Calvin Coolidge was, and how often he made me laugh. Why, my very first recollection of him was filled with laughter!

I was a teacher at the Clarke School for the Deaf in Northampton, Massachusetts. One summer morning, I was watering the flower garden, and for some peculiar reason, I happened to look up. There, in a nearby window, I saw a young man shaving. His face was covered with lather, his suspenders hung at his waist, and the top of his union suit was open at the neck. He was also wearing a derby hat. The sight of this tickled me, and I laughed aloud. Perhaps he heard me, since he turned to look out the window. Spying a young lady, he did the gentlemanly thing: he tipped his hat and continued shaving. I was hysterical!

It turned out that we had mutual friends, and not long afterwards, we were "formally" introduced and began a very proper Victorian courtship. As we made the rounds of Church socials, picnics, card parties, dances and the latest innovation at the turn of the twentieth century, ice cream parlors, I began to realize some of the fine and endearing qualities Calvin had to offer, not the least of which was his very deep, albeit unspoken, affection for Miss Grace Goodhue. Me.

My story is very much like Eliza Johnson's, in that it is no story at all.[1] Like Eliza, my entire life was being a wife and mother, which was what was expected of

> [1]**LUCY HAYES**
> *If you asked us—at least most of us—if, when we married our husbands, we ever thought we would be First Lady, you would get a resounding "No!" You would also get the same response if you asked our husbands if they thought, when they married, that they would ever be President.*

nice young ladies. I expected to be First Lady as much as Eliza did. Not at all. Ever!

Both my parents discouraged our courtship. It wasn't that they *disliked* Calvin. He came from decent people, was educated at Amherst College, and was modestly successful as a young attorney. They just thought him unsuitable for their very vivacious (and I was!) daughter. My parents wanted me to be happy, and couldn't conceive it possible with such a "cold clam" as they called him. So they decided to dissuade us by complaining about *me*. "Why Mr. Coolidge," my father said, "Grace can't even bake bread!" "I can buy bread," Calvin drawled, "I want Grace." My mother insisted that I spend a year at home with her, learning to be a good New England wife: cooking, mending, keeping house—and baking bread.[2] Her purpose was not to instruct me on everyday chores; she wanted to put time between us so we could change our minds. Calvin didn't. I didn't. And I was never more than a mediocre housewife and plain cook.

> [2]**CAROLINE HARRISON**
> *Being a good homemaker is not merely developed from practice. One needs to have some acumen—and love—for it.*[3]

> [3]**BETTY FORD**
> *I'll bet if you took a survey, very few of us were really "dedicated" home-makers.*

Once we were married, Calvin decided to augment his modest living by becoming active in local politics. He ran for a minor office and was elected. People admired his honesty, his conservatism (we lived in a *very* conservative area of the country) and his loyalty to his political associates. He was one of them. They knew it and he knew it. He could speak for the interests of western Massachusetts without even thinking about it. And never a breath of scandal tarnished his reputation.

His rise in Massachusetts politics was so slow and inconspicuous that I was barely aware of his activities. I had been told he was a fairly good public speaker (when he actually chose to speak) but I had never heard him. So one evening, when he was on the program for a local meeting, I put on my hat and coat. "Going out?" he queried. "I thought I'd go listen to your speech," I said. "I've never heard you, and people say you are quite good." "Best not," he said. That was the end of that. I stayed home.

I was obedient like Crete Garfield and Frances Cleveland. If my husband said no, it was no. It was unlike me to contradict. It was also unlike him to accept contradiction.

So Poppa (I started calling him that when our boys were babies) advanced from Alderman to Mayor of Northampton to State Legislator, and I developed my own routine. I started taking brisk hour-long walks every morning. I believed in fresh air and exercise. (Poppa had little interest in either.) I also did my own housework, laundry and cooking, just as my mother instructed.[4]

I suppose this is as good a place as any to mention that we were the only presidential family that never owned a house.[5] When we were newlyweds, we began renting half of a two-family house, appropriate enough for a young couple starting out. But when John and Calvin Junior came along, and Poppa's political career was rising, I wanted our own home. "The boys will need more room," I said, "and the town Mayor should have a more presentable house." "No need," Calvin decided, "there's room enough." So that was the end of that. We rented.

I must make a small digression. Most of my immediate predecessors mentioned their "entertaining" skills.[6] It was customary then, as it is now, for rising political figures to host their colleagues periodically. A great deal can be accomplished in social settings. I know that. And since I was very outgoing and enjoyed company, I offered many times to give a dinner party for some of Calvin's associates. But Poppa was about as comfortable in "society" as he was standing on his head. "Don't think so," he said. And that was the end of that, too.

But I was a contented person. I filled my very happy hours being Mrs. Coolidge. I was active in our Church and once the Great War started, I helped out at the Red Cross on a regular basis. I had many friends in town, and we exchanged visits and luncheons—all the usual things ladies did then. I also corresponded with several old sorority sisters from my college days.

Ah, another digression and a tidbit for posterity! I was one of the original founders of Pi Beta Phi sorority, which I believe was the first one in the country. I was active in it all my life. My original "sisters" and I started a Round Robin correspondence that lasted forty years—maybe more. This way, we'd catch up and keep up with the events in each others' lives. Like

> [4]**MARY LINCOLN**
> *I did all our cooking when we lived in Springfield. I had no experience before our marriage, but I bought a recipe book and became fairly adept. Mr. Lincoln always loved my white almond cake the best.*

> [5]**BESS TRUMAN**
> *Technically we never owned a house either. We lived with my mother, in a house my grandfather built. It didn't become ours till she died. By that time, we were living in the White House.*

> [6]**NELLIE TAFT**
> *A politician's wife needs to be socially adept. Frankly, any man who chooses a political career should only marry a woman who can complement his ambitions.*

I said, I made friends easily and kept them forever.

It's astonishing how very little I knew about Calvin's career. I actually had to read in the newspapers that he was running for the State Legislature! It was not lack of interest on my part. I was always interested in my husband's work—and I was always interested in life in general. But Calvin told me I mustn't bother myself with complicated politics. If it appeared that I felt hurt or left out, he would buy me a new hat. I had dozens of hats.

Deep down, Calvin loved me dearly, and I knew it. He just had little regard for my "education." Actually, he had little regard for any woman's "education" unless it was artistic. And if it *was* artistic, he would acknowledge the ability, and be completely baffled by the art. The truth was that he didn't respect a woman's intelligence. When Edith Roosevelt and Nellie Taft and the Wilson Wives wrote their chapters, it was obvious that their spouses respected and admired and enjoyed the company of women. Not Poppa. If he enjoyed company at all (other than family), it was a small select group of men. Not that you could tell he was enjoying himself. He'd nurse a beer for an hour, smoke one cigar, nod to everyone, and go home. But Calvin insisted that politics was man's business.[7] In fact, all business was man's business.

[7]**NELLIE TAFT**
Will got to know the Coolidges quite well—both as ex-President and as Chief Justice. He said many times that the best political decision Coolidge ever made was marrying Grace.

So was paying the bills. Poppa kept a watchful eye on our bankbook. Public servants were paid pittances, especially in the state legislature, which was considered a part-time position of honor. Calvin's law practice was small. Our income did not encourage extravagance, which, knowing Poppa, is amusing just in thought! Clothing got used and mended. When Poppa went to Boston, he bought a second-class train ticket. When he stayed in Boston, it was in a second-class room of a second-class hotel. When our sons approached their teens, they shoveled snow and delivered newspapers—the same as thousands and thousands of other boys. And I made casseroles and warmed-up leftovers, just like thousands and thousands of other wives. It was a simple life. I was happy.

Ask me what I thought about women's suffrage! As you'd expect, when Calvin was "agin it," I was "agin it." When he finally decided it was a key political issue, we both became "for it." With Calvin, it was not a conviction; it was politics. He considered himself a representative of the people. He voted what *they* thought; he would not originate.

Oh, he was always ambitious, but he always set reasonable, achievable goals. Being Mayor. Being a state legislator. I'm not sure how or why he was elected Lieutenant Governor. He was anything but the typical glad-handed politician that Massachusetts usually chose (and, of course, the Harvard crowd viewed his "education" the same way he viewed mine). I believed he thought that a term or two as Lieutenant Governor might help his law practice, if nothing else. We began spending more time in Boston, since I was expected to accompany Lieutenant Governor Coolidge to many public events. It was about then that Poppa started appreciating my "political value." I had always loved people, and to my delight, the feeling was usually reciprocated.[8]

My "education," faulty though it might have been, had always included current events, literature and art, and the new moving pictures that were becoming so popular after the Great War. And baseball. Since both my sons played on school teams, I developed a keen understanding of the game and was an ardent supporter of the Boston Red Sox till my dying day. Believe me, in a room full of Massachusetts politicians, an "intelligent" discussion about the Red Sox always broke the ice and helped me make new friends! Calvin began to take another look at his wife and discovered that she was indeed, a political asset.[9] I'm not saying this from conceit; it's just that so many people said so, there may be some truth to it. Naturally, being the unsophisticated woman I was, it took me longer to absorb it, but I finally came to the same realization. Where Calvin was dour, I smiled; where he was taciturn, I was loquacious; where he was ill-at-ease, I exuded the confidence of a person with absolutely no agenda. And where he was "Calvin Who?" I was "that delightful Mrs. Coolidge."

> [8]**DOLLEY MADISON**
> *Grace truly is the daughter of my heart. She is right in sensing that people always respond to those who sincerely like them. Everybody loved Grace!*

> [9]**NELLIE TAFT**
> *Will adored Grace, and often said that if it weren't for her, Calvin wouldn't get elected dog-catcher.*

Once Poppa concluded that I could socialize for him, his ambitions grew. He set his eye on the Governorship. I don't think Poppa ever dreamed beyond that. I, on the other hand, never dreamed. I just kept my hat handy for wherever the road led, and indeed, it led to the Governor's Mansion. We moved in, but since we were Coolidges, we continued to rent our half of the two-family house in Northampton. "Won't be in Boston forever," Poppa said. "We'll have to go home sometime."

The months following the Great War were traumatic for returning veterans, particularly in the cities. At first there were a great many men and few jobs, but as industry grew rapidly to accommodate them, there was a mad rush for the high wages being offered. The Boston Police Force took notice of the discrepancies in pay, and demanded more money. This was a *Boston* problem, and Poppa was ever mindful to keep his nose out of other people's affairs. He sympathized with the policemen (who definitely deserved higher wages), and he strongly encouraged the Mayor and City Council to resolve their problems promptly and fairly. Unfortunately, the Boston fathers arrived at such an impasse that the policemen went on strike, causing the expected havoc. When the Governor finally had to act, he declared that it was unlawful for "anyone, anytime, anywhere to strike against the public welfare."

That one brief Coolidge-like sentence elevated Poppa from an obscure State Governor to a national figure. Our lives would be forever changed—even if we never changed a bit!

When Poppa was nominated as the Republican Vice Presidential candidate in 1920, it was a total surprise to everyone, ourselves included. Few had ever heard of Harding. Even fewer ever heard of Coolidge. But then, no one ever heard of the Democratic candidates, James Cox and Franklin D. Roosevelt either. It was the first election where women were allowed to vote, so naturally I voted for Calvin—and Harding.

A few words about the Hardings. Being a people-lover by nature, I was prepared to like and befriend our new president and his wife. On the rare occasions we were together, I was cordial and friendly. Mrs. Harding, for some reason known only to herself, disliked me intensely.[10] Her attitude, while polite, was distant. So we went our own way, doing what Vice Presidential families had always done: socializing and "filling in" when the First Family was unavailable. "Gotta eat somewhere," Calvin remarked as we were inundated with dinner invitations. Since dining "out" meant less expense to our grocery budget, it met with Poppa's sense of thrift. Curiously, the very remoteness of his nature, coupled with his occasional pointed, pixilated and completely unexpected humor, made him a big hit in Washington.[11] They liked us!

[10]**FLORENCE HARDING**
I thought the Coolidges were hopelessly provincial and socially inept. They were also dull as dishwater. I was not the only one who thought this way.

[11]**DOLLEY MADISON**
I am sure your infectious grin and charm helped more than you realize.

216

Politics was a man's business, like Calvin said, and I had no business drawing conclusions. But we *both* noted that Washington thrived on "society" rather than the "men's club" atmosphere of Boston.[12] Women were invited everywhere, and we were having a fine time. "It is not hard to be Vice President," Poppa said. In the 1920s, the Vice Presidency was still the empty honorarium that was conceived by our forefathers.[13]

> [12]**ELEANOR ROOSEVELT**
> *I noticed that atmosphere when Franklin was Assistant Secretary of the Navy under President Wilson. Everyone was very social and gossipy. I hated it!*

> [13]**ABIGAIL ADAMS**
> *John always said the Vice Presidency was the worst position ever devised by the mind of man. He was right. It was an empty shell.*

Many years later, long after both Hardings were in their graves, it was suggested that Florence Harding was jealous of me. I was twenty years younger, and I still had my youthful looks and vitality. She had aged visibly. I could make the plainest clothing look stylish, and I fear no matter what she wore, she looked hopelessly dowdy. I made friends easily and quickly; she was always an outsider. And, most important, I had the obvious love and devotion of my husband and sons. She was alone. After hearing that litany of reasons, any unkind feelings I may have harbored for Mrs. Harding immediately disappeared when I considered her unhappiness.[14]

> [14]**FLORENCE HARDING**
> *No comment.*

When President Harding died, we were visiting the Coolidge family farm in Vermont. We went there as often as possible, since Father Coolidge was near eighty and we had always been very close. We were totally unprepared. Harding's previously reported illness had been considered minor. They said he was recovering.

At midnight, an automobile pulled up to the house and there was a terrific banging on the door. When my sleepy father-in-law opened it, a telegraph messenger blurted out the shocking news. Within a quarter hour, several other cars drove to the house, carrying reporters and local dignitaries anxious to bear witness to the momentous occasion. We dressed hurriedly and came downstairs. Father Coolidge was a notary public, and thus legally qualified to administer the oath of office. It would have taken hours to arrange for a local judge. So in the early hours of the morning, in the little gaslit parlor, with his hand on an old family Bible, Poppa was sworn in as our 30th President. Then he shook hands with the dozen or so people who were crammed into the tiny parlor, and we went back to bed. "What else is there to do at two a.m.?" he said.

Modern "Second Ladies" receive a broad education in the duties expected from our nation's leaders and their spouses. I had very little knowledge or experience in those things. Mrs. Harding never asked me to assist her, and my own hosting abilities were untested, since we never entertained on a grand scale. Poppa was just as inexperienced as I was, but he did offer some wise (at least I thought it wise) advice: "Don't try anything new, Grace."

But it was *all* new to me. I had always done my own housework and cooking. Now I was a "manager." I had to plan huge formal affairs for hundreds of dignitaries as well as small dinners for the most important people in the world. I had a long list of requests to fulfill and personal appointments. Plus hundreds of letters to answer every week. I had to oversee a full White House staff, yet maintain a home-like atmosphere for our family. I was overwhelmed!

> [15]**DOLLEY MADISON**
> *It is very much in Grace's character to remember to thank the people who helped her.*

I suppose this is as fine a time as any to say a few words about the wonderful people who help run the White House.[15] First Families come and go, each with their own habits and peculiarities. The staff, however, remains. They provide not only the transition, but the knowledge of what must be done and how to do it. Most of the First Lady's job is flawlessly channeled by dozens of unseen public servants who manage everything from ironing napkins to making sure the Marine Band knows every national anthem in the world. They made my life very easy.

We Coolidges were an odd First Family for the "Roaring Twenties." We didn't roar. We were still old-fashioned Victorians. My hems were raised only slightly—a decent level for a middle-aged woman. We obeyed the Prohibition laws, although we did not agree with them. (Calvin liked a beer or whiskey on occasion—"to be social," he said.) He did not like to impose his morality on the world. Poppa believed that Prohibition was bad because it encouraged a lot of good people to disregard the law. Our teenaged sons, while enjoying the current fads and entertainments, were certainly not allowed to run wild.

Frankly, I don't know how Poppa would have managed without me. I don't mean to sound vain, but surely our dinner parties would have been oppressively dull. After Poppa made the customary greeting, all fell silent. It was always left to me to break the ice and start conversation. Not that I minded. The country roared with personalities! Sports figures! Babe Ruth, the former Red Sox pitcher who became a Yankee outfielder. (I never did forgive him for his desertion!) Movie stars and Broadway performers. Al Jolson! Mary Pickford! Charlie Chaplin! They all made their way to the White House to have their picture taken with the President. Calvin always obliged. He thought it was good for the people to see him in less formal situations. I loved hosting them, since it made for delightful conversation.[16] Poppa never found them to his liking—not even my own personal favorite, Will Rogers. The only celebrity he really enjoyed was the young aviator, Charles Lindbergh, and we were both thrilled when he married the daughter of Calvin's old Amherst friend and classmate, Dwight Morrow.

> [16]**ELEANOR ROOSEVELT**
> *Franklin enjoyed hosting celebrities, but I can't say it was to my taste. I always preferred people of more substance than movie or radio personalities. And I knew nothing about sports.*

First Ladies always have a formal portrait painted. I had never posed for a painted portrait before. It is a beautiful full length, youthful impression of me, wearing my favorite red dress—posing with Rob Roy, our white collie. Poppa always took an uncommonly active interest in my appearance, and despite his legendary thrift, always encouraged me to wear expensive clothes. He wanted me to wear *his* favorite dress, which was white. Mr. Christy, the artist, protested, saying that red was a perfect balance of color for the white dog. "Wear the white dress and dye the dog," Poppa said, conceding the argument. As it turned out, it's one of the most popular First Lady portraits. I loved it! Mr. Christy captured the real Grace Coolidge.

Every First Family knows there is a great price to be paid for the Presidency. Our younger son was the price we paid. Forgive me, but we both would have been eternally happy and grateful to forego the White House and keep the child.

> **JANE PIERCE**
> *Amen to that.*

> **MARY LINCOLN**
> *Amen to that.*

It should not have happened. Our Cal was a healthy, active boy of sixteen, with a winning smile (like mine) and a dry humor (like his father). He was playing tennis and developed a blister. Common enough. But the blister became infected, and the infection poisoned his blood and in less than a week, our boy was dead. Penicillin was still a few years away.

About that same time, Father Coolidge also passed. Matters of state prevented Poppa from being in Vermont to say goodbye to the man he loved and revered above all others.

For a man as undemonstrative as Calvin, those twin losses pained him more than can be imagined. Of course I mourned our son. I sat for hours with our pastor. I shed tears as I answered the thousands of letters of condolence I received from strangers. And I cried and cried as I "remembered" young Cal with our close friends and his classmates.[17] I became fiercely protective of our remaining son John, who I would shortly "lose" to marriage. Poppa disappeared into the deep silences of his nature. I think I was the only one who knew the depth of his grief.

> [17]**EDITH ROOSEVELT**
> *When Quentin was killed in action during the Great War, it comforted me deeply to share memories with his young friends and classmates. I kept in touch with some of them for the rest of my life.*

In 1928, Calvin was hugely popular. He had easily won a term of his own in 1924. Since his first "term" was only the remaining months of his predecessor, he would be, by tradition, eligible to run for a "second term" on his own, and was likely to win. But Poppa simply announced, "I do not choose to run." That was it. He never amplified or explained further.

He had not discussed his decision with me. He never discussed politics or business with me. I never even knew his daily appointments or if and when my presence would be needed. I just kept my hat handy for whatever arose. But as time went on, I sensed the true reason he "did not choose to run." In his own sense of New England Puritan morality, knowing everything has a cost that must be paid, I believe Calvin calculated the cost of his father and his son as the price for his "first" term. He would expect a price for a "second" term as well, and if anything had happened to either John or myself, my dear, quiet, uncommunicative, very loving husband could not have borne it. "Too expensive," he most likely thought.

The Coolidges, history seems to agree, were a lucky couple: In at the right time and out at the right time. As the country entered the Great Depression, Poppa became more and more depressed—the cancer that was discovered in his stomach notwithstanding. He feared that his innate sense of status quo had allowed the economy to run amok. I cannot comment on this. I don't know the answer. I do know that Poppa did the very best job he could, according to the tried and true principles of centuries of forefathers. It was the only way he knew.

I lived on quietly in Northampton for nearly thirty years after Calvin's death. I even tried a few new things. I flew in an airplane. I went to Europe. But mostly I visited with old friends, and, of course, spent time with my son

John and his family. I reactivated my interest in the deaf and I became a dedicated and active trustee for the old Clarke School. I lived each day as I always had: optimistically, pleasantly, and as productively as my health allowed. Perhaps I could have done more. But nobody ever asked me to.

LOU HENRY HOOVER
1874-1944
First Lady: 1929-1933

I was so certain my place in history would be secure! I would be a shining beacon to generations of women! After all, I was a frontier woman from California when the West was full of glamour and pioneer gumption and adventure. I could ride, shoot, hunt, fish and survive like the best of 'em. My father was the town banker and we were fairly prosperous; I had "breeding" and a college education. Not to denigrate the accomplishments of my predecessors, but my education was legitimate—not an advanced finishing school or teacher's training.[1] I graduated from Stanford University, which, as most people know, is one of the finest institutions in the country for science and technology. I was a degreed geologist.

> [1]**LUCY HAYES**
> *Everything in its time. When I went to college, we were trained in subjects suitable to our sex. Each generation has its own idea of what is suitable.*

It was at Stanford that I met Herbert Hoover, who was a senior when I entered. After my graduation, we married. Bert traveled all over the world as a mining engineer, and I went along and helped him in his work. We circumnavigated the globe at least three times in the first six or seven years of our marriage—with two babies in tow! Bert was an exceptional engineer and administrator, and quickly rose in responsibility and income. I frequently drafted the reports and analyses for him, and he relied on my knowledge and judgment. After all, I was a geologist. I knew the subject.

Developing a mine, particularly in remote areas of the world, is like building a city from scratch. You must provide transportation systems, homes, food, schools and services for the workers and their families—sometimes hundreds of miles from civilization. Since I had a natural ear and learned languages easily, I became the intermediary for the "native" contractors; making sure things were done promptly, properly and at the expected cost. My pioneer upbringing accustomed me to some of the related deprivations of remote locations, so I was in charge of setting up schools and cottage-industries for sewing and cooking and laundry and whatever could be concocted for entertainment. What Bert was to the mine, I was to the families of the miners. We were an excellent team; a true partnership, like John and Abigail Adams.[2]

In 1902, there was an uprising in China known to history as the Boxer Rebellion. Antagonism against "foreign" influences provided the spark. We lived with English, German, French and other American families in a mile-square compound. It rapidly became a war zone. Bert was a natural leader, and we found ourselves at the center of innumerable meetings and emergency sessions. It was a frightening experience! Here we were, thousands of miles from civilization as we knew it, barely able to communicate, and people were shooting at us. We barricaded our compound with sandbags, pooled all our food, water, fuel and other resources and even turned our little infirmary into a make-shift hospital. I became an expert in make-shift. I made rounds every day, going everywhere, checking on everyone's welfare, trying to be as useful as I could. That the incident passed within a few weeks with few casualties was a miracle, as far as I was concerned. But the lessons I learned in adapting resource to necessity stood me in good stead for the rest of my life.

> [2]**ABIGAIL ADAMS**
> *Not too many First Families were "partners" in that sense. The Franklin Roosevelts and the Lyndon Johnsons. And the Clintons.*[3]
>
> [3]**SARAH POLK**
> *And the Polks!*

A dozen years later saw us happily ensconced in London. Bert had prospered extremely well as a mining consultant. Some of his enterprises would provide us with a comfortable living for the rest of our lives, and we were still under forty. Our sons were thriving; we were building a home in California, and I was actively involved in a half-dozen worthwhile charitable activities. I had even found time to translate (with Bert's help) an ancient mining treatise from its original Latin. The book was published and became a "best-seller," at least in mining circles. Bert let me keep the royalties, since while our names were listed as co-authors, I did most of the work. He was the first to admit it. His Latin was poor.

Then the Great War began in 1914, and thousands of American citizens were stranded in Europe. Ships and trains cancelled business and civilian passage. Each country only honored its own currency. London was chaotic, between the War and all the Americans who were pouring in with no baggage, no money and nowhere to go or stay.

One of our friends at the American Consulate asked Bert to help. He agreed at once. Within three hours he telephoned me to meet him downtown "with all the money we have in the house." This amounted to about 500 pounds (around $2500 then) which he began lending to our countrymen in 2 and 3 and 5 pound increments, so they could buy food and lodging. He required only a hand-written note to secure the "loan."

I immediately set to work organizing committees to set up nurseries at the railroad stations. We called everyone we knew to provide diapers, milk and food for the children. People donated tables and chairs, games, toys and books. Dozens of women and young girls volunteered to be "nannies for an hour." Some stayed for weeks.

While Bert was coercing London banks to honor American letters of credit and arranging safe transport home for marooned Americans (a political as well as financial exercise), I sat on a dozen committees to help in the interim. We contacted restaurants and grocers to provide affordable meals, accepted and distributed donations of clothing, established play-schools and dormitories, started a make-shift hospital and recruited doctors and nurses to volunteer their services. And we solicited and collected financial contributions, disbursed them and accounted for them accordingly.[4]

Once that furor abated (and, I want to note, every dime of our personal "loans" was repaid!) another crisis loomed even greater. The German Army had decimated Belgium, and millions of people were starving. Literally. We did not have to be asked to help this time. We volunteered immediately. Bert and I reactivated all our resources to try to feed, clothe, shelter and provide fuel for an entire nation. It was a massive and unprecedented undertaking. While Bert arranged for shiploads of supplies, I criss-crossed the Atlantic several times on my own. My first concern was to place our sons in school near my family so they would be safe. But my second thought was to make Americans aware of the Belgian plight. I embarked on a schedule of speaking tours and personally raised more than $200,000—in 1916![5]

By 1916, Bert was well known on both sides of the Ocean. In addition to all my committee work, it fell to me to assume hostess duties. Hardly an evening passed without our entertaining a wide variety of guests. How we were able to summon all this

> [4]**PAT NIXON**
> *I have always thought that Mrs. Hoover was one of the most under-rated Ladies. Perhaps her innate dignity led to a perceived aloofness, but she was a marvelous woman!*

> [5]**LUCY HAYES**
> *It amazes me how adept the modern ladies are as speakers. I was asked to chair groups, or say a few words on occasion, but I had no confidence in my ability to hold the attention of an audience. I dreaded it.*

> [6]**ELEANOR ROOSEVELT**
> *Good health and plenty of energy are two of the greatest blessings for any First Lady—or President. I was fortunate in inheriting Uncle Theodore's vitality, and I was seldom ill.*

energy I will never know—but then again, we were still fairly young.[6]

We were financially comfortable, a far cry from Bert's youth, which was only slightly above poverty, so we could afford the trappings of society as well as donate our time, services and more often than not, provide personal funds when needed.[7] Bert believed that if one was fortunate enough to be financially independent, he had the obligation to help those in lesser circumstances. I agreed. Bert never took a dime of salary in more than fifty years of public service. But I digress.

> [7]**JACQUELINE KENNEDY**
> *The Hoovers were, to be blunt, "loaded." There have been a few wealthy Presidents, but Herbert Hoover was the only one who earned the wealth entirely himself. No family money or property was ever involved.*

When America finally entered into the Great War, President Wilson summoned Bert to come home and manage the Food Administration in America, to conserve, increase production and feed the world. Of course we responded at once.[8] Despite living abroad for nearly twenty years, we were, first and foremost, Americans.

> [8]**EDITH WILSON**
> *Woodrow and I both liked and admired the Hoovers. We also thought they were Democrats.*

By the end of the War, Herbert Hoover's name and reputation was known nationwide. Politics summoned. Bert was not inclined toward party politics, not then, not ever.[9] I'm not even certain if or how Bert voted during those years we were abroad. My guess is that he was an old "Bull Moose" Progressive Republican, if one needs to pin a label on him. He was by nature a conservative man—yet he was always progressive in his outlook. He wanted to harness all our burgeoning technologies for the benefit of mankind. Serving

> [9]**LOUISA ADAMS**
> *John Quincy Adams was also disinclined toward party politics. He always tried to remain above the pettiness of factions.*

as Secretary of Commerce appealed to him enormously. His administrative talents were used to their maximum, and he attracted some of the best and brightest people to work with him, including Bob Taft, Nellie's boy. A fine, young man.

We maintained two homes: the house in California and a townhouse in Washington. I crossed the country regularly to keep an eye on the house—and on the boys, who by then were attending Stanford University. I also became active in Republican Women circles. By that time women could vote. Had I been in the country during the "teens," I would have been an active suffragist. I certainly had the intelligence to cast a responsible ballot!

> **NELLIE TAFT**
> *I was a little too old to march with the suffragists—and my health was still impaired from my stroke. But, like Abigail Fillmore, I sympathized.*

> **ELLEN WILSON**
> *I always favored women having the right to vote. Woodrow and I discussed it frequently—long before he was President.*

> **EDITH WILSON**
> *I was always against Women's Suffrage, and even when women did get the vote, I never voted. I always thought it unseemly.*

> **ELEANOR ROOSEVELT**
> *I opposed Women's Suffrage early on. I was a sheltered young matron who thought as I was told to think. As I got older, of course, I realized the foolishness of such thinking.*

My main interest, however, was the Girl Scouts. If anyone goes to Girl Scout Camp, they go to "Camp Hoover." It was not named for my husband. It was not named for J. Edgar Hoover. Or the vacuum cleaning people. It was named for me. I had discovered the Girl Guides in England, and thought it was a superb organization, providing useful occupation for a young girl's time. My own interests in camping and pioneer skills drew me immediately. Scouting also offered useful domestic and cultural activities and a dedication to service. When I was asked to be National President of the Girl Scouts, I was deeply honored. It was not merely a prestige position like Caroline Harrison and the D.A.R.

> **CAROLINE HARRISON**
> *I beg your pardon?*

No offense, Carrie dear, but your position *was* an honorarium.

My Presidency was a serious commitment. I chaired meetings, devised programs, supervised activities, and I was delighted to lend my name, support and prestige. I traveled extensively and gave willingly of my time and personal funds. I was an activist long before Mrs. Roosevelt.

Bert was Secretary of Commerce for eight years: through the Hardings (whom we did not care for, did not respect, and whom we eventually grew to pity), and through the Coolidges (whom we respected only slightly and thought dull and flat). Florence Harding was completely out of her class and

Grace Coolidge was sweet, but inept and hopelessly bewildered.

> **FLORENCE HARDING**
> *Not everyone can be as wonderful as Lou Hoover. Being "Mrs. Snooty" never appealed to me.*

> **GRACE COOLIDGE**
> *She <u>was</u> a little full of herself, now, wasn't she?*

> **FLORENCE HARDING**
> *For someone so proud of her "frontier" life, she turned into the biggest "Eastern" snob of them all!*

When Bert was elected President in 1928, I expected to come into my own. Was there any other First Lady so well qualified? I was certain to rank right up there with Abigail Adams and Dolley Madison. How could I miss? I would do more than accept bouquets and host tea parties for women. I would sponsor cultural and humanitarian programs. I was *born* to be First Lady!

I thought to myself, "What a fine example I will be!" I knew Nellie Taft wanted to leave her mark, and I pitied her stroke and incapacity when she lived in the White House. But it fell to me. I was the educated one. The serious scholar. The first-class administrator. The one who could handle all the ceremonial and functional duties in my sleep...plus! I would be that active lady.[10]

> [10]**NELLIE TAFT**
> *I knew and admired Lou Hoover! Whatever I was unable to accomplish, I was sure she would fulfill for me!*

But then came the Depression. It was no more Herbert Hoover's fault than the man in the moon's. The signs had been a long time coming. Bert was always cool toward Coolidge, and a Jeremiah about the economy. He was sure it was a castle built on sand. Coolidge didn't agree.[11] Or if he did, he kept quiet about it. Bert worked tirelessly to the very best of his considerable abilities, but he wasn't an *outgoing* man. He had a shy nature, and loathed the very thought of having to

> [11]**GRACE COOLIDGE**
> *Poppa had some suspicions about the economy, but he believed in business. Businessmen told him that the boom would continue. I think he believed because he wanted to believe. And perhaps also because he didn't know how else to deal with it.*

227

defend himself. He was accustomed to receiving accolades for his great humanitarian services. It was a brutal blow for him to bear the brunt of hard times. It nearly destroyed him completely to have people actually think that he didn't care about the poor and destitute! He was crushed that shanty-towns were called "Hoovervilles!" How dare they? After all he had done for War Relief and famine! It was so unfair!

As I see it, Bert had two major failings as a politician: He lacked the heart and stomach to tackle his enemies, and he lacked a flamboyant imagination. He played by the rules. He'd stretch them if he could, but he'd never break them. I had similar failings.

We both strongly believed in helping people help themselves. If we helped the employ*ers*, it would take care of the employ*ees* in the long-term.[12] Offering handouts was against the American free-enterprise philosophy. That should be a job for the family. For the churches. For organizations like the Salvation Army and Good Will.

> [12]**NANCY REAGAN**
> *Is this "Reaganomics" or what?*

It wasn't that we were unaware or unsympathetic to the needs and tragedies of the working people. Never! I couldn't begin to tell you how many people we helped from our own pockets.

But for all our abilities and achievements, Bert and I lacked the so-called "common touch."[13] We were uncomfortable. We always believed that speeches before prominent people were more valuable than speaking to the masses. Prominent people had the wherewithal to help and contribute. The masses could only applaud.[14]

> [13]**LADYBIRD JOHNSON**
> *Lacking the common touch is one thing—but the Hoovers were rigidly anti-contact with the "plain folk." They had a bell rung every time they would be in the corridors, and the White House staff would have to duck into a closet so they could avoid being face-to-face with either of them.*

We firmly believed we should continue to entertain graciously at the White House since it projected the image of success and hope. Most of the expense was paid from our own funds, since Bert returned his salary to the Treasury.

> [14]**ELEANOR ROOSEVELT**
> *And vote.*

We behaved in the only way we knew how to behave: With dignity and hard work. And no one, *absolutely no one*, worked harder as President than Bert. He rose early and retired late. I rose early and retired late. Every meal was a working meal, breakfast included. I insisted that the staff must be seamless and unobtrusive in its serving procedures. I didn't want Bert or our guests to be disturbed or distracted.[15]

> [15]**LADY BIRD JOHNSON**
> *Lou had this system of hand signals so the staff could fill the glasses or clear the soup plates. Never a word was spoken to them.*

Bert seldom took time for himself or the family. I worried about his health; we knew the toll the Presidency had taken on President Wilson. I was determined that Bert have some relaxation so I found some property a few hours from Washington at a lovely spot in the Maryland mountains, near a fine trout stream. We both loved fishing. I decided to purchase it. The Department of the Interior built a small cabin for the President to use as a weekend retreat. It was near the Rapidan River, so we called it Camp Rapidan, and went there as often as possible. When Bert's term ended, we donated the camp to the government. Roosevelt called it "Shangri-La" and went there a few times. I don't believe the Trumans ever used it.[16] Then, when Ike became President, he rediscovered it and renamed it, and Camp David it has been ever since. Courtesy of the Hoovers.

> [16]**BESS TRUMAN**
> *Neither of us cared for camping. Harry "discovered" Key West, and as for me, there was no place like home!*

But the Roosevelts—Franklin and Eleanor—broke all the rules. Bert became a villain and I disappeared completely. Lou Who? For all my hopes and expectations, like Nellie Taft, I am as anonymous as Jane Pierce.

> **LUCY HAYES**
> *That's why we're doing this book, darling. To give us this opportunity to be known!*

I was never quite sure why Franklin Roosevelt hated my husband so much.[17] He had supported Bert during the '20s. I believe he went on record more than once saying that he thought Herbert Hoover would make a fine president. But somehow, Franklin Roosevelt developed an intense dislike for Bert. Actively or tacitly, Roosevelt

> [17]**ELEANOR ROOSEVELT**
> *The times were so desperately hard that I think Franklin thought it was good politics to have a "villain" for the Depression. Personally, I thought Mr. Hoover was ineffective, unimaginative and tactless. Ditto for his "missus."*

made Bert shoulder the "blame for the Depression." Bert, true to his fine character, never complained and differed with FDR on issues only; never on personalities. He had far too much respect for the Office of President to demean it. I, on the other hand, admit to lesser character, and loathed Franklin Roosevelt with all my being.

I will never forgive him for the dam. Never.

Hoover Dam was begun in Boulder, Colorado during the early '20s when Bert was Secretary of Commerce. This was more than a pet project; it was one where Bert could truly use his immense knowledge and experience. It was the largest public project ever undertaken up to that time, employing thousands of people in hundreds of trades and disciplines. It was brought in on time and even a little *under* budget! Bert adored that dam and pored over every detail of its construction. It was going to be called Hoover Dam from the start. Bert deserved it!

I don't know whatever possessed Franklin Roosevelt to change its name to Boulder Dam. It was wrong. It was cruel and unfair. And it was unnecessary. It was only a name, for heaven's sake! What purpose was served by changing it except to satisfy Roosevelt's personal venom?[18] Bert was more deeply hurt by that callous action than just about anything else. It was his "baby"; the project he loved best! He was not being penalized for his faults, but for his virtues. And Bert, gentleman that he always was, never said a word. I thought it was despicable! But then again, Roosevelt was always capable of despicable acts.

And even though I had died by that time, I bless Harry Truman for restoring Hoover Dam to its rightful identity and for allowing Bert, in his aging retirement, to continue to be useful, and redeem his sterling reputation.[19]

[18]**ELEANOR ROOSEVELT**
That was nasty on Franklin's part, I suppose. We didn't always agree on everything.

[19]**BESS TRUMAN**
Harry always thought that Herbert Hoover was a fine man who got a raw deal from history. He was grateful that ex-President Hoover was available to help in those terrible days after the War when Relief in Europe required experienced administration. Harry said no one else could have been better! They became good friends.[20]

[20]**LADY BIRD JOHNSON**
The Presidential pension is the only money Hoover ever accepted from the Government. When Congress voted a pension to Harry Truman, who had no retirement income at all, Hoover believed it would embarrass "his friend Harry," whom he liked and admired, to decline the pension. I think he gave the money to charity.

I could say I loathed Mrs. Roosevelt as much as I did her husband, but I cannot do that. I admit to some envy; after all, her voluminous activities dwarfed my Girl Scout efforts, and her tireless energy totally eclipsed mine. She also served twelve years to my four. Eleanor destroyed every pretension I had of being the "First-Lady-To-Admire," but I grew to respect her. She deserved every accolade she received. I was, without question, a far better White House hostess and mistress. But Eleanor didn't care for the formal role. She pioneered her own course and left her own unique and indelible mark.

I, on the other hand, did the very best I could under the circumstances. In another time, under other conditions, I might have succeeded with my lofty goal of being the first "modern" First Lady. Instead, I am merely thought of as another unknown non-entity. More's the pity.

ANNA ELEANOR ROOSEVELT ROOSEVELT
1884-1962
First Lady: 1933-1945

When Lucy Hayes first asked me to be a part of this endeavor, I declined. After all, I said, this book is supposed to be for and about the lesser-known Ladies. So much has been written about me, a good deal by my own hand, there is nothing left to tell; my activities and philosophies are well known. But Lucy said that Mrs. Truman and Mrs. Eisenhower must be included—and rightly so—so I'm obliged to participate. I promise to keep it very brief and to the point.

Like Mary Lincoln, I can state the essentials quickly. I was born in New York City, orphaned at ten, raised by an assortment of eccentric relatives, and, following a traditional "finishing school" education, did volunteer work in the Settlement Houses of New York's Lower East Side. I married my 5th cousin Franklin, and after fifteen years of fading into the wallpaper, became active in politics to help improve social conditions. When my husband, crippled with polio, became President, I became his eyes and ears and legs. When he died, I continued actively on my own for the rest of my life.

About My Parents. My father Elliott was Theodore Roosevelt's brother. He died when I was ten. I adored him, but since he was ill for most of my childhood, we spent very little time together. Once I was grown, I learned that he had been addicted to alcohol and laudanum and needed to be separated from the family. He was the only person in my youthful memory who truly loved me and my dying wish was to be united with him in Eternity. I had no such wish about my mother, who died when I was six. She was beautiful and elegant, but remote. I certainly did not inherit her beauty, but I suppose I inherited her remoteness. It was always easier for me to care about general causes than about specific individuals.

The Sagamore Side: Uncle Theodore, whom I loved and admired, felt a responsibility for my upbringing. I was invited every so often to visit his family when I was a child, but I was totally unathletic and left far behind in their games and adventures. I loathed bugs and snakes, and was indifferent to leaves and rocks and small animals—all of which was indispensable to my Sagamore cousins. Cousin Alice was my own age, but she hated me and made me miserable. They meant well, I'm sure, but I was never at home there.

About Franklin. I liked Franklin always. I believe he liked me. But we had different personalities that became more apparent as time went on. I was more serious. Nobody ever called me a barrel of laughs, either. I gravitated to like-minded companions. Franklin, on the other hand, had an outgoing personality, and needed levity in his friends, most of whom bored me. We were a fine balance for each other. I focused on the should-be's; he on the could-be's. Together we accomplished a great deal.

NANCY REAGAN
Just out of curiosity, what did Franklin think of your friends?

You would have to ask him.

About My Marriage. I bore six children in ten years, and lost one. That was common. But if a woman decided to have no more children, there was only one way to prevent it: separate bedrooms with the door closed.[1] "Nice" women were not even supposed to know that contraception existed, let alone have access to whatever methods were available.

---

[1]JACQUELINE KENNEDY
I remember my mother-in-law telling me that after nine children, she wanted no more. And good Catholic that she was, her door was locked.

I suppose if a man is denied conjugal privileges in his prime, he will be tempted elsewhere. In my naïveté, I assumed that if I could do without, so could Franklin. Of course that was foolish. This does not mean that I approve. It also does not make it less painful. It is merely a fact of life that one must accept.[2] I don't know nor do I care to know the exact details of what passed between Franklin Roosevelt and Lucy Mercer. The only important thing is that it was never the same between Franklin and me again. Many years passed before I realized and

---

[2]FLORENCE HARDING
I imagine Eleanor assumed that her husband would go to "those places." I imagined that, too. We were such fools.

---

acknowledged my own stubbornness and sanctimoniousness. Franklin made many efforts to try to repair the damage. I never relented.

Perhaps it was for the best. I was free to channel my energies into much more productive endeavors. If I had stayed home as a traditional and dutiful wife and mother, I believe I would have died of despair.

About Mamma (pronounced the French way, Mi-MAH). Cousin Sallie (she was my distant relative) was a formidable woman. The sun rose and set on Franklin, her only child. She was against our marriage from the start. I was neither wealthy nor socially prominent. I was also not even slightly pretty. According to her, I had very little to offer.

> [3]**LOUISA ADAMS**
> *I could probably say the same about my feelings toward Abigail, except for the affection. I never felt any.*

I was in awe of her, harbored deep resentments, became tolerant, and finally had a bit of affection for her, in that order.[3] As I developed a life of my own, the unimportance of her approval became proportionate to my accomplishments. She never understood me, and few people can approve of things they cannot understand.

About My Children. I loved my children dearly, and would have gladly given my life for any one of them. But I never cared for the company of children.[5] I found them tiresome and demanding. But my mother-in-law, on the other hand, adored "mothering" and spoiled them terribly. I couldn't fight Franklin's illness and absence, five demanding children *and* Mamma working against me at every opportunity. It was too much. She won.

> [5]**JANE PIERCE**
> *It is God's purpose that a woman bear children and raise them. It is her highest duty in life.*[6]
>
> [6]**BARBARA BUSH**
> *Oh give it a rest, Jane!*

I tried to be a good mother when they were small, but I think a good mother is a happy mother, and I was neither.

When the children were grown, I found it much easier to enjoy their company. I like to think that I welcomed a long, *long* succession of sons- and daughters-in-law with open arms and sincere friendship. The fact, however, that our five children had eighteen marriages amongst them speaks volumes.

But I was there for every one of them when they needed me. I was never too tired to answer their letters—or the sweet crayon notes from my grandchildren. I would fly across the country at a moment's notice to be at their sick bed. No birthday, anniversary or special occasion passed unnoticed, ungifted or unacknowledged—and I needed no reminders. When the War came, and all four of my sons were in uniform, I wept uncontrollably for hours because I was certain they wouldn't all return.[7] All four survived, and I thanked God every day for the rest of my life.

> [7]**EDITH ROOSEVELT**
> *I lost one in the First War. Two more in the Second. But then again, there were thousands more like me.*

About Val-Kill. When Franklin and I married and the babies started coming in rapid succession, my mother-in-law took complete charge. We lived in *her* house at Hyde Park and *she* ran the household. When Franklin and I became estranged, it was *she* who demanded that we remain together rather than create a scandal. When Franklin contracted polio, he spent months at a time seeking treatment in Warm Springs, Georgia. I developed a life of my own. If having a life of my own made me happy, than Franklin was happy. He loathed acrimony. So did I.

Mamma was appalled by my unconventional activity with unconventional friends and I was uncomfortable inviting them to Hyde Park, where she was so obviously disapproving. Fortunately Hyde Park was a large piece of property, and we had a substantial income. So, with Franklin's encouragement, I had a cottage built some distance away, which I called Val-Kill. There I could relax, invite friends and hold meetings. In short, I had my own home. Of course, when Franklin was home, I stayed at Hyde Park.

About Privacy: I was a Victorian. I was born in 1884. Private things were private, and people respected it.

JACQUELINE KENNEDY	LADY BIRD JOHNSON
I doubt that anyone had her privacy invaded more than I. I spent more than thirty years fighting a losing battle to have a normal life.	*It seems that the favorite scenery today is everyone else's dirty laundry flappin' in the breeze.*

I do *not* agree that everybody needs to know our personal trials and tribulations. Do not look to me for gossip.

In the years since my death, I am appalled and offended at the amount of intrusion and speculation given to my personal life. I was fortunate. I had numerous friends, both male and female. It is true that some of my close friends had what was called at the time, "Boston" marriages. I knew it and chose to ignore it as unimportant to our friendship. To assume that my knowledge and continued association made me party to that behavior is erroneous. By that same reasoning, since many of my friends were Jewish, it would have made me a secret convert. I was not. It is a sorry state of affairs when rude, offensive and scandalous connotations are drawn![7] End of subject.

> [7]**DOLLEY MADISON**
> *I agree! There are volumes of correspondence between Jemmy and Thomas Jefferson. They considered themselves "intimate," and used that phrase often. But no one would ever give it an "immoral" connotation.*

As promised, I have kept my chapter brief, but I am pleased to add whatever I could. This volume is for our lesser-known Ladies and I do not wish to detract from their own glories.

ELIZABETH (Bess) WALLACE TRUMAN
1885-1983
First Lady: 1945-1953

There are only a few First Ladies who had a "perfect" marriage. Some had fine marriages, most had decent marriages, and I suppose Louisa Adams and Florence Harding had unhappy marriages. But only a very few of us had "perfect" marriages. John and Abigail Adams. Theodore and Edith Roosevelt. And Harry and me.

So what makes a "perfect" marriage? Not just love, not just liking each other, but having every major character trait compatible. It makes the whole greater than the sum of the parts. You can't even think of John Adams without Abigail. And no one who knew Theodore Roosevelt could ever picture him without Edith to balance his life. Despite his first marriage, fate must have meant for Theodore and Edith to be together.[1] And of course, us.

> [1]**EDITH ROOSEVELT**
> *I always believed that Theodore would have been bored silly by his first wife.*

I don't ever remember meeting Harry. I always knew him. He said he met me in Sunday School when we were five years old, but I don't remember it. But from the start, we were always in the same class in school. Harry was from a farming family outside of Independence, Missouri, and the Wallaces—me—lived in a big sprawling Victorian house right smack in the center of town. Harry was timid about being beneath us socially and economically, but I never thought about it much. My mother, on the other hand, never forgot it. She considered the Trumans one step above trash. Harry was never good enough for her daughter. But if the Prince of Wales had come a-courtin', he wouldn't be good enough either. Even when Harry was President of the United States, he was still "farmer Truman" to my mother.

I guess one of the reasons that Harry and I had a perfect marriage was that he had to love me *very* much to put up with my family the way he did for so long. And when I say long, I mean *long*! He courted me for years, and we lived with my mother until he was President. And then *she* lived with *us* in the White House. She lived to be nearly ninety. And through it all, Harry never lost his sense of decorum, courtesy and humor when it came to Madge Wallace.

I would never have said this on earth, but my mother was a very nasty and difficult woman. She didn't like Yankees, she didn't like Negroes, she didn't like the Irish, or the Eye-talians, or Catholics or Jews. As a matter of fact, I don't recall her ever liking anyone. For sure I never recall anyone ever liking her. She was the type of woman you could always rely upon to make a tactless, thoughtless, and totally inappropriate remark.

I spent my entire life trying to conceal the fact that my father took his own life when I was eighteen. In those days, suicide was a shameful skeleton in the family closet.[2] My father had incurred some "serious business reverses." That was the story we admitted. David Wallace had been one of the

> [2] **ELEANOR ROOSEVELT**
> *I never knew how much I had in common with Bess Truman. I suppose our differences were more obvious than our similarities.*

handsomest and most charming men in Independence and my mother married him despite her parents' objections. In actuality, Papa drank, and he had problems holding a job. My mother demanded to live the way she had been raised. The Gates family, her side, was one of the most prominent in the Midwest. Perhaps he shot himself that awful day for the insurance money to provide for mother, my three brothers and me. Maybe he just couldn't bear Mother any more. I don't know. But it was a very long time before anyone in our family could face the neighborhood. My mother never really did again.

I, on the other hand, was outgoing, athletic and popular. I had a lot of friends—boys and girls—and every intention of going to college or maybe business school. But when Papa died, it was left to me as the eldest, to hold our family together. Because of the Gates' social prominence in Independence, it would have been scandalous for me to work. I stayed home after high school, helped "manage" the house (we always had a couple of servants) and "socialized." I went to card parties and picnics and concerts—the usual. And I helped my brothers finish their education, marry and get the hell out of that house, except for my youngest brother, Fred. He was only five or six when Papa died. He lived with Mother and me long after I was married. He had problems like Papa; he drank and had a hard time holding a job. Believe me, between my brother's problems and my bitter, harping mother, it's a wonder Harry ever came back after the first time he called on me. But, if there was one thing about Harry, he was tenacious.

Even though he and I went all through school together, we seldom ran with the same crowd. He said I was *always* his sweetheart, but while I liked him well enough, we didn't begin courting till we were well into our twenties. He'd come by and we would go walking, or, after he bought that horrid wreck of a car he was so proud of, we'd go driving. We'd seldom sit in the parlor or on the porch, since my mother made it rather uncomfortable for "that Mr. Truman."

> [3]**ELLEN WILSON**
> *We "eldest" sisters were always the responsible ones.*

I expected to remain single. My mother couldn't live alone, and there were few—if any—people who could possibly live with her. I would stay.[3] Funny, however, even when my courting days progressed through my late twenties, and then into my mature thirties, I didn't feel like the proverbial old maid. I had a beau. Harry Truman doggedly and faithfully came by.

We had a long courtship. A *very* long courtship. Maybe fifteen years or so—and that was *after* we started courting in earnest! Harry didn't have the money or the prospects to provide for a wife. He still had to take care of *his* mother and siblings. (Mama Truman was a delight! The siblings were so-so. But who am I to talk?) I think I always knew that Harry and I would be married one day, sooner or later. It was later. *Much* later. When WWI broke out, Harry was well past thirty, and we were still "unofficially" engaged. He decided to enlist. My mother thought he was nuts and said so. I backed Harry's decision, although for once, I happened to think my mother might possibly be right. I wanted to get married then and there, but Harry was adamant. He didn't want to leave me a widow, or worse—saddled with an invalid husband. I said we waited this long, a little longer wouldn't matter. He came back in one piece and we got married.

Captain Harry couldn't be kept on the farm after he saw Paree, and in the

> [4]**ELEANOR ROOSEVELT**
> *I never realized how much I had in common with Harry, either. He lived with a demanding mother-in-law and so did I.*

one and only major argument of our lives, I told him that we absolutely had to live with my mother.[4] When I peeled him off the ceiling (and he was a man of legendary temper), I told him point blank that if I had to choose between him and my mother, obnoxious though she was, I would choose her. She needed me. Harry could find someone else if he wanted, but there was probably nobody in the world other than myself who could care for my mother. Harry didn't want anyone else. He bought the package.

It's hard to believe that Harry and I spent not only our courtship and most of our marriage in my mother's house, but we managed to raise our daughter Margaret in that trying atmosphere, with no real harm done. And I heard Harry complain long and loud and colorfully about a lot of things, but after that day, he never said an unkind word about my family. He *must* have loved me very much.

Harry's involvement in politics was accidental. He needed a job, and one of his army buddies was the nephew of the Democratic political bigshot.

They thought Captain Harry would be a good candidate for County Administrator, or "Judge" as they called it, because he could bring in the veteran vote.[5] The bigshot had a questionable reputation, however, and Harry was not about to ruin his good name. But the "Boss" agreed to let Harry be his own man, and he kept to his bargain. Harry was never asked to do anything illegal or immoral or against his conscience.

> [5]**CAROLINE HARRISON**
> *Ben's political involvement was accidental, too. He was an administrator, rather than a candidate, but his War record would bring in the veteran vote, which it did.*

I liked politics—sort of. Harry loved it! He took to it like a duck to water, and it was about that time that the "perfect" part of our marriage started.[6] I kept busy raising our little girl and looking after my

> [6]**LADY BIRD JOHNSON**
> *Lyndon was a duck in water when it came to politics. I liked it too. I liked it a lot!*

family, being a homebody and playing bridge with the girls. I was happy. I did "women" things. I had no other ambitions. Politics, being a "man's business" at the time, was exactly what Harry needed in his life. It got him the hell out of the house. He did "men things." He had a regular poker game at one of the local hotels. They'd stop for a bourbon or two. I never worried about him. The games were for very small stakes and he never lost more than a few dollars. And while he certainly enjoyed a drink or two with the boys, I never *ever* saw him drunk. He was happy. He got the respect from his peers that he never had living in my mother's house. Politicians seldom socialized in their homes then, and even if they did, Harry would never have brought anyone into a house where his mother-in-law and brother-in-law sat at the head and foot of the table.

Early in our marriage, even before politics, Harry had a partnership for a few years with a Jewish war buddy of his named Eddie Jacobson. They liked each other and were friends. Many years later, Eddie remarked that during those years Harry and Bess never once invited him for dinner. He said he didn't think Harry was anti-Semitic, but that I probably was. Not so. I didn't care about his religion. But my mother certainly did, and we lived with her. We couldn't lock her in her room in her own home when we had guests, and Harry believed that he was sparing Eddie Jacobson—and us—from needless embarrassment by keeping the door closed. We seldom had visitors—other than family, or my bridge club.

When Harry was 50 (and remember, we were both nearly forty when we finally married), he was once again going to be unemployed. He had been County Judge as long as the law allowed, and he decided he wanted to run for the U.S. Senate. The "Boss" said no. "You're a nice guy, Harry, but nobody knows you outside the County, and there are a half-dozen other good candidates." Fate, I suppose took a hand. Every one of those half-dozen other good candidates dropped out for one reason or other.[7] Harry was still available. I suppose the "Boss" finally figured it wasn't their year, and Harry could be a throwaway. Harry jumped in with both feet, and crisscrossed the state like a lady's corset. He went everywhere, spoke everywhere, kissed every baby, shook every hand and milked a few cows along the way. My mother minced no words in telling me I was married to a lunatic. I worried about what he would do after he lost. But since nobody told Harry that he was a sure loser this time, he had faith in his campaign ability—and to everyone's surprise, and I mean *everyone*, he won. My husband the farmer-shopkeeper-county administrator was now a United States Senator. And he'd earn more money than we ever had before![8]

He took a small apartment in Washington, and we both semi-commuted. I'd go there for a few weeks, then he would come back to Independence for a few days. I actually started to like Washington. The Congressional wives were friendly, and once they found out I played a mean game of bridge, I was invited to a lot of card parties and luncheons.[9] But I still had time on my hands, with Margaret in school and only a small apartment to care for, so I started helping out in Harry's office. I handled his "personal" mail, and acted as escort for visiting Missourians. It was a pleasant time. I liked it a lot better than I thought I would. The next session, we took a larger apartment, and even invited my mother to stay with us. In Washington, Harry could sit at the head of his own dinner table. But I went back to Independence as often as I could. Home still tugged at me. I always liked familiar surroundings and I missed my old friends and neighbors.

Harry's Senatorial career took a long time to blossom. He was tainted by the Boss's unsavory reputation, but, true to form, Harry proved that he could handle the job and be his own man. He was diligent about every committee

> **[7]FLORENCE HARDING**
> *There were at least a half-dozen better qualified candidates than Wur'n in 1920. Fate does indeed play a hand in politics!*

> **[8]NELLIE TAFT**
> *Amazing! The rest of us complained about how little public servants are paid, and the Trumans thought they were in a gold mine!*

> **[9]MAMIE EISENHOWER**
> *I was an avid card player as well. The '30s and '40s were full of card-playing women. There wasn't much else for us to do. Our husbands wouldn't let us work. Not that I ever wanted to work...*

assignment, and made it a point to become an expert on all the nuances of the job. By the time the Second World War was underway, he had gained the sincere respect of his peers. When Roosevelt named him as vice president for his fourth term in 1944, it was a complete surprise to all of us. Roosevelt had generally ignored Harry for the most part; there was never any familiarity between them.[10] Harry and I were both nervous about it. We wondered if the President would be able to survive a fourth term. He had aged visibly. My mother decided FDR was insane, and said so. I don't think she voted for him.

> [10]**EDITH WILSON**
> *I think FDR looked at Harry Truman the same way as Woodrow looked at FDR in 1920: A nice fellow, but a light-weight.*

A week after a very quiet inaugural, Harry was invited for lunch with the President, and came home noticeably shaken. Roosevelt didn't look well at all, Harry said, and while neither of us talked about it further, we were alarmed. A month later, Harry called and said in a very strained voice that I was to get Margaret immediately, take a taxi to the back entrance of the White House, and "wear something dark." I didn't have to have any pictures drawn. Harry—my Harry—was President of the United States. It was a chilling thought.

Mrs. Roosevelt moved out very quickly.

> **EDITH ROOSEVELT**
> *It took Ida McKinley a couple of weeks.*

> **FLORENCE HARDING**
> *It took me a couple of weeks, too. I was anxious to leave.*

> **ELIZA JOHNSON**
> *It took Miz Lincoln a whole month to move.*

> **JACQUELINE KENNEDY**
> *No one was more anxious to leave than I!*

Before she left, she offered to guide me through my first (and last) press conference. She was an expert and gave them weekly. After those busybodies asked me stupid questions like what Harry ate for breakfast, or did I know how to tango, which was none of their business,[11] I decided then and there that Mrs. Roosevelt's shoes were much too big for me to fill, and I preferred my own houseslippers anyway. And in the back of my mind, I feared they might dredge up the scandal of my father's death. No press conferences.

The years I spent as First Lady were the worst in my life. Our "perfect" marriage was

> [11]**BETTY FORD**
> *Oh pooh! Those are harmless questions, and they do serve a purpose. They humanize the First Family.*

nowhere near perfect. I was miserable. The Secret Service commandeered the house in Independence, built fences, installed telephones and telegraph wires, moved furniture, and stationed people everywhere. We were afraid to make a move. For sure we couldn't sit on our own porch in the evening. For sure my friends couldn't just pop over to say hello. I fumed. My mother fumed.

So we invited her to stay with us in the White House, and offered her the most prestigious room in the place: the Lincoln Bedroom. But she was a recalcitrant Rebel, and refused to go near anything associated with that damnyankee Lincoln.

I had made up my mind from the outset that I would do whatever was expected of me, do it cheerfully and to the best of my ability, but I'd be damned if I was going to turn myself into somebody I wasn't. I gave the luncheons, I hosted the receptions, I bought more clothes and hats than I ever had in my life—and grew more homesick by the day.[12] Harry, despite the headaches of the Presidency, was having a wonderful time! So was Margaret. Fortunately she was old enough to fill in for me during my increasingly frequent trips back home.

The best thing I can say about living in the White House is that we didn't live in it long. Shortly after Harry assumed office, the creaking floors and shaky chandeliers indicated serious structural damage. When the leg of Margaret's piano protruded right through the floor—or the ceiling, depending where you were—the Army Corps of Engineers did an emergency survey, said that the place wasn't safe to live in, and immediately relocated us across the street to Blair House. That suited me better, but I still didn't like being First Lady.

I didn't get involved with the renovations. Harry did.[15] He always loved history and enjoyed those kinds of projects. In between all the crises that he faced on a daily basis, working with the engineers was relaxation for him. And, bless him, knowing how much we both loved to sit outside on a pleasant evening,

> [12]**ABIGAIL FILLMORE**
> *I wonder if Bess ever wished she could "retire to her rooms" like some of the early Ladies who didn't want the job.*[13]

> [13]**PAT NIXON**
> *I doubt any 20th Century Lady would be happy cooped up in her room. What we missed the most was the freedom of anonymity!*[14]

> [14]**HILLARY RODHAM CLINTON**
> *I missed my jeans and my car and being able to go to the mall by myself!*

> [15]**JACQUELINE KENNEDY**
> *It's probably just as well that Bess wasn't involved. Her taste was very provincial, and at least Harry had enough sense to leave everything to the professionals.*

he had them put on a balcony, just for us. We used it as often as possible.

When he decided to run for re-election in 1948, he dragged Margaret and me on his cross-country whistle-stop campaign. Every hour he made me come out and smile and wave. Harry was a cat in cream, and for his sake, I tried to smile, but more and more, I realized that I was a housewife who wanted nothing more than to be in her own house. By the end of the trip, if I had to listen to myself and Margaret being called "The Boss" and "The Boss's Boss" I was going to scream. But Harry said that while I heard it a thousand times, the people never heard it before—and they liked it. Harry won the election in the biggest upset since Joe Louis knocked out Max Schmeling.

While Harry was President, we were definitely not perfect. We were very imperfect. I was unhappy and uncomfortable, and not the kind of support Harry needed with all his pressures. I stayed in Independence more than I stayed in Washington. I suppose I'm ashamed of myself for not rising to the occasion—as distasteful as it might have been to me.

I guess the only thing posterity will remember about Bess Truman is my attack on a battleship with a seemingly unbreakable bottle of champagne. I was angry and humiliated by the event, especially with all those newsreel cameras rolling. Naturally, as soon as I got back, I told my husband who immediately demanded a copy of the film. The President of the United States had no intention of letting his wife be the laughing stock of the nation! When we saw the film, Harry was beside himself! I don't think I ever saw him laugh so hard. The tears ran down his cheeks, and Margaret rolled on the floor in hysterics. There I was, whacking away at that ship with a bottle that absolutely refused to break. Bess Truman, the best batter on the girls' softball team, unable to break that damn bottle! It was very, *very* funny. And we all realized that no one was laughing at Bess Truman; they were laughing at a funny situation—no matter who was swinging that bottle! I guess my legacy to the country is a good chuckle. Others have done worse.[16]

During our long retirement years, the "perfect" returned. My mother had died while Harry was President, and willed "her" house in Independence to us, so we finally had our own home. Harry continued actively in politics and wrote several books. I picked up my bridge club

> [16]**NANCY REAGAN**
> *That newsreel clip is a classic! It is a wonderful thing to be able to laugh at yourself!*

and friendships where we left off—just as if I had never been away. Margaret married and blessed us with four grandsons, who were the joy of our old age.

But the best part was that we both lived long enough to see Harry's reputation and esteem as President grow and grow, until he is surpassed only by the damnyankee Lincoln and the insane Franklin Roosevelt. We both got a chuckle out of that.

MAMIE DOUD EISENHOWER
1896-1979
First Lady: 1953-1961

When I was eighteen—or was it nineteen?—I saw the most beautiful young man I had ever seen in my life. He was more than six feet tall—nearly a whole foot taller than I was—and he stood straight as an arrow, lean and strong. He had blond hair, a twinkle in his eye, and a grin that could melt steel and light up the entire neighborhood. That was Ike—Dwight Eisenhower—and from the first moment I saw him, I knew that more than anything, I wanted to be Mrs. Ike. Unfortunately—at least as far as my family was concerned—my "Adonis" was a mere second Lieutenant in the United States Army—a far cry from what they expected for their little girl. Besides, I was entirely too young.

I could have been the model for the pretty, spoiled china-doll little girl of the early 20th Century. My father, having made a comfortable fortune as a Kansas businessman, retired at thirty-six for health reasons, and moved us to Denver where we had a fine home in one of the best sections of town. My sisters and I had the best of everything—the prettiest dolls, the fanciest party dresses, the most popular dancing school, and every newfangled toy or diversion available. Even our own pony cart.

Like Lady Washington—(we generals' wives must stick together)—I did not enjoy my lessons—nor was I especially good at them[1]—and I found every excuse in the book to avoid them. I can't say I was a "homebody" either, since I never was taught to cook or sew. And, of course, I was never expected to do housework. A touch of rheumatic fever when I was very small spared me from having to do anything that might tire me. I suppose because I was petite and cute and flashed a smile that could charm the spots off a pinto pony, I was allowed to get away with my willfulness. Like I said, I was spoiled.

> [1]**JULIA GRANT**
> *I enjoyed my lessons just fine, and was an excellent student. I was also a good cook, and could sew quite nicely.*[2]
>
> [2]**MARY LINCOLN**
> *Yes, yes, yes. Julia Gee was good at everything.*

But when I met Lt. Dwight Eisenhower—recently graduated from West Point—I knew my heart was lost to him forever. My parents' objections to his career prospects and my "youth" were no match for Mamie and her lost heart. Besides, they adored Ike. Just about everybody did. So we had a brief engagement, and were married.

Ike dutifully took me to Abilene, Kansas, to meet his family. I was understandably nervous, and, wanting to look my best, wore my favorite "traveling" outfit, my perkiest hat and brand new high heeled shoes. I don't think Mama Eisenhower ever saw high heeled shoes before, and while she was sweet and welcoming—we eventually became good friends—she must have wondered what farm boy Ike could possibly have in common with this citified little slip of a thing. Ike's five brothers adopted me immediately, and I always fit in with all the Eisenhowers.

Our first home—there would be a couple of dozen of them—was three small rooms at a hot, dusty army outpost in Texas. I was determined to be the best junior officer's wife in the entire Army. It took me two whole days to realize that there wasn't much to do in three small rooms out in the middle of nowhere. So I bought a cookbook and fancied myself whipping up delicacies and serving them in grand style. Unfortunately, I never got the hang of following recipes—probably my willfulness—since it reminded me too much of the lessons I hated. I would always be an indifferent cook; Ike, however, became a first class barbecue chef! He loved to cook!

Then I turned my attention to making curtains, and even bought a sewing machine. Again, I was adequate, but lost interest early on. Then, to keep me from complaining about how bored and lonesome I was, Ike decided to teach me to drive a car—which acquainted me with Ike's famous temper. My sweet, genial, ear-to-ear smiling husband turned into a monster! He hollered. I cried. He melted. I eventually learned to drive, but I was never very good at that, either. But then again, those early cars were complicated to maneuver, and Texas roads—at least out where we lived—were non-existent.

ELEANOR ROOSEVELT
I learned to drive from necessity. I was probably one of the world's worst!

LOU HOOVER
I was one of the first women in our community to drive a car. I mastered it easily and was always an excellent driver.

NELLIE TAFT
I would have loved to drive a car, but after my stroke, it was considered dangerous for my health. Besides, I was getting too old.

LADY BIRD JOHNSON
I can just imagine these ladies behind the wheel of an old Model-T back in the nineteen-teens, complete with dusters and goggles! It must have been hysterical!

A brief aside about Ike's famous temper. The higher he rose in rank, the hotter his temper became. He liked having his own way. A word about *my* famous temper—I had one, too. I liked having *my* own way. We loved each other dearly and deeply, but we were not the quietest couple in the world. Most of our quarrels arose because of my loneliness. Ike was away so much, and I, with limited interests or talents of my own, had too many unoccupied hours.

Then I discovered something I was good at—finally! I was good at making friends and being social—just like Ike. Everybody liked Ike, and everybody liked Mrs. Ike. I became friendly with other officers' wives—who were as lonely and bored to death as I was—and we made our own entertainment. Sandwiches, lemonade and sugar cookies require very little skill, so I easily took my turn as luncheon hostess. I even cut the crusts off the bread and cut the sandwiches into little triangles to be festive and fancy. I began enjoying army life and my new friends.

Then Ike was transferred and we had to move—something we did more times than I can count—and I think we lived in every kind of dwelling except maybe an igloo! I learned to be an *excellent* mover. I could be ready—bag and baggage—at a moment's notice. I could pack and unpack in record time, and turn an empty house into "home" by supper. I stored the cartons and crates between moves, and had specific ones for my good china and crystal. I don't think anything was ever broken. And wherever we went, I made new friends. I learned to play mah jongg—which was all the rage—and we both learned how to play bridge—I was very good at it; Ike was even better. He was always a good card player. When canasta became popular, I mastered it with ease.[3] Ike thought it was a "woman's game," so he never bothered to learn.

Then our darling baby Icky was born. Doud Dwight Eisenhower—the sweetest, brightest, happiest and best-loved child you could imagine. Ike couldn't wait to come home every evening to play with the baby. Icky had a box full of toys, and hardly a week would pass without Ike bringing home

---

[3] **HILLARY RODHAM CLINTON**
It's incredible how much time some of the early 20th century ladies spent playing cards. What a waste![4]

[4] **PAT NIXON**
Not so. For a great many of us it was an important social skill. It gave us something to do in an age when we weren't supposed to work, and our husbands' success freed us from doing housework. I always enjoyed playing cards.[5]

[5] **BESS TRUMAN**
I would have been lost without my bridge club! Those girls were my lifelong friends.

another set of blocks or wooden trucks. Life was grand!

Then came that awful dinner party. We had been invited out, and arranged for a local girl to stay with our three-old son. We didn't know—and *she* didn't know—that she had been exposed to scarlet fever. Icky sickened in three days, and worsened so rapidly that the doctors could do nothing. When he died, it scarred us forever. I was inconsolable. I cried for weeks. But Ike's grief was inward. He loved that boy with his whole heart, and something died in him when we lost that little child.[6]

> **[6] EDITH ROOSEVELT**
> *When Quentin—our baby—died in France during the First War, he was barely 21. I am convinced that it shortened Theodore's life as well, since my husband survived Quentin by only a year.*

Ike and I began drifting. We turned away from each other—mainly because we didn't know how to turn toward each other. He buried himself in work. I couldn't comfort him. He couldn't comfort me. It was a very dark time in our lives. Our marriage was in trouble. The wife of Ike's Commanding Officer suggested that I rekindle our marriage. "You mean I should vamp Ike?" I asked. "Absolutely," she advised. So I went out, bought some stylish new clothes and had my hair bobbed. The hairdresser gave me a whole new look—bangs on my forehead. Ike said I was the cutest thing he ever saw. The bangs stayed for the rest of my life. But Icky's memory also stayed forever, and to his dying day—even through the War—Ike always sent me flowers on the day Icky died.

Not long thereafter our son John was born. We loved him dearly, and he became the joy of our lives—giving us a million reasons for pride and happiness.[7] As for me, I became a worrier. I worried about every cold, every chill, every ache or pain, every bellyache, every scratch—and I worried every time Ike was away. Poor John. I suppose I smothered him with my concerns. I was a first-rate worrier.

> **[7] PAT NIXON**
> *We knew John Eisenhower very well, since his son married our daughter. We could think of no finer man to call "family."*

We moved just about yearly between the Wars—and I discovered yet another thing I was good at! To my utter amazement, I became thrifty! Me! Spoiled Mamie, who had everything she ever wanted! Army promotions were few and far between, and Ike was "Captain" Eisenhower for years, and "Major" Eisenhower for even more years. It had nothing to do with his *ability*—it all depended on avail-*ability*—and seniority. It was the Depression, and few people gave up steady army positions, so few promotions were available. We considered ourselves lucky that Ike had a job. My mother would slip in a few dollars for "mad money" with her letters, which I never told Ike about. But I learned to be a careful shopper. I wasted very little, and found ways to save a dime here and quarter there. I'd carpool with other officers' wives, and sometimes we'd even buy in bulk—to split the cost. You see, I had a goal; I wanted a house. After ten or fifteen moves, it becomes tiresome. I wanted a home of our own—so I could throw away the crates and cartons—and put the furniture in a *permanent* location. But when you're in the Army, you follow orders. We kept moving.

When the Second War broke out, Ike was depressed thinking he'd have to "sit it out" at a desk job—like he did during the First War. He was on General Marshall's staff, and the General had become very dependent on *finally*-Colonel Eisenhower. Naturally, while I wanted whatever Ike wanted, the thought of my husband being a high-muckety-muck in Washington was not hard to accept. I liked being in Washington. I had a nice group of friends and we found things to do. But most importantly, Ike would be safe. He would come home every night. But General Marshall gave Ike the field command he had always wanted, promoting him to "General." Then everything changed. Ike was not just any old field commander, he was the *premier* field commander. The highest of the muckety-mucks!

I tried to console myself thinking that high-muckety-muck generals are always miles behind the front lines and I needn't worry.[8] Hah! I was an expert worrier with a vivid imagination! Ike was flying constantly—I was petrified to fly—and planes were being shot down constantly. He was headquartered in London with bombs and air-raids and Lord only knew what else. Our son John was at West Point, due to graduate on June 6, 1944.

> [8]**MARTHA WASHINGTON**
> *I suppose I was fortunate that I could spend time with the General at Winter Headquarters.[9]*

> [9]**JULIA GRANT**
> *And I spent time in the field with Ulys.*

(Ike was scheduled to be the commencement speaker, but he had other plans that day and had to cancel.) John and his classmates would be shipped out to the front lines right after graduation. I had *plenty* to worry about. I lost nearly thirty pounds from worrying myself sick—and I was small to begin with. I was skin and bones!

I also had much too much time on my hands. I was alone—both my men gone—with a modest apartment that required little care. Most of the time I "socialized" and played mah jongg with my little crowd of officers' wives—consoling each other and trying to put on a brave face. Then I began receiving invitations to luncheons, teas, and the latest rage, cocktail parties. They were cheaper than dinners. Everybody wanted to invite Mrs. High-

Muckety-Muck General Ike.

Cocktail parties were a prime source of gossip and rumor, so soon enough I learned that Ike had an attractive "lady driver" in London. As a matter of fact, Ike mentioned his "lady driver" in his letters to me on occasion. I thought little of it at first—Ike was twice her age. Gossip started. Ike was burdened and lonely. He was also good looking and personable. Gossip continued. I started worrying, despite Ike's reassurance of his love and devotion. I found myself enjoying a Manhattan, and then two—and then three. Then the gossip started about me. I immediately stopped going to cocktail parties, and developed a taste for ginger ale. I never had more than a single cocktail from that time on—although the gossip about both of us continued for the rest of our lives and even into eternity.

I never for a moment believed that Ike's relationship with his "lady driver" was more than platonic or fatherly. We wrote to each other nearly every day, and I never sensed that his heart was divided. Ike grew up on "duty, honor, country," which to him, also translated to "wife, home, family." I never had any reason to doubt Ike's word, so I never doubted. Well, maybe I worried just a little. He wrote of his love and his loneliness, but mostly about the anguish and the awesome responsibility he bore for so many young lives that would be lost, and the oceans of tears that would be shed for them.

I shopped for him continuously—sending him the kind of soup and crackers he liked, and the pajamas and slippers he needed, and the western magazines he enjoyed. Shopping wasn't easy—gas was rationed and it was hard to find anything! I wrote him of all the goings-on in Washington. I was always running into old friends, and friends of friends and I knew those chatty things were exactly what Ike needed to hear: that "real life" as we knew it, was still going on—and "real life" was what we were fighting for. Above all, I tried *not* to show my anxiety about him, about John, about the gossip, and about the fact that I weighed less than 100 pounds and caught cold so often.[10]

But the War was won and our soldiers came home. New York gave Ike its most tremendous and spectacular ticker tape

[10]**BETTY FORD**
Mamie was always inclined to cater to herself a lot. She'd take to her bed if she sneezed twice.[11]

[11]**EDITH ROOSEVELT**
A good fitness program would have done wonders![12]

[12]**ELEANOR ROOSEVELT**
It wouldn't have hurt if she made herself a little more useful during the War. Everyone else was busy. Mamie really was spoiled.

parade—with all the trimmings! Miles of veterans marched. Just about every band in the State marched. Every high-muckety-muck politician marched. Ike insisted that I ride in the car with him, instead of just having a place of honor on the reviewing stand.[13] It was my proudest hour. Ike was sharing his glory with me, and, as he said privately, he was sharing it indirectly with all the wives, mothers and sweethearts in the country. He grinned and waved! I grinned and waved!

> [13]**NELLIE TAFT**
> *When I insisted in riding in the carriage with Will for his inauguration it was a novelty. No wife had ever done that before.*

I had a special secret reason for grinning: Ike was eligible to retire—and we would finally, *finally* have a house of our own. He had written a best-selling book about the War and was in great demand as a speaker. Finances were no longer a concern! Mother didn't need to send me "mad money" anymore.

There was talk about Ike running for President. He refused. But when he was offered the Presidency of Columbia University, he couldn't refuse. Robert E. Lee became a college president when he retired, Ike reminded me. Besides, Ike loathed politics. He was a man of principle and action, not words and runaround. I wanted to look for a house immediately, but once again, the job came with accommodations: A luxury apartment. I started looking anyway, and finally found a wonderful old farm in Gettysburg, Pennsylvania, which we both loved at first sight. We bought it, but it was a good thing I kept the crates, since were destined *not* to live there for a good many years. In 1950, President Truman asked Ike to go overseas as head of newly-formed NATO, to help Europe rebuild and protect itself. We went to Europe, where we were greeted and treated like royalty. [14] It was my first real look at the difference between the "royal treatment" and how decimated Europe was. It made a lasting impression.[15]

> [14]**JULIA GRANT**
> *When Ulysses and I went abroad after his Presidency, we were also treated like royalty. In my wildest dreams, I never thought I would dine tête-à-tête with Queen Victoria!*

By 1952, politics was not calling—it was demanding! We hadn't been formally affiliated with any party, although we both leaned toward being "nominal" Republicans. But *everybody* liked Ike—Republican or not—and we were swept into the White House in one of the biggest landslides in history. One more job with a house. But this time it was

> [15]**EDITH WILSON**
> *We got the royal treatment after the First War, but neither Woodrow nor I really were exposed to the devastation.*

different. This time, we'd have a home away from the White House. Architects and carpenters and plumbers and decorators were called in! I was in my glory! Ike was staggered about how much money "thrifty Mamie" was spending, but I didn't care! I had my house! I escaped to Gettysburg as often as I could.

<table>
<tr><td>[16]**GRACE COOLIDGE**
Who nobody remembered...</td></tr>
</table>

It had been a generation since a really popular First Lady—Grace Coolidge—graced the White House, no pun intended.[16] Lou Hoover had died and was barely remembered in the '50s. Eleanor Roosevelt was too political—and she seldom really "hosted." Bess Truman always looked like she was being imposed upon.[17] Even at my age, I was certainly better looking and had a better figure than my predecessors (once I had put back some "happy" weight)—and I was glad to

<table>
<tr><td>[17]**BESS TRUMAN**
...Which I was.</td></tr>
</table>

be the nation's hostess. Women copied my hair-do, and "Mamie" bangs became the rage. Ike was everybody's genial grandpa—so I was everybody's grandma. I was the epitome of "mom in an apron." It would never have dawned on anyone that I was less than a marvelous cook! People were asking for my recipes! What a laugh! We sent them Ike's favorite steak marinade.

Having my own house, having my beloved husband, having a fine son and his growing family—what more could I want? I didn't need to be First Lady to be happy. I was already overjoyed! I hosted, attended, accepted bouquets—sometimes a dozen a day—and was more than glad to speak a few words at Veterans conventions or Gold Star Mothers groups. What was so terrible about that? I had a wardrobe full of pretty things, had breakfast in bed whenever I liked—which was all the time—and merely had to snap my fingers and my requests would be granted. I even painted our White House bedroom pink—my favorite color. (Ike never liked sleeping in a pink bedroom, but that was too bad. Pink it was.) I could be "spoiled Mamie" again. I didn't want make any other mark as First Lady except as Ike's wife. That was enough for me!

<table>
<tr><td>[18]**PAT NIXON**
I think that was the first time a Vice President ever "assumed" some of the presidential duties for a still-living president.</td></tr>
</table>

Then Ike had a heart attack; I refused to leave his side. This time I was really scared. It wasn't Mamie's usual worry-wart fretting. I was afraid he would die before we could be just "Ike and Mamie" on the farm in Gettysburg. I moved into the hospital with Ike, but unlike Edith Wilson, I made absolutely no attempt to organize his presidential priorities.[18] There was a Vice

President. He could take charge. And on that subject: I was always fond of Pat Nixon, and respected her husband. Ike's relationship with Dick Nixon was pleasant, but not close. They hadn't known each other prior to the '52 campaign, and Dick was a little too "political" for Ike's ecumenical taste. As time passed, however, we grew to appreciate Dick's acumen and capacity for hard work. It was Ike's dying wish when our grandson David married Julie Nixon—even though we both thought they were much too young at the time!

But Ike recovered and even served a second term. Then we finally went *home* to Gettysburg. Our retirement was idyllic—and I'm not being "gushy." It was truly idyllic. We had guests often. Famous people—old friends. Best of all, our family and grandchildren! Ike wrote books and accepted more honors. I went along for the ride and made friends in town. Ike played golf; I found a canasta group. He painted; I shopped. We played bridge and watched TV. He barbecued steaks and I tossed the salad. We were Ike and Mamie on the farm—as normal a blueberry pie family as you could want!

There is only one more thing I might add for posterity—my own "conjecture." History has always wondered why Ike "fell out" with Truman—especially when they had had a cordial relationship for a long time. Some people thought it was because Ike decided to run as a Republican. Couldn't be. Truman might have been disappointed, but he was a professional politician; he would have understood. Other people thought Ike was miffed when Truman "fired" General MacArthur. Ike was stunned, but Truman had reason. Besides, Ike never cared for General MacArthur anyway.

No, I think there was a personal reason, although we never discussed it: Ike knew about all the gossip during the War—his so-called "romance" with his lady driver, and my so-called "drinking problem." He wrote it off for what it was: gossip. But around 1952, I think it came to his attention that one of the prime "spreaders and believers" of those nasty stories was none other than Senator-and-then-President Harry Truman. [19]

> [19] **BESS TRUMAN**
> *I don't know about the spreading, but I do know Harry believed the rumors. So did I. I still do.*

If that *were* the case, Ike would have never forgiven him.

The Author's Epilogue

"Ladies…" is a book of voices. They are voices seldom heard, consigned to the silence of historical neglect. They are voices telling their stories, or, as Lucy Hayes instructed, whatever they want, in order to give a glimpse of a real person between the birth-and-death dates in the almanac. The intention is for the reader to hear their uniqueness, their individual styles, their individual ways of expressing themselves.

"Ladies…" is a book of economies. What is included, what is omitted and where, demands some difficult choices. Seventeen Ladies lost children; four had husbands who were assassinated; another five had assassinations attempted. Scarring experiences for all. Avoiding redundancies and tedium is challenging; thus some Ladies dwell, some gloss over, and some avoid the references entirely. Times and events needed to be compressed, condensed, and combined.

"Ladies…" is a work of fiction. Purely conjecture. Naturally, it is based largely on historical fact, whether it pertains to the individual First Lady, her husband the President, or a compilation pertinent to the time in which they lived. Some of the conjecture is significant: Abigail Fillmore being secretly supportive of women's suffrage; Sarah Polk's regret for sitting for nearly fifty years. Some is minor: Andrew Johnson being a "poor shot." But in an effort to make our unknown and under-known First Ladies come alive, the chief aim is to make each conjecture plausible.

Can I prove that Abigail Fillmore supported women's suffrage? Of course not. But Seneca Falls is in upstate New York and she lived in upstate New York. The dates coincide. She was an ardent reader and interested in current events. (A fact.) She would have been aware of it. (A conjecture, but reasonable and likely.) As a former teacher, she certainly would have been intelligent enough to form a personal opinion. It is the author's opinion that she would have supported higher learning for women, if nothing else. It is certainly a plausible conjecture.

The conjecture about Andrew Johnson being a poor shot, for example, is also plausible. He was a tailor by trade and a politician by profession. He lived in a town. He would have had little reason or opportunity to become an expert marksman. Again, plausible.

"Ladies…" is full of such conjectures, whether they are factual, emotional or a combination. How Edith Roosevelt actually felt about Alice Lee, Theodore's first wife, is historically documented: She believed he would have grown bored with Alice. That Edith was deeply hurt when Theodore married Alice can only be assumed, since she never discussed it. But it is a legitimate assumption, eminently plausible.

How Mary Lincoln actually felt about the country's generosity toward

Lucretia Garfield is also a conjecture. But it is well documented that Mary was always worried about her finances and resentful that rich Republicans didn't come to her aid. Her anger at Crete's "largesse," while not an historical fact, is certainly plausible.

By crossing through "eternity" to enable First Ladies (including the Moderns) to talk to and about each other, the device is essentially to please the reader, and occasionally to interject some information or comment that might otherwise be lost, boring or pedantic. Allowing Lou Hoover and Eleanor Roosevelt to chime about driving a car during Mamie Eisenhower's chapter seems fitting. It humanizes them. To have various ladies banter about their illustrious genealogies during Caroline Harrison's chapter offers some truths—but it is basically for fun.

The reader may note a lack of depth in the discussions about the three great moral issues of the 19th and early 20th centuries: slavery, temperance and women's suffrage. This is because the Ladies themselves were basically centrists. Slave holding Ladies were truly kind, but unrepentant. "It was how it was." None were abolitionists—not even the ones who believed it to be morally wrong. Lucy Hayes is the only Lady to speak on temperance, since she was historically involved. The other Ladies, while they may have been personally temperate, did not espouse prohibition. And none of the Ladies, not one, was a suffragist.

Mamie Eisenhower was the last First Lady to be born in the 19th Century. She was the last First Lady to wear long dresses as an adult. She was the last First Lady to assume a completely traditional role of tea parties, ceremonies and bouquets. With the anomaly of Eleanor Roosevelt, a woman before her time, First Ladies from Jacqueline Kennedy on, were their own persons, who devised their own job descriptions and agendas.

Television and magazines, air travel and instant access has thrust modern presidential wives into major prominence, with or without their personal inclination. The Women's Movement of the mid-20th Century has broadened their opportunities and afforded them their own bully pulpits. They have all risen admirably to their tasks, which have become full-time jobs. Unelected, unpaid and unsolicited to be sure, but jobs just the same.

To exclude the modern First Ladies would cause a gaping 50-year vacuum. To include them with their own chapters would be impossible. We know them too well; there is nothing to conjecture. Commentaries seem the appropriate venue for them—and they are done entirely with affection and respect.

They all had a wonderful time writing their stories.

FSF

DESTINY OF A WAR VETERAN
by Sal Atlantis Phoenix

Destiny of a War Veteran depicts the life of a conscientious veteran. The subject matter of thestory is serious and tends towards the realistic side of the aftermath of war. The story is about the analysis of the human soul lost in fantasy and in reality, about submission and rebellion, and about philosophy and tyranny. The story is vivid with images, and complex and rich in characters. It is an intriguing tale that defines the socio-political scenarios.

Vietnam War veteran Joe is tempted to participate in Middle Eastern and international politics, compelled with insinuated illusion of establishing freedom and democracy. The subsequent effects of the human tragedies engulfed from the political scenarios devastate him, and he seeks refuge beyond the realm of humanity.

Paperback, 188 pages
5.5" x 8.5"
ISBN 1-4241-8005-8

About the author:

Sal Atlantis Phoenix, a veteran of life and a conscientious citizen, is a playwright and fiction writer. His lifelong experience convinced him that "…with all its sham, drudgery and broken dreams, it is still a beautiful world. Be careful. Strive to be happy."

THE ASSASSIN WHO LOVED HER

by Janet M. Henderson

In *The Assassin Who Loved Her*, journalist Jennifer Long wants two things: to become a great writer and to fall in love. Her dreams come true when she writes about a serial killer called the Assassin who stalks, threatens, and torments her for exposing his motives in the media.

Tim, the pilot, brings Jennifer financial security. Jason, the actor, brings her fame and fortune. John, the former FBI agent, brings her protection and intrigue. But Jennifer must survive murder, deceit, heartache, and grief before she finds true love, happiness, triumph, and relief.

From Chicago, to Washington, to Hollywood, to Portugal, Jennifer fights for her life and career. Her story will make you laugh and cry. It'll make you believe in love. It'll make you hope and pray she wins. With a fairytale beginning and a Hollywood ending, it has everything a good novel should have! Read it and love it!

Paperback, 276 pages
6" x 9"
ISBN 1-60610-424-1

About the author:

Janet M. Henderson teaches English in the City Colleges of Chicago. She was born in Chicago and, as the daughter of a U.S. Marine, grew up in Virginia, North Carolina, California and Hawaii. Her first novel, *Lunch with Cassie*, received excellent reviews from Writer's Digest. She lives in Chicago.

THE SCARLET "P"

by Ron Sullivan

The Scarlet "P" is a novel centered in the affluent town of Paradise Valley, Arizona, a bedtime community of Phoenix where business professionals, sports figures and captains of industry reside. The peace and security of the town is shattered by the death of four young ladies out jogging or playing tennis. They are savagely murdered and their bodies mutilated.

Detective Don Graves of the Paradise Valley Marshal's Office leads the multi-agency investigation to identify and arrest the monster that was responsible for the killings. Amy Brady, an assistant DA working the case, becomes romantically involved with Graves and helps with the identification and capture of the monster.

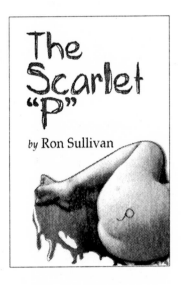

Paperback, 163 pages
5.5" x 8.5"
ISBN 1-60474-392-1

About the author:

Ron Sullivan was born and raised in White Plains, New York, and has lived in the Phoenix, Arizona, area for over thirty years. The father of six children, he has recently retired from residential real estate and has now fulfilled his lifetime ambition to become a novelist.

ABYSS OF INSANITY

by J. Michael Beck

John Thomas Parker is a man pushed to the edge of sanity. He has just discovered his wife is cheating on him and he is hurling down a dark path that will change his world forever. He begins looking for a companion in the wrong place at the wrong time. He meets Marcy, a lovely woman apparently working the streets as a prostitute. However, Marcy has a secret that will pull John into an abyss of evil, where murder and ruined lives surround him. His and Marcy's fate may rely on others to figure it out before it is too late.

Paperback, 335 pages
6" x 9"
ISBN 1-60610-092-0

About the author:

I have thirty-three years of law enforcement experience, beginning with the military, state and city police and twenty-one years of federal law enforcement. I have a bachelor's degree in criminal justice and currently work as an investigator completing federal background investigations. I have worked alongside men of honor and had the misfortune to be associated through my work with some men so filled with evil I could never create a character who could live up to the real bad guys. I put my years of law enforcement into this novel. The best and worst of mankind are represented in these pages. —J. Michael Beck